Who Owns Tomorrow?

Also by Richard Worzel

The Only Secure Job:
Changing from Employee to Entrepreneur

The Next Twenty Years of Your Life:
A Personal Guide into the Year 2017

Facing the Future:
The Seven Forces Revolutionizing Our Lives

Who Owns Tomorrow?

7 SECRETS FOR THE
FUTURE OF BUSINESS

Richard Worzel

VIKING
CANADA

VIKING CANADA
Penguin Group (Canada), a division of Pearson Penguin Canada Inc., 10 Alcorn Avenue,
Toronto, Ontario M4V 3B2

Penguin Group (U.K.), 80 Strand, London WC2R 0RL, England
Penguin Group (U.S.), 375 Hudson Street, New York, New York 10014, U.S.A.
Penguin Group (Australia) Inc., 250 Camberwell Road, Camberwell, Victoria 3124, Australia
Penguin Group (Ireland), 25 St. Stephen's Green, Dublin 2, Ireland
Penguin Books India (P) Ltd, 11, Community Centre, Panchsheel Park, New Delhi - 110 017, India
Penguin Group (New Zealand), cnr Rosedale and Airborne Roads, Albany, Auckland 1310, New Zealand
Penguin Books (South Africa) (Pty) Ltd, 24 Sturdee Avenue, Rosebank 2196, South Africa

Penguin Group, Registered Offices: 80 Strand, London WC2R 0RL, England

First published 2003

1 2 3 4 5 6 7 8 9 10 (FR)

National Library of Canada Cataloguing in Publication

Worzel, Richard, 1950-
    Who owns tomorrow? : 7 secrets for the future of business / Richard Worzel.

Includes bibliographical references and index.
ISBN 0-670-04355-9

    1. Business forecasting. I. Title.

HD30.27.W67 2003   338.5'44   C2003-903255-8

Visit the Penguin Group (Canada) website at **www.penguin.ca**

"The reason I can see farther [than others] is that I stand on the shoulders of giants."

—SIR ISAAC NEWTON

This book is dedicated to those writers on whose shoulders I stand. They—unknowingly—shaped my interest in reading, writing, and thinking, and thereby helped me find my way into this future.

THEODOR SEUSS GEISEL ("DR. SEUSS")
Who made words and reading seem like a delightful game.

ROBERT A. HEINLEIN
Who enticed me to become a passionate reader, showed me the value of critical thinking, and gave me a taste for speculating about the future.

GEORGE W. GOODMAN ("ADAM SMITH")
Whose delightfully puckish prose and insights into humanity and the stock market helped me decide on my first career, and kindled within me a desire to express my thoughts as gracefully as he does.

ROBERT M. PIRSIG
Whose writing persuaded me to seek quality in all things, and helped me refine my writing skills and my purpose in life.

NEVILLE J. NANKIVELL
Who, when he was managing editor of *The Financial Post*, invited a young stock-market analyst to try his hand at freelance writing, encouraged me to write a regular column, and helped me produce my first book, from which my career as a speaker and professional futurist eventually developed.

My thanks to them all.

Contents

An Open Secret
The Strategic Importance of the Future

"I think there is a world market for maybe five computers."

—THOMAS J. WATSON, FOUNDER OF IBM, 1943

The future will catch us by surprise.

We expect that tomorrow will be pretty much like today, but that's not the way it will be. Instead, the future is going to be dramatically different from the present for many reasons, including the pace and acceleration of technological change; the range of technologies that are becoming important; management and leadership changes and challenges; the massive demographic shifts we are beginning to experience; the geopolitical and global economic transitions that are changing the face of the world; and the ebbing of power from large organizations, both corporate and government.

The future of business, therefore, will offer greater vulnerability coupled with increased opportunity, as Thomas Watson's comment illustrates perfectly. First, he was dead wrong. He made the faulty assumption that computers were going to remain as expensive and hard to use as the ponderous, handcrafted behemoths of that time. Despite this, he didn't permit IBM to get stuck in his mistake. He and the company changed their minds, altered their strategy, and went on to dominate the computer industry until the 1990s. Have you considered what mistakes you might be making about the future? And are you allowing yourself to get trapped by them?

Five years from now the world will be transformed, and the differences pose a threat to those who are unprepared, even as they offer riches to those who can capitalize on change. Knowing where the changes are coming from, and how they will affect business, the consumer, and government, will make it substantially easier to prepare. That's the purpose of this book—to offer a road map of the future to make planning easier and more successful.

What do we actually mean when we talk about "the future"? A lot of people expect me and other futurists (as well as economists, politicians, and anyone else involved in the prognostication business) to "tell the future" for them. The unspoken assumption is that there is only one possible future, and that if I were a true future-teller, I'd just read their palms and tell them what lottery ticket to buy. It doesn't work that way.

There are an infinite number of possible futures that spread out before us, and it's impossible for me, or anyone else, to pick out the specific, detailed future that is guaranteed to happen. Any assessment of the future is a guess, although some guesses are more educated and more reasoned than others. Accordingly, knowing (or guessing) the future is not important; every specific prediction has a high probability of being partly or completely wrong, as happened with Thomas Watson's prediction about the future of computers.

What, then, is the point of contemplating the future? The purpose is to plan intelligently for an uncertain outlook. Contingency planning, for example, takes into account a range of possibilities, assesses the most likely ones, and prepares for those with the highest probabilities. Moreover, the process of planning is more important than the plans themselves.

There's a possibly apocryphal story of a famous general known for his meticulous planning. Once a reporter asked him, "General, is it true that no battle plan survives contact with the enemy?"

"Absolutely correct," snapped the general.

"Then, sir, why do you undertake such meticulous planning when your plans are going to be worthless once the battle starts?"

"Because it allows me to improvise with greater intelligence," the general replied.

Everyone deals with uncertainty, no one knows what the future will hold, and there are going to be unexpected surprises that affect all of us. If you've contemplated a range of possibilities, and decided ahead of time how you'll respond to them, then you can respond more quickly and with greater depth of preparation when reality unfolds. In a world where the competition for jobs, profits, and survival are escalating rapidly, this kind of advance preparation will mean the difference between success and failure.

This book is intended to be a resource, not a bible that dispenses the final truth. You can use it in whichever way works best for you. If you like starting at the beginning, reading through the middle, and ending at the end, do just that. If you like browsing around, selecting things here and there, as you would with a library or a cafeteria, feel free. If you cherry-pick, then go back for details, the book is designed to help you do that as well. This book is structured around the seven issues that I believe are crucial for the future success of any business operating today. Each of the first six secrets relates to a number of broad aspects of tomorrow. As a result, two chapters are devoted to each of these secrets. The final secret I want to hand to you is a toolbox that will allow you, just like the meticulous general, to improvise with greater intelligence.

Each of the seven secrets relates to at least one vignette, which is a story about the future that illustrates the principles of that secret. The purpose of these vignettes is to give you a sense of what it will be like to wake up in tomorrow's world and experience it for yourself. I've found over the years that people sometimes have a hard time imagining what the changes I describe will be like, or how they'll work. Vignettes seem to fill that gap.

As you read through the book, however you do it, you may disagree with some or all of my thoughts about the future, and like or dislike the vignettes that I present. But even if you disagree, you should still find my work useful if it raises questions that help you explore and prepare for tomorrow.

In many ways, the best way to deal with the future is to identify the right questions, rather than to seek simplistic right answers. A good question will allow you to explore an issue in many ways, and adapt to unexpected changes, whereas a simple answer has a tendency to blindfold you to other possibilities.

So, let me start by exploring the most dangerous mistake you can make in tomorrow's world: failing to pay enough attention to the only real asset your organization has.

Optimize Your Most Important Asset

"Every major company says that people are their most important asset. What, then, do they gain by downsizing?"

—JOHN DIEBOLD, AUTHOR OF *AUTOMATION* (1952)

1

The War for Talent

Most organizations treat their people as if they were disposable, replaceable, interchangeable parts: warm bodies to be hired when things are busy and downsized when demand slows. Suzanne Sutter, a top executive with U.S. retailing giant Cole National, which has outlets in Canada, summed up this approach well. Cole, she commented, used to treat its sales staff "just like a box of Kleenex: if one left, another would pop up."[1]

This is dangerous behaviour on many different levels. The first and most obvious is the direct cost of hiring and training people. Marriott International, one of the smartest companies in the hospitality trade, found that one of its fast-food subsidiaries hired 27,000 workers to fill 8,800 jobs in a single year.[2] A recent survey by the National Retail Federation, an advocacy organization that is U.S.-based but also represents international retailers, found that annual turnover for full-time staff in U.S. retailing was an appalling 74 percent, and for part-time staff reached a truly dreadful 124 percent.[3]

Staff turnover is incredibly expensive. Studies across U.S. industry sectors, for example, show that staff replacement costs range from 50 percent to

150 percent of annual payroll for salaried staff. Even replacing burger flippers costs about US$500 apiece, while replacing a software engineer can cost more than $100,000, counting everything from lost production time to recruitment and training of replacements.[4] So the most visible cost of hiring and firing people shows up directly on the bottom line. But the greatest cost is losing the loyalty and commitment of your people.

The Only Important Asset

Peter Drucker, the acknowledged master of management studies, notes that the traditional factors of production—natural resources, labour, and capital—are no longer important. What are important are "knowledge workers." Drucker was using this term as early as 1959 to describe people who rely on knowledge rather than skills to perform their jobs. In a recent essay, he commented: "The management of knowledge workers should be based on the assumption that the corporation needs them more than they need the corporation. They know they can leave. They have both mobility and self-confidence. This means that they have to be treated and managed as volunteers."[5]

Yet most companies today organize themselves along the lines of the Prussian General Staff model of the 19th century: a rigid hierarchy that was designed to maximize the talents of a few intelligent people at the top and to use the bulk of the people in the pyramid as little more than worker bees trained to follow orders. This model gives maximum status and ego gratification to the people at the top, treating them as stars or superstars, but is drastically out of date and poses a real danger to organizations that intend to survive.

Most readers will nod and accept the truth that employees are important, and that a command-and-control hierarchy is no longer the best structure, yet believe that this isn't a problem in *their* organization because they "empower" their people. Fortunately there's a litmus test: since money represents power and authority, how much influence over departmental budgets do front-line workers have? The less say they have in

Leadership is not about maximizing the abilities of the top person. It's about creating an environment where everyone reaches their maximum potential.

how money is spent on the front line, the stricter the hierarchy and the less likely it is that companies are maximizing the abilities of their people. If budgets are created centrally and imposed from above, your organization is a command-and-control hierarchy no matter how management describes it. But this isn't about budgets and money: it's about inspiring people to bust their butts for the company.

Maximizing a company's people means maximizing the contribution of every individual in the organization. This flies in the face of current conventional thinking. Until very recently, what made boards of directors and shareholders salivate was the superhero CEO, the one who could fly in and take charge, like Lee Iacocca with Chrysler, Lou Gerstner with IBM, or "Neutron Jack" Welch of General Electric, who could force a company to perform. And, obviously, if such people could perform superhuman feats, they had to be paid like superheroes. No compensation was too obscene.

There are two major problems with superhero CEOs. First, they're scarce and can't be manufactured to order. And second, *companies* don't perform, their *people* do. Leadership is not about maximizing the abilities of the top person. It's about creating an environment where everyone reaches their maximum potential in support of the company's goals and philosophy. Great leaders inspire people to greatness; they don't drag companies across the goal line by themselves.

So if the difference between a good company and a great company is the difference in the quality and performance of their people, how did we get into a situation where we thought that the performance of a few people was important, and all the rest were just spear carriers and scenery? Why have we moved to a workplace where no one feels secure and everyone looks out for themselves rather than the company? And what do we do about it?

The Pressure to Be Nimble

The world is forcing companies to become nimble, to adapt to change, focus on opportunities quickly, and respond before competitors do. Moreover, the skills a company needs can change, seemingly overnight. In the mid-1990s, it was suddenly crucial for companies to have Internet presence, which meant they needed people who could create websites using HTML (Hypertext Markup Language), and who understood the arcana of e-commerce, a thing that had never existed before. Since the supply of these people was small and their perceived value enormous, the prices they could command went sky-high, until it cost billions of dollars to buy dot-com companies in order to acquire their founders and the niches they had created. By late 2001, this urgency had vanished like a fog. Companies awoke with horror, realizing that they had wasted enormous amounts of money not only on people with a narrow range of skills that were no longer in great demand, but also on the largely worthless things these people had created. Skill sets change so rapidly that today's superstar can become tomorrow's redundancy.

As the pace of business has picked up, businesses have responded by re-engineering themselves more frequently and more extensively than ever before. It's almost as if companies feel they can change direction, change their market appeal, or even change their luck by changing their people.

A generation ago, white-collar employees who worked hard, kept their noses clean, and were loyal to the company could be reasonably sure of steady work, chances for advancement, and pensions on which to retire. It was an unwritten contract: loyalty in exchange for security. That unwritten contract has been torn up, and the uncertainty that used to dog only assembly-line workers now pervades all jobs in the workplace, up to and including superstar CEOs. Today the unwritten contract is more like: "We reserve the right to lay you off at any time that suits our profit picture. In exchange, we accept that you may quit at any time to take a more lucrative job elsewhere." This creates uncertainty for everyone. Yet this new contract not only seems to be acceptable to most businesses, but is actively applauded by Bay Street and Wall Street; in the short run, stocks typically go up when companies announce mass layoffs.

But I maintain that managements that institute widespread layoffs are admitting one of two things: either they weren't doing their jobs by weeding out unsuccessful employees on a regular basis; or they weren't paying enough attention to their customers, and have been caught by a change in the market with large numbers of people with the wrong skills. Either way, they are trumpeting their incompetence, and the numbers largely back me up. A 1998 report by the American Management Association indicates that U.S. firms that went through large-scale layoffs were unable to sustain any increases in productivity or profits. Indeed, only about a third produced long-term gains in shareholder value, so that the only thing that most layoffs succeeded in doing was to create smaller companies, not more productive or more profitable ones.[6]

Moreover there are other, largely unrecognized, costs of layoffs, starting with something called survivor's sickness. According to consultant David Noer, of Greensboro, North Carolina, employees who remain behind after layoffs often feel angry, depressed, or fearful, so that they are unwilling to take risks. They also worry that they will be the next to be cut, and often devote their energies to looking for a new job.[7] Worse still, a 1995 study by Deborah Dougherty of McGill University and Edward Bowman of Pennsylvania's Wharton School shows that downsized firms lose their innovative edge, in part because downsizing breaks up the informal relationships and networks that innovators within an organization use to win support and resources for new products. As a result, the pace of innovation slows.[8]

Meanwhile, although companies maintain the power to hire and fire, the overall balance of power has been shifting out of their hands and into the hands of the skilled worker.

The Rise of the Knowledge Worker

Knowledge workers need to be treated and managed as volunteers, said Peter Drucker. They have what companies need: the ability to transform the world with what they know. What's more, they're aware of their power, both collectively and individually. When you couple that with the disappearance of corporate loyalty, you have a prescription for instability. Companies need knowledge workers, and it costs enormous amounts of money to find and attract them, but companies no longer strive to hold on to them. Knowledge workers have become hired guns, with you for a good time, not a long time, as *The Economist* noted in 2001:

> *McKinsey, a consultancy, argues that the key battle of this century is the war for talent: the war to hire and retain the best people. Mr. Drucker's knowledge workers are a demanding lot. They are less and less likely to want to work full-time for one company, seeing no reason to pledge their loyalty to an organisation that can no longer reciprocate the favour.*[9]

Knowledge workers make up the fastest-growing segment of the workforce today, even as more traditional segments, such as factory workers and service employees, shrink as a percentage of the total. In North America, knowledge workers are already a force to be reckoned with; in the United States, they account for fully a third of the workforce, outnumbering factory workers by two to one. Within the next 20 years, knowledge workers will comprise about 40 percent of the total workforce in all developed countries.[10]

So not only are knowledge workers becoming more powerful, but a steadily rising percentage of every company's workforce will fall into that category. For companies that won't learn, and continue to treat their workers as replaceable parts, this is the worst possible news. Knowledge workers will use such companies as rest stops along their self-directed career paths. Such companies will spend more and more time and money on recruiting and replacing knowledge workers. Projects will be disrupted as crucial individuals leave with scant notice. And the workers who are left in a seriously downsized organization might be termed "sludge"—a residue of workers who lack the confidence or the skills to leap to a more hospitable company. So companies that want to be nimble, those that try to leap from worker to worker in their pursuit of the future, will find instead that it is the knowledge workers who use them as stepping stones, while the companies sink under the weight of their own personnel policies.

The final aspect of the growing power of knowledge workers is demographic. The baby boomers, born between 1947 and 1967, constitute approximately 35 percent of the Canadian population and just over 50 percent of the labour force. The leading edge of the boomers are now in their mid- to upper-50s, and thus among the most senior—and experienced—people in their organizations. Statistically, people start cutting back on their working hours in their mid-50s, either for reasons of deteriorating health or because they can afford to. This means that over the next 20 years, the single biggest group of workers, and those with the greatest amount of knowledge and experience, will start leaving the workforce. Of course, the departure of the highly paid boomers will also leave room for younger people to advance within organizations, and it will free up a great deal of salary room.

However, from the point of view of skills and maximizing the talents and abilities of your workforce, the departure of the boomers is going to tear an enormous hole in your organization and leave great gaps where knowledgeable people are needed but frankly unavailable. This is already evident among doctors, nurses, university professors, and teachers, for example, and will shortly become painfully apparent among skilled tradespeople such as plumbers, carpenters, electricians, and furnace repair people. This trend will spread to every industry and almost every segment of society; companies will find themselves desperately seeking knowledge workers in specific areas and finding none available.

So knowledge workers do now, and will increasingly, hold the whip hand, and companies that do not pay attention to this power shift will find themselves rapidly being left behind by firms that pay special attention to recruiting and retaining the brains that they need.

There remains one last factor to consider before I describe what you can do in response to this problem, and that is to ask: What constitutes a knowledge worker?

What's a Knowledge Worker Anyway?

The term "knowledge worker" has evolved since the late 1950s, and is now often used to imply a knowledge of technology, but the original and more general meaning is more accurate. Everyone knows things. Indeed, any worker is able to function solely because he has some form of knowledge, even if it's something as simple as how to pick up boxes on one side of a warehouse and deposit them safely in the right location somewhere else.

As a result, I disagree with the basic concept. I don't think knowledge is crucial, and believe that the term "knowledge worker" is misleading. If knowledge were the real key to success, there would be no Ph.D.s driving taxicabs, and a university degree would be a guarantee of affluence, which it clearly is not. You must have knowledge, but knowledge by itself does not make you successful or valuable. You need a much more complex set of human attributes to succeed.

First, you must have *relevant* knowledge. Being an expert on the fiction of Ernest Hemingway won't be of much value if you're developing a new detergent. And the relevance of knowledge is transitory. The world changes so quickly that knowledge that is relevant one day may be vastly devalued shortly after, as with my earlier example about HTML programmers. This means that a knowledge worker who wants to remain in demand must be constantly updating her knowledge and testing it against the marketplace to make sure she remains relevant. Knowledge is an asset that must be built up constantly or it will erode rapidly.

The relevance of knowledge also means that post-secondary education may not be necessary for someone to qualify as a knowledge worker,

> *If knowledge were the real key to success, there would be no Ph.D.s driving taxicabs, and a university degree would be a guarantee of affluence, which it clearly is not.*

and that knowledge workers are not restricted to the professions or even to white-collar work. Higher education can provide a theoretical framework, plus a depth of knowledge in a given field that is difficult to amass through experience alone. But if knowledge is valued purely on relevance, then *how* you acquire knowledge is unimportant. Indeed, a blue-collar worker will often have specific knowledge that is more relevant, even if less academically profound, than his white-collar boss.

Next, knowledge in isolation is not enough; it must be placed in context and be used with purpose to give it meaning and value. An abstract, purely academic knowledge of the human genome is sterile on its own. As a means of understanding how disease attacks the health of a human being, and as a tool to use in defeating such attacks, though, such knowledge will be invaluable. So knowledge in one field must be connected to other, related fields and deliberately applied with an objective in mind. In fact, I consider understanding to be vastly more important than the possession of mere facts.

Finally, you must put what you know into action, which requires self-confidence, conviction, energy and initiative, and the desire to achieve something worthwhile. The best field commanders in the military are not necessarily the ones who know the most about tactics and strategy, but the ones who actually perform in the heat of battle. The same is true of knowledge workers: they must be able to apply their knowledge, and be prepared to bet that their actions will be successful.

In the corporate world, creating this willingness to act is often described as motivation, as if it were a kind of ointment that could be applied to everyone, but it's actually much more profound than that. Indeed, companies that set out to *motivate* their people are often disappointed with the results. Getting people to jump up and down and to shout and pump their fists will provide some catharsis and emotional satisfaction, but the effects frequently dissipate by the time the employees get back to their desks. In fact, at the root of the enthusiasm that managers are so keen to conjure up are the Greek words *en* ("within") and *theos* ("God"). Enthusiasm comes from the concept of "God within," or, less literally, "to be inspired."[11]

Instead of looking for some sort of universal snake oil to create motivation, corporate managers need to understand the unique inner drives of the individuals working for them, to learn what's important to them, and to help them accomplish their goals using the company's goals as their vehicle. This is a tall order, requiring sensitivity, insight, a genuine interest in the individuals involved, polite persistence, and compassion. This approach is more difficult, yet much more likely to succeed than treating people as production tools that all get turned on the same way.

Indeed, as a professional speaker I'm often asked if I'm a "motivational" speaker, because managers are looking for this universal "ON" switch to motivate higher sales and productivity. I reply that, no, I don't believe you can slather on motivation like suntan lotion. Instead, I tell them that I'm an informational speaker, but that this often achieves the desired result because it allows employees to realize solutions to problems that have kept them from achieving what they want.

So a knowledge worker is someone with knowledge that is relevant to the task at hand, who constantly upgrades and updates her knowledge, who can place it in context and understand its implications to other areas of knowledge, and who has the desire and courage to act to achieve the company's goals in order to achieve her own. This may sound rather academic, but understanding knowledge workers is the key to understanding how to attract, retain, retrain, and harness their internal enthusiasms to produce the constant, creative miracle that companies now need to survive and thrive.

How to Optimize Your Only Real Asset: Your People

The Stayer family of Sheboygan, Wisconsin, founded and built Johnsonville Foods, a maker of premium-priced sausages. By 1980, the company was successful by most yardsticks, with sales growing by 20 percent a year. But the CEO, Ralph Stayer, was worried about the future; his concerns and the insights those concerns provoked were to lead to one of the great success stories of management–worker relationships. In 1990, Ralph Stayer wrote an article for the *Harvard Business Review* in which he discussed the struggles he had along the way. In that article, he neatly described the central issues of the war for talent:

> *What worried me . . . was the gap between potential and performance. Our people didn't seem to care. . . . I [eventually realized] that I didn't directly control the performance of the people at Johnsonville, that as a manager I didn't really manage people. They managed themselves. But I did manage the context.*[12]

Executives don't manage people; people manage themselves. What executives do is create the context within which employees make choices on how they will act. I'll come back to Stayer's comments, but let's start by talking about the context your company creates.

Know Who You Are, Know What You Stand For

Values are the compass that helps an organization keep all of its people going in one direction. Moreover, common values create harmony and a sense of purpose within an organization.

A company that intends to survive and prosper for decades will see its products change; its people come and go; and the location of its offices, its logo, its name, and almost everything else about the organization altered as time and events unfold. But what keep an organization going in a focused direction are the values that underlie these changes. It is these shared values that give purpose, so that necessary changes don't become merely random reactions to transient events.

This steadiness of purpose has two primary advantages. It becomes an organizing principle that causes the changes to build on each other, to compound returns like a good investment. And it infuses the people who work for an organization with a mission, a goal bigger than merely working for a paycheque; it gives them a

Executives don't manage people; people manage themselves.

sense of shared destiny. Values become something that people can become dedicated to.

Ironically, it doesn't matter as much *which* values an organization espouses so much as having everyone in the organization agree with those values. It can be helpful if the values are big and inspire people, if they are something people are proud of and can talk to their friends and neighbours about. But it's more important that the values are shared within the organization.

Nordstrom, the American retailing chain, has a shared set of values revolving around providing extraordinary service for customers in pursuit of extraordinary sales, profits, and personal income. The company's hard-charging dedication to customer satisfaction is primarily selfish: Nordstrom wants to sell more and make more than any other retail chain in the world. This is not a grand, altruistic goal that will be enshrined for the ages. But it does infuse the people who work there, and gives Nordstrom a yardstick by which to hire and fire people: if you share our values, and want to bust your butt to make a bunch of money, then you're a "Nordie." If that's not for you, then we wish you luck somewhere else.

Johnson & Johnson, the New Jersey–headquartered manufacturer of health- and medical-related products, has long held the philosophy that its primary business is to help improve the health of the people who use its products. As a result, when seven people in the Chicago area died in 1982 because bottles of Extra-Strength Tylenol had been laced with cyanide, the company wasted no time in warning consumers not to use any Tylenol product, and recalled roughly 31 million bottles of Tylenol with a value of more than US$100 million. There was no hesitation within the company— it was the right thing to do, and has become the gold standard by which corporate responsibility is measured. That kind of ethic attracts people of a like mind, and repels people who think only of profit.

Both companies know what they stand for—and that helps them act when problems arise, because the people who work there know what they're supposed to do.

If People Are the Most Important Asset, Then Hiring Is the Most Important Skill

The builder's rule of thumb of "measure twice, cut once" is widely overlooked by corporations in their recruiting and retention policies, but is crucial to a successful organization. Candidates should be carefully considered, not just for the skills they possess but also for the attitudes that they bring to work. Indeed, research done by James Heskett, Earl Sasser, and Leonard Schlesinger of the Harvard Business School indicates that skills are far less important than attitudes.[13] Skills can be taught. Attitudes come with the individual, and individuals whose attitudes don't fit with the company's values are not going to be as happy or as productive as those whose attitudes do.

A good example of this is ISS, a Danish firm that cleans offices. In its hiring and training, it stresses the importance of maintaining the firm's stringent cleaning standards. It then suggests that prospective employees who are uncomfortable with these strictly enforced standards may not be happy working for the company, and encourages them to leave. If this sounds counterintuitive, it may help to know that not only does ISS have a retention rate that is five times higher than the industry average, but it is known for the loyalty of its clients.[14]

Another equally important aspect of recruiting is knowing whom not to recruit. Most people want to do well, to strive and achieve, and to be successful within an organization. There is a small minority, though, who feel a sense of entitlement, carry a chip on their shoulders, and who will create unhappiness and disharmony around them. Regardless of their skills and talents, they are more costly than they are worth, for they will disrupt your organization.

If you accept that great companies are great because they have great people, then a company's most critical decisions relate to the people it hires and keeps. Accordingly, the recruiting process should be one of the most carefully thought out of the entire organization, as should the evaluation of existing staff. This becomes especially important when a company decides it needs to downsize.

Letting large numbers of people go is inherently destructive, as discussed earlier, and letting unproductive staff go should be done continuously, individual by individual, rather than en masse. But what makes mass downsizing worse is how most organizations go about it. Senior executives in such situations typically behave like cowards and decide that they will cut 10 percent of all employees, across the board.

The builder's rule of thumb of "measure twice, cut once" is widely overlooked by corporations in their recruiting and retention policies, but is crucial to a successful organization.

They see this as being fair. But the difference between merely competent employees and the best employees is enormous. Accordingly, if management must downsize, it should go through a process of evaluating individual employees with an eye to keeping the best and most important people, even if this means that some divisions lose more people than others. Measure twice, cut once, because finding great people is the hardest—and most important—part of building an organization.

Continuous Training Replaces Job Security

Earlier I commented that knowledge is an asset that must be constantly built up, or it will erode rapidly. Knowledge workers know this, and are eager to stay current. Moreover, employers who recognize that the value of their people depends on how much relevant knowledge the employees have also know that continuous learning is crucial to the ability of their organization to compete. Herein lies a mutually beneficial common goal: employees want training, and companies need it.

Yet many companies are reluctant to invest heavily in training when the average employee may stay less than three years. Worse, they see money spent on training as a potential benefit for a competitor. But in being blinded this way, they're missing the forest for the trees: training not only helps make their people better, but works on several different levels to increase employees' loyalty.

First, since training costs money and increases the value of the employee, the employer is sending a powerful message, saying, in effect, "You're an important part of our future. That's why we want to invest in you." People want to feel needed, and investing in relevant training does that.

Then, too, appropriate training makes people more effective. Study after study has shown that people want to do well, to achieve, and go home at night feeling fulfilled. Giving people better intellectual tools and teaching them how to use them becomes a win-win relationship: the company benefits from having more productive employees. The knowledge worker benefits from being more effective, feeling better about himself, and improving his performance—and hence his chances for promotion.

Next, studies have shown that one of the main reasons why people leave organizations is that they dislike their working environment. A particular irritant is the perceived low quality of co-workers. Investments in training raise the level of all workers and increase the sense that you are working with serious, worthwhile people.[15]

Finally, training is replacing security as the trade-off for loyalty. Companies that offer training are saying, in effect, "You know we may have to let you go if the economy turns down, or the market changes, and we know that you may leave for a better job somewhere else. But if you work hard while you're with us, we can enhance your marketability by upgrading your skills." Indeed, Sumantra Ghoshal of the London Business School and Christopher Bartlett of the Harvard Business School believe that this is the implicit new formula between management and worker: loyalty in exchange for enhanced employability.[16]

To cap it all off, even if your people do walk out the door, training is still worth the money. In 1994 the electronics manufacturer Motorola, headquartered in Illinois, estimated that it netted a return of US$33 for every $1 it invested in training.[17]

Making your people more valuable, then, makes your company more valuable—and probably encourages your people to stay.

The Bottom Line

At the end of all the analysis, the single best way to attract the knowledge workers you need, to entice them to stay, and to get the most out of them can be reduced to a single word: respect.

On January 1, 2000, *The Wall Street Journal* published an interview with Peter Drucker, discussing many aspects of the future of business. What caught my eye were his comments about the way companies treat their people. Drucker teaches a Saturday-afternoon course in management, to which top companies from around the United States send some of their best people. At the time of the interview, his class had 78 students, all from upper-middle management, and this is what he had to say about them:

> *The companies don't send them to us unless they are the most successful, most promising people. And their bitterness about their management and their companies is unbelievable. They feel the financial people treat them like peons. What really offends them most is that the financial people think they can make them happy by bribing them [with high salaries and stock options]. . . . The answer is respect. . . . Look, who is the most successful in attracting and holding good people? The nonprofits. The satisfaction has to be greater than in business because there is no paycheck.*[18]

Money's important, don't get me wrong. But money is more often a reason why people leave than why they stay. You can insult people by paying them too little, but you can't normally handcuff them merely by paying them a lot. This sentiment is echoed by Michael O'Malley, of management consulting firm William Mercer, in an *Economist* article: "Although employees may leave for more money, non-monetary factors are often more important, says Michael O'Malley. . . . Companies that try to 'buy happiness' often end up with 'a deal culture where everything is for sale and everything can be bargained.'"[19]

So if respect is worth more than money, how do you produce it? Fundamentally, it means expecting people to produce valuable results, giving them the tools to do so, getting out of their way so they can get on

When management says, "Where you know best, you make the decisions. If you want our help, ask."—that's respect.

with it, listening to what they have to say when they're finished, implementing changes they recommend, and then recognizing their accomplishments. After all, if you hire them to do a job, you should let them get on and do it.

Earlier I talked about Ralph Stayer and Johnsonville Foods. As a result of his efforts to get his people to care about their work, Stayer transformed the company from one that merely hired people and used them, into one that was actually run by those same people while he acted more as a management consultant than a CEO. The Stayer family still owns the company, and as it's privately held, it's impossible to know just how well it's doing. But their website says "today Johnsonville Sausage is the [United States'] largest manufacturer of fresh sausage products including bratworst and Italian sausage."[20] Not rocket science, it's true, but not bad for a company that started as a butcher shop in 1945.

Johnsonville production-line employees perform the quality control on their products, answer customer complaints and give "make good" coupons where they believe warranted, analyze the production process and implement improvements, set employee performance standards, and can have fellow employees fired if they fail to perform up to peer-established standards. The compensation system is a base salary, plus performance bonuses that are set according to an employee-designed and -administered process. The human resources department has been eliminated, to be replaced by a learning and personal development team responsible for helping all employees upgrade their skills. The company has an educational allowance that individual workers can use as they see fit, whether the courses are relevant or not. Over time, though, more and more employees have used this allowance to concentrate on job-related skills.[21]

But the Johnsonville Foods formula was developed by them for their company. What worked for them might not work for you. The key factor in their success is not the final result, but that ownership allows—encourages—the changes to happen. Implicitly and explicitly, management says, "Where you know best what's going on, you make the decisions. If you want our help, ask." That's respect.

In his *Harvard Business Review* essay, Stayer said something that I think is key to the whole issue of optimizing the value of employees:

> *Helping human beings fulfill their potential is of course a moral respon-*
> *sibility, but it's also good business. Life is aspiration. Learning, striving*
> *people are happy people and good workers. They have initiative and*
> *imagination, and the companies they work for are rarely caught*
> *napping.*[22]

That's what most employers dream of for their knowledge workers, but are they willing to pay the price to get it? Compare what Stayer said about his employees with what Drucker said about the members of his Saturday class, then decide for yourself which system works better, and which is more expensive.

2

HR and the Human Cost of Change

Change is hard on organizations, but can be devastating to individuals who are thrown out of work. What will be particularly cruel in the years immediately ahead is that companies will be eager to find people with just the right skills at the same time that talented people who don't happen to have in-demand skills will be anxious for work. It's going to be a strange and uncomfortable world, with companies desperate for people and people desperate for jobs, yet no matchups between the two. Eventually this will produce a qualitative shift in the way companies think about and treat their employees. This shift is not yet in evidence, as the following vignette demonstrates.

Miriam is 37, the mother of two boys aged 12 and 15, and worried. She works at the Hamex Appliance Factory in Berthierville, Quebec, northeast of Montreal, assembling food processors. Hamex is a "white label" manufacturer: the small household appliances it produces are sold under the brand names of a variety of Canadian and American retailers.

Miriam is worried by rumours floating around that the plant is going to close and production moved to a new factory in Mexico, which would allow Hamex to export to the United States duty-free under the North American Free Trade Agreement (NAFTA). She doesn't have strong educational qualifications—only a basic high school diploma—and was lucky to get a job at the Hamex factory in her hometown after her divorce seven years ago. She has gradually worked her way up, while increasing her pay and getting regular performance bonuses for her steady work and low rate of defects. But she knows that there must be another mother in Mexico who is just as anxious to have her job, and who will make about a fifth of Miriam's wage. Even if Miriam were willing to accept wages that low, she couldn't live in Quebec on that little money.

This morning management is going to make an announcement— hence her anxiety as she drives into work. She parks her car and goes into the plant, finding the friends with whom she has shared coffee, games of gin rummy, and Friday evenings at the local tavern. They're all edgy and nervous—and their anxieties aren't soothed at all when the Hamex CEO walks into the plant and steps up onto a wooden box so everyone can see him.

"I'm very sorry to have to tell you that the plant is closing in four months," he begins—then stops as a loud murmur runs through the crowd, part angry, part sad. "My father built this business and this factory, and we've done everything we can to try and save it. But we can't. Our customers are telling us that we need to cut our prices substantially, or they'll take their business elsewhere. Their customers, the consumers who buy appliances, are comparison shopping, both in person and on the Internet, and our appliances are no longer the best buy."

"How about if we cut our wages?" one of the older workers yells.

"We looked at that," the CEO says, "and we were going to ask you to do that, and we were going to cut our own salaries by the same amount to show solidarity. But then Deal-Mart, our biggest client, came to us and told us that either we were going to have to cut our prices by 23 percent or they were going to buy offshore. There's no way we can cut wages by enough to produce that big a price drop."

"So what are you going to do?" the older man asks.

"In the short term, we're subcontracting our production to a factory in China, and . . . " There's another outburst, this time of surprise. "I know you all thought we were moving to Mexico. But China is cheaper. Even with higher tariffs into North America, China's much cheaper. So—reluctantly—we're closing the plant and starting production there. Eventually we'll build a new plant, a joint venture with a Chinese company.

"I'm sorry. You're not only my employees, but many of you are friends and all of you are family. The only alternatives we had were to move production to China or go out of business. We'll see that everyone is treated fairly. There'll be a severance package that is as generous as we can make it, and we've hired an outsourcing company to help you look for other work. Good luck, and God bless you all."

Now Miriam is really worried. She looks around, sees the same stunned looks on everyone's faces, and realizes that they are all going to be competitors for the few jobs available in this region for semi-skilled labour. How is she going to support her boys?

Although Miriam's story is fantasy, it's real in every important detail. So-called i-commerce—using the Internet to shop for price and features—has dramatically increased consumer knowledge and clout. Marketers are responding by cutting prices, so that the cost of consumer goods is in a downward spiral with no real end in sight. At the same time, globalization has created a world market for labour, so that unskilled, semi-skilled, and highly skilled workers alike are in competition with people around the world. When employees like Miriam are up against workers with comparable skills in Mexico or China—especially China—they're going to lose out because wage levels are much higher in Canada or any other developed country.

Of course, lower consumer prices mean a higher standard of living for all working Canadians because when things cost less, you're able to buy more of them. And, on balance, Canadians are better off as a result of global competition. But the rewards are not distributed equally, so there are going to be winners and losers in the process. Miriam and people like her will be losers unless they can get training that allows them to transform themselves from semi-skilled labour into some form of knowledge worker.

So, in terms of the future of business and its effects on the society in which we live, the important questions are: Why is this happening? What will it mean for our individual and collective futures? And what should we do about it, as individuals worried about our own employment prospects, and as companies worried about the ability to attract and retain the right workers?

Why Is This Happening, and Why Now?

Globalization—the trading of goods and services over global distances— has been emerging for hundreds of years. The Hudson's Bay Company, for instance, was formed in the 1600s for the express purpose of trading between North America and Europe. What is new about globalization is how important it has become to each of us, and the speed with which it is changing our lives.

When the Asian economic crisis developed in 1998, the economy of British Columbia went into recession because of its integration with the Pacific Rim countries. This is a clear-cut example of the importance of globalization to Canadians. Moreover, stories like Miriam's are happening all over the developed world, with lower-skilled workers being displaced by workers in poor countries who are paid much less for comparable work. Economically, there's no reason why these jobs should stay in Canada. We have no right to deprive workers in other countries of the jobs if they can perform as well but for less money. And there's no compelling reason why

We have no right to deprive workers in other countries of the jobs if they can perform as well but for less money.

Canadian consumers should pay more for the goods and services they buy in order to keep such jobs here. This would amount to a tax paid by the many to benefit the few.

North American companies have been putting a lot of energy into automating in recent years as a way of cutting costs and keeping factories open, to the point where Canada and the United States have surged into the lead in the deployment of robots in manufacturing.[1] Such efforts have generally been quite successful, and North American manufacturing output continues to grow from cycle to cycle. The increased automation, though, means that, even with the rise in output, North American factories need fewer people, and manufacturing employment is declining.

It's no longer just manufacturing and blue-collar workers who are experiencing this "creative destruction," to use economist Joseph Schumpeter's phrase. Architects in Mexico, for example, who make about one-quarter what American architects make, are competing for major projects, undercutting their American counterparts in price, and happy to be getting the work. Telemarketing and customer service for all kinds of industries are increasingly being done abroad, especially in India, where virtually every educated individual speaks English. In fact, some North American companies train Indian workers to speak with a North American accent, and the Internet allows them to keep current on such flourishes as local weather, sports teams, and news, so that they sound as if they work nearby.[2] Time differences mean that assignments calling for typing, data entry, and similar clerical skills can be transmitted over the Internet and performed overnight, so that when North American workers arrive at their desks the next morning, their notes from the previous day are ready.

Moreover, India specifically has become a hotbed for computer programming and software. India has the world's second-largest population, as well as an enormous number of well-educated people who speak English and are talented in math and science, so software is a logical industry. As a result, many multinational companies are moving software development to India, which means that programmers in North America are not getting that work.[3]

So globalization and the Internet don't just drive down the cost of appliances. They are also radically changing the future for skilled and professional people.

Then There's China . . .

The most important development in manufacturing and the global labour markets is the emergence of China as an economic powerhouse. China has been called the world's factory floor because of its vast working population. As China modernizes its economy, opens it up to global trade, and institutes free-market reforms, Chinese industry is bursting onto the world stage and disrupting the operations of almost every industry. At first, Chinese industry produced cheap, low-quality goods, much as Japan did in the early years of its industrialization. Now, however, with technology transfers from other countries, Chinese industry is rapidly developing the sophistication and quality control of a developed country. And with the vastness of China's population, many of whom have reasonable educations, plus its elite, who get world-class educations, China can provide workers at all levels. It has everything from cheap factory-floor workers to cutting-edge researchers who will lead the world in their specialties, especially in fields where developed countries have ethical or moral concerns, such as genetic engineering and stem-cell research.

Normally what happens with a rapidly industrializing country is that as more and more people go to work in new industries, the price of labour goes up. This is what happened in the so-called Asian-tiger economies such as Japan, South Korea, and Taiwan: wages gradually moved up towards rich-country levels, and the need grew for industries requiring more than just cheap labour. However, because China is so huge, labour remains cheap and plentiful even though national industries are booming.

As a result, virtually every multinational manufacturer in the world is either now producing in China, or has plans on the drawing board to do so. They have no choice, because they would otherwise find that their costs were higher than their competitors'; they would be priced out of the market and would eventually go bankrupt. Moreover, China is building modern, state-of-the-art factories, including the latest in automation where appropriate, so that North American companies will be competing head-to-head with Chinese companies that use similar technologies but pay their workers much lower wages.

What Does This Mean for Our Future?

Complete globalization—the eventual integration of individual national economies into a unified, worldwide marketplace—is something that will happen only once in history. Assuming that globalization continues, it will yield a one-time boost in economic activity that has the potential to allow every country in the world to experience rich-country standards of living. Not only will we be able to feed, clothe, and house every living human being, but we will be able to supply education and comfort to everyone as well. That doesn't mean it will happen that way. What does happen will depend in large part on the competence of governments, and on local and global politics.

Yet the progress of globalization is neither a smooth nor a sure thing. In the 1920s the world was largely headed towards exactly this kind of integration, and the globalization dividend that we are now experiencing should have happened 80 years ago. Instead, it was interrupted by one of the most damaging trade wars in history, which, along with incompetent fiscal and monetary policies, triggered the global Depression of the 1930s.

This could happen again if nations turn protectionist. Indeed, countries are responding to the declining employment in manufacturing in much the same way as they have responded to declining employment in agriculture: they are looking for ways to cheat on trade rules in order to protect domestic jobs, urged on by self-serving corporations, unions, and narrow-minded protectionists. In this they are joined by the anti-globalization movement, the protesters who oppose the forces of globalization. I'll have more to say on this subject in Chapter 12.

If This Is Exploitation, Bring It On!

One of the greatest criticisms of globalization is that the goodies are not shared equally, that the rich gorge and the poor don't even get crumbs. The anti-globalists complain that jobs are destroyed here while workers in poor countries are exploited to line the pockets of the already obscenely rich. Meanwhile, the argument goes, corrupt multinationals, intent on nothing but profit, create an environment where governments compete with each other to embrace the lowest possible standards so that they can attract or retain industries and jobs—the so-called race to the bottom. All of these are either half-truths or just flat wrong.

It is undoubtedly true that the wealth created through increased trade is lumpy, that it is not shared out equally. And it is true, as I said before, that there are clear winners and losers. Yet the overall result is that entire societies and national economies win, and that the vast majority of people in participating countries, including Canada, win as well. Moreover, anything else is worse, not better.

This can best be seen in countries where the changes are most dramatic: the poor countries that become less poor through trade. A recent study by the World Bank examined the differences between poor countries that embrace globalization and trade and those who resist it. The results are unequivocal: of 24 countries that opened their national economies to trade and international competition, all of them saw increases in the quality of life of their people. The three billion people from these countries saw a 5-percent annual growth rate in their per-capita income through the 1990s, compared with 2 percent for rich countries. This was a significant increase in growth from the 1960s, when these same poor economies grew at an average of about 1 percent a year. As a result of higher incomes, these countries experienced increased life expectancy, decreased infant mortality, and higher education levels for their children. If this is exploitation, bring it on.

Then there are the two billion people in poor countries that avoided globalization in the same period, attempting to isolate and protect their economies from foreign competition. As a group, they experienced a decline in economic activity and income per person, and their education levels lagged behind their more globally oriented counterparts. Clearly globalization works in favour of poor countries.[4]

As for the race to the bottom that some fear, meaning the deteriorating standards in health, welfare, and environmental standards, it ain't necessarily so. In 1998, for example, a *Globe and Mail* editorial noted that the Organisation for Economic Co-operation and Development (OECD) had found that those poor countries that became a part of the global economy usually had stronger unions, better wages, higher labour standards, and tougher laws against practices such as the use of child labour than those that kept their borders shut to trade. "Why do standards rise instead of fall when countries trade?" the paper asked. "Partly because better-off, more aware citizens demand it. Partly because trade brings in the money to pay for it. And partly because of that much-maligned animal, the transnational corporation."[5] On this last point, Turkey's experiences are typical. The wages paid by multinational companies in 1999 were 124 percent higher than the Turkish national average, and the number of people employed in such companies expanded by 11.5 percent a year, compared with less than 1 percent a year for domestic companies.[6] Who's exploiting whom?

What about Disappearing Jobs Here?

So if globalization is good for poor countries, doesn't that mean it comes at the expense of rich countries? Aren't we suffering from the migration of jobs from Canada to China, say? No, because trade is a positive-sum game:

it's possible for all countries to win. Poor countries win because they get new jobs that pay more, and their economies expand. Rich countries win because we get rid of low-paying jobs with little chance for advancement, and our economies develop new, higher-paying jobs with more opportunity. Statistics Canada was quoted in 1998 as saying that new job creation in the Canadian economy "has been in industries and occupations that tend to pay higher-than-average weekly wages, while the major employment losses tend to be concentrated in low-paying industries and occupations."[7]

And yet higher standards of living and better jobs come at a price. First, there are people like Miriam who are unlikely to find another steady job that pays as much. If she doesn't retrain and find a new profession that involves more sophisticated work that can't be done more cheaply by a counterpart in a poor country, she will probably never find steady employment again. And since most unionized labour is in blue-collar industries, especially manufacturing, unions tend as a group to be opposed to globalization; it's their members' jobs (and the unions' existence) that are threatened.

The second cost is uncertainty. What we have lost is the employment-for-life guarantee of earlier generations, where if you were loyal, worked hard, and kept your nose clean, the company took care of you before and after retirement. Today, employment is a transient thing, and uncertainty affects everyone. For instance, the average job tenure for American men aged 35 and over has been decreasing steadily since 1983, and the average 32-year-old American has already had nine different jobs.[8]

Moreover, the fastest-growing segment of the employment market is made up of temporary workers, also called the contingent labour force. Once again, let's look south as a leading indicator of what's going to happen here. Even in the palmiest, high-tech days of the late 1990s, California, home of Silicon Valley and the epicentre of the high-tech boom, experienced more growth in temp jobs than any other industry. In fact, the temp industry in California added as many jobs as the software and electronic-equipment industries combined.[9] In 2001, the staffing services

No one, including governments, can protect you or your company from change.

company Manpower Inc. was the largest employer in the United States, and the number of temp workers in the U.S. now exceeds the number of workers in the manufacture of automobiles and aircraft combined.[10]

The reason for this dramatic increase in temporary employment is that it gives companies flexibility that they don't have with employees: it's easy to fire temps. According to David Autor, an economist at the Massachusetts Institute of Technology (MIT), efforts to create legislative safeguards "to protect workers against unjust dismissal have fostered the growth of jobs that offer less job security and lower pay."[11] Attempting to protect jobs, whether from foreign competition or rapid change, in fact destroys them. No one, including governments, can protect you or your company from change.

So what can and should we do instead?

Where Will This Lead Us?

Earlier I said we would witness a qualitative shift in the way companies and workers interact with each other. This will come because companies need good people more than they need specific skills, especially since good people can learn new skills. Accordingly, companies, out of their own selfish interests, will strain to find ways to hold onto their carefully recruited, intensively trained people by means that would seem almost bizarre today:

Alana finishes up an order for a custom-made sofa, giving the final details to Cyrano, her computer butler, then instructing him to send off appropriate files to the customer, manufacturer, and accounting. Once she's done that, she checks for messages, and finds one from her boss, Helen, who says she needs to see Alana as soon as possible. Alana asks Cyrano to check with Helen's computer butler. He reports

back that Helen is free right now, so Alana gets up from her desk and walks over to Helen's office.

Helen asks Alana to close the door, then comes straight to the point: Alana's job is going to be phased out over the next 12 months. Helen is quick to assure Alana that there's nothing wrong with her work. "Our software has become so sophisticated," Helen explains, "in part because of you, that it can now be used by clerical workers in India to perform the customer service and support function that you've done up until now."

Alana looks thoughtful, then comments that she thinks that would be a mistake, that much of what she really does is to understand the customers' concerns and provide hand-holding and troubleshooting when problems arise. Then she shrugs and asks Helen what job management has in mind for her. Helen looks uncomfortable and says there's no immediate prospect of another job at the company, which is why she wants to chat. She calls up Alana's work profile, which is excellent, along with her battery of psychological test results and profiles, and the two women start reviewing how Alana has developed as an employee. Alana is proud of her advancement, and not especially worried. If Hamex Home Supply can't use her, she is known well enough in the industry that she won't have any problem finding another job, although she'd prefer to stay here.

She and Helen look over a computer-generated organizational chart of Hamex, based on the actual activities of its employees, both here in Quebec, and in Tennessee, China, and India. Alana asks Helen if she could have a few days to consider her options and come back with a proposal for a new job. Helen looks relieved and immediately agrees, because that's what she had hoped Alana would say.

Three days later, Alana comes back with a new job proposal to work as a troubleshooter between customer service and manufacturing. She shows Helen her analysis of the customer complaints and employee feedback on Hamex's operations over the past 24 months, and shows that there are some cultural differences between the two groups of employees. In fact, Alana suggests that, if her first insights prove correct, she might be able to come up with a "best practices" process patent that could be sold to other companies. Helen works through Alana's analysis, sees the friction point Alana has identified in the company's operating flow, and agrees that this is worth pursuing. She says she'll forward it to the management committee, which is composed of other employees, with her endorsement.

Management committee approves a 12-month trial, with one condition. The committee notes that Alana's proposed new job requires knowledge of manufacturing techniques and statistical quality control. While Alana has qualifications in this area, they are 12 years old and not as complete as the committee would like. The committee asks her to take an online, just-in-time course in conjunction with her work. The company will pay for the course, with the proviso that if she chooses to leave Hamex before the end of the 12-month experiment, she will pay a pro-rated portion of the course cost. The committee also notes her identification of a possible process patent, and stipulates for the record that she is the originator of the idea. Since Hamex will be paying her a salary to do the work on this patent, she and the company will share any net royalties 50:50, after recovering marketing and legal costs, which the company will front. Since these provisions all seem reasonable, Alana accepts—and has a new job.

This vignette reflects how employer–employee relationships will evolve within the next 20 years. Jobs will appear and disappear with changes in management philosophy and the marketplace, and with the emergence of new technologies and new sources of labour. However, employees will be asked to move to different jobs, or even help invent new ones of value to the company rather than being dismissed when their jobs become unnecessary. Good, versatile people are too valuable to discard merely because the work they are currently doing is no longer needed. As a result, human resource departments will offer employees a range of analytical tools to assess their own capabilities, the company's operations, and the needs of the marketplace. With these tools, plus their familiarity with the company's market and customers, knowledge workers will be in a position to apply their expertise to identify new opportunities.

Meanwhile, the company will be saved the costs of laying people off and hiring new ones. In the second vignette, Hamex did not have to pay severance to Alana, saved the cost of recruiting a new person, will improve production and decrease defects, and might wind up with a new source of revenue through a patent. Most importantly, both Alana and the company have deepened their relationship and further fostered their loyalty to each other. It doesn't always work this way: sometimes employees can't come up with a credible new job and are laid off. But they are almost always given the opportunity to find new work of value to both parties and provided with whatever help the company can give to make it successful. Hamex employees appreciate this, and jobs with Hamex are sought after, giving the company an advantage in hiring high-quality people at all levels.

Some background qualities of this future world need further elaboration, because they reflect where we are going and how we need to get there:

1. Training is going to be a constant in the future. Everyone will continually seek to upgrade their skills and abilities, and employers will encourage them to do so. Most of the cost of training will be borne by employers, but they may require employees to pay part of the cost, particularly if the employee leaves shortly after finishing a course. If employees stay, then the company will more than recoup the costs of training through increased productivity and employee satisfaction and loyalty.

2. More and more of the training will be computer-assisted and take place just in time. There will be no need to transport people to distant locations, which ties up valuable staff and trainers for days on end. Instead, much of the necessary learning will take place through

computers, and include person-to-person contact via Internet-based video-conferencing and online chat groups with trainers and peers. Moreover, this kind of learning means that retention and comprehension will rise dramatically, because people will have immediate opportunities to apply skills as they learn them.

3. Computers and automation are affecting the job market in surprising ways. Routine physical and clerical work is being rapidly automated, displacing the workers who used to push paper or do repetitive jobs. Yet this also implies that non-routine work that can't be done by computers or robots is becoming more important. Most of this work has to do with human interactions, such as customer service and support, leading and managing teams, and communicating within and between companies. The IT revolution is making people skills ever more important—which means that it becomes ever more important for people who want to stay employed to develop such skills.

4. Employees in developed countries will need to become more agile mentally in order to help companies define their collective future. At present this is a job almost exclusively reserved for management, but front-line workers often see and understand more of what's going on in their areas than management does. Accordingly, companies will need to find ways of harnessing and encouraging the specific insights of their people, rather than assuming that all original or strategic thought comes only from the top.

5. Finally, workers will need to take more responsibility for planning their own careers, whether they expect to stay within a company or jump to other employers. This means that individuals will also need to make sure they have skill sets that are current and valuable, and that they are learning new things of value to potential employers.

The Film-Production Model

The way work is done in the future will often resemble the way a feature film is produced today. A person or group of people, either within a company or freelancers working on their own, will have a concept for a project. This person or group will line up backing for the idea and arrange financing for it by projecting the rates of return and supporting the projections with detailed analysis. Once they have the necessary backing, the project's producers will recruit the talent they need, including stars, camera operators, carpenters, caterers, and so on, or they will delegate the responsibility for recruitment. Then they'll produce the product or service, market the hell out of it, have a wrap party, and move on to the next project, assembling a new team and starting all over again.

There are two fundamental ways that companies can adapt to this model. The first way is to assemble contract or temporary workers on an ad hoc basis for each project and hope that they can find the specific talents that they need each time. This gives the highest degree of flexibility, but also means that they may not be able to get just the right people, and may have to pay up if they want specific individuals.

The second way is to develop what might be thought of as a repertory company, assembling a cast of actors that keep changing roles as the company moves from production to production. Then, as the demands of the marketplace change, people adapt to new roles and learn new things that enable them to fill these roles.

The most likely result will be a combination of these two: each company will have a core of long-term, key employees, complemented by contract workers for specific bit parts. But companies that don't find a structure that allows them both flexibility and the ability to hang onto their best talent will lose market share.

What about the People Who Aren't Talented?

Whenever I talk to an audience about the future of work, someone always comes up afterwards and asks what's going to happen to the people who don't have the ability to cope with this kind of quicksilver workplace. I usually make them very uncomfortable by saying, "What you're really asking is: What about the dummies?" They deny that that's what they mean, but that's the nub of it.

My reply to this indelicate question is that the vast majority of people are much more capable than we normally believe. Moreover, there are more kinds of abilities than the classic academic/intellectual abilities that our schools educate for and grade. I recall that when I was in high school, I was always top of my class in math, while my friend Wayne fell more into the "dog ate my homework" category. Yet when we worked on cars in shop class, I was the dummy and he was the genius.

The world of tomorrow will require people who have creativity and the ability to innovate. It won't necessarily require the kind of academic brilliance that gets kids an A in trigonometry. Moreover, companies will have a vested interest in seeing their people develop their skills and then helping them to exploit their abilities. Further, our society has an even greater need to help all citizens find what they are best at, and to assist them in pursuing a career through those abilities. This is why education, for both children and adults, is going to be the crucial strategic activity for all countries and all societies in tomorrow's world. Countries that do a good job of helping their people identify and exploit their own talents will become rich and will have the ability to provide assistance to those who have difficulty. Countries that do a bad job or persist in applying rote learning like a coat of paint in assembly-line school systems, without taking account of the needs and unique abilities of each individual, will get progressively poorer over time. Eventually, they'll become too poor to be able to help the rapidly growing number of chronically unemployed.

For at the end of the day, there are going to be people who cannot find or hold onto jobs. There will be people—as already happens in Europe because of its rigid employment laws—who have no hope of employment, because they have no skills worth enough to pay for their lifestyle in a rich country. These people could easily become a burden on themselves and on society. How many of them there are in our country, and what proportion of our society they form, will determine Canada's place in tomorrow's world.

Countries that persist in applying rote learning like a coat of paint in assembly-line schools will slide into poverty.

I don't like this conclusion, and people often get angry with me for voicing it, as if I were to blame for letting it happening. But it's the truth, and we ignore it at our individual and collective peril.

But helping people find and exploit their talents is only the first secret. The second deals with the mindset of the organization that will lead to either success or failure in tomorrow's world.

Demolish the Status Quo

"Business success contains the seeds of its own destruction. . . . When the curve shifts and a different set of skills are needed, the past selection process has gotten you a management that is not in tune with the new one."

—ANDY GROVE, CHAIR AND CO-FOUNDER OF INTEL CORPORATION

3

The Opposite of "Smart" Is Not "Dumb"

Companies are in danger.

Far from being the threatening multinational monsters that the anti-globalists love to hate, big corporations are vanishing with increasing rapidity, and their clout is diminishing. By 1983, one-third of the Fortune 500 companies listed in 1970 had disappeared, whether through bankruptcy, merger, or acquisition.[1] A later repeat of this study showed that only 40 percent of the Fortune 500 companies listed in 1980 still existed as separate entities in 1995.[2] In the 10 years from 1989 to 1999, the worldwide market share of the top five companies in each of the computer hardware, software, and long-distance telephony industries slipped by 15 to 30 percent.[3] In 1970 the top three automakers and the top three television networks in the United States collectively owned approximately 90 percent of their respective markets. By 2001, their market share had dropped to about 50 percent.[4]

What of the steady drumbeat of mergers, signalling the creation of ever-bigger behemoths to squeeze money out of workers and consumers? According to *The Wall Street Journal*, the biggest mergers in history occurred in the decade of the 1990s, but took place in distribution industries such as oil, telecommunications, and financial services, whose products had become commodities and whose margins were under pressure. These mergers "signaled erosion rather than accretion of economic power."[5] Moreover, a broad range of studies dating as far back as the 1890s indicates that mergers rarely improve corporate efficiency or profitability, even in situations where they result in near-monopolies.[6] The power that companies seek through mergers usually eludes them.

I believe that corporations today are feeling threatened by a rapidly changing world, and that mergers are a knee-jerk attempt to bulk up in response. I also believe such efforts are misguided and largely doomed to failure. Instead of trying to get *bigger,* companies should be trying to get *smarter,* which is a more difficult, but less expensive and more rewarding, process. To put it bluntly, size doesn't matter like it used to.

Why is this happening? What's leaching power away from big organizations, and where is it going? What are the implications for the way an organization is run, for the leaders chosen to run them, and for the people who work in them? Let's start by discussing where power is migrating and defining what "smart" means.

Where Has All the Power Gone?

Mao Tse-tung once said that power grows from the barrel of a gun. I used to believe that power grows from the barrel of a television camera. Both statements are true, but neither is complete. Implicit in them is that power is drawn from the people, which has been a truism in government since the days of the European philosophers whose ideas helped spark the American Revolution. However, modern technology is shifting the locus of that power, so that it no longer needs to be collected and exercised through institutions. It now flows directly to individuals because people can now communicate directly with each other and the world, and knowledge is more accessible than ever before.

The effects of this on business are direct and forceful. Nike, Inc., was considered one of the world's best marketers. The quality of its shoes was good, but the quality of its marketing was legendary. It had muscle, clout, and market share. Then it was blindsided by protesters who tarred Nike with exploiting sweatshop labourers in developing countries. This would puzzle any traditional marketer: where, in the feature-benefit equation of North American footwear, does the welfare of developing-world labourers fit?

The answer lies in who holds power. When communications media are scarce and expensive, then advertisers control the channels and the message is what the marketers want it to be. When there is an explosion of channels, communications media become cheap and anyone can exploit them. At that point, a company like Nike isn't just competing with other companies that make shoes, but with anyone and everyone who has something to say. The treatment of developing-world labourers becomes more important than having Michael Jordan's silhouette on the side of your sneakers.

Next there's the rise of i-commerce, using the Internet to research competing products before buying anything through traditional channels. As we saw in the last chapter, i-commerce has made it simpler for customers to compare your offerings with those of your competitors. The net result is that customers are more critical; less forgiving; more demanding on price, quality, and service; and more powerful than they were.

Does this mean that the ants can always defeat the elephants? No, it doesn't, but it has levelled the playing field enormously, and it does mean that the elephants have to be much more wary about what they do. It also means that, with more competition for the hearts and minds (and wallets) of the general public, it's harder for any company to get its message across in the way it wants.

Of course, as consumers take to the Internet to criticize and complain about service flaws, poor products, abusive labour policies, and generally to vilify companies, companies are fighting back with lawsuits on issues of slander or copyright and trademark infringement. But if you start on the defensive by threatening people who call you a bad guy, it's an uphill battle to persuade the public to buy from you.

Losing control over the channels of communication and the access to knowledge and information isn't the only way companies are losing power. The pace of change is accelerating, increasing the number of decisions you need to make every year. Even if you manage, through superhuman efforts, to make the same percentage of good decisions, you will still end up making a growing number of bad decisions. This means there are more opportunities for competitors to steal your customers, further diluting your market clout.

I'll have more to say about communications and the speed of change later on, but for the future of business, the implications are clear. It's harder and harder to defend a significant market position. Control is largely gone, and the ability to influence markets and consumers is being diluted. Power is migrating from big organizations, including governments, and being dispersed to individuals. This means that being big may still have advantages, but being smart is better.

What Do I Mean by "Smart"?

Big companies have resources that small companies cannot match, so it would be easy to conclude that "smart" implies big. That's a mistake. Meanwhile, most of the job creation of the past 20 years has come from small companies, and even multinationals seek to imitate their agility. From such observations it would be easy to conclude that "smart" means small. That, too, is a mistake.

"Smart" in the context of the future of business means being clear about who you are, what you believe, and what your abilities are; being more sensitive to changes in your defined market, and able to adapt to shifts in customer needs and expectations faster and more effectively than your competitors. In a word, it means choosing to *respond* to change, rather than *react* to it. Reacting implies being unprepared, caught by surprise, and producing inferior results. Responding implies having anticipated problems and being prepared not only to cope with them but to exploit them. Reacting is like driving a car while keeping your eyes fixed on the rear-view mirror. Responding means driving with your eyes trained far down the highway, after you've consulted a map and created a plan for the trip.

Which brings us into the realm of vision. Vision has fallen into disrepute of late, in large part because the excesses of the 1990s stock market led people to the conclusion that visions are fantasies and what's really needed is hard-headed thinking by tough-minded managers without regard to such fuzzy concepts as "vision." That's blaming the victim for the crime. I would argue that the excesses of the stock-market bubble were the result not of too much vision but of too little vision and too much wishful thinking.

The telecommunications companies' belief that any investment in optical fibre would be justified, regardless of cost or market demand, is perhaps the most dramatic example of wishful thinking masquerading as vision, and has led to an overcapacity that won't be soaked up for years, possibly decades. Some companies, such as Bell Canada and CanWest Global Communications, had similar fantasies about "convergence," thinking that by overpaying for old assets in mature industries such as publishing and broadcasting, and bolting them onto "new media" enterprises, they could create new empires with mystical synergies that would somehow turn "old" into "gold." Then there were the Internet companies, this generation's prize lemmings, who believed their own news releases and led millions into financial suicide by proclaiming that business plans were bunk and profits were pointless. These are all examples of delusions, not vision, and at the time I commented that these companies would wind up in tears.[7]

But, other than saying "I told you so" (which is always gratifying), my point is that vision is not a warm and fuzzy toy used by management consultants to entertain the troops on corporate retreats. Vision, planning, and preparation for the future are crucial arts for companies who want to own tomorrow. Vision is a necessary tool to becoming future-smart.

In 1991, two graduate students, James Collins and Jerry Porras, wrote a paper, "Organizational Vision and Visionary Organizations," for Stanford University's Graduate School of Business. In it, they asked 170 American

CEOs to identify the companies they thought were most visionary. Collins and Porras then ran an experiment in which they calculated what would have happened if they had invested $1 in each of these companies, starting in the 1920s. If a company didn't exist that far back,

The stocks of visionary companies outperformed the Wall Street averages by a factor of 50:1.

they invested the dollar in a savings account until the year it came into existence, and then invested the accumulated proceeds in the company. This portfolio of visionary companies outperformed the Wall Street averages by a factor of 50:1.[8]

Collins and Porras performed a follow-up study to determine what it is that makes some companies more successful than comparable competitors over the long term. Between 1988 and 1994, the two men asked 700 American CEOs to name the firms they most admired, and culled a list of 18 visionary companies from the replies. With two exceptions—Sony and Wal-Mart—all of these companies had been in existence for more than 60 years, almost 50 percent longer than the average large American company of that period. They compared these 18 companies with competitors in the same markets and of comparable age, and, to their surprise, found that the visionary companies did not concentrate on maximizing shareholder value, profits, or earnings per share, but focused instead on awareness of their community or environment, and had a strong sense of their identity, of who they were and what their purpose was.[9]

Their work was studied by Arie de Geus, a futurist who worked for the Royal Dutch/Shell Group, and who produced a study for Shell about what differentiates companies that survive over the long haul from those that fail. His comments on the work of Collins and Porras were succinct: "Visionary companies display a powerful drive for progress that enables them to change and adapt without compromising their cherished core ideals."[10] I'll have quite a bit more to say about the practical use of vision, planning, and preparation in Chapter 13, towards the end of the book. But vision is only a tool in the hands of smart companies. This leaves the central question still up for grabs: What is "smart"?

The Opposite of "Smart"

Let me start by saying that the opposite of "smart" is not "dumb." Being dumb is usually fatal for a company, it's true, but the proper antonym for "smart" in business is "lazy." And let me be clear that when I say "lazy," I mean intellectually and emotionally lazy. Many lazy executives work long hours but don't try to find better ways of doing things. They just put their heads down and do what they've been doing, or what's simplest, even if it takes years of hard work. Moreover, they rule with their egos, not their intellects. They'd rather be the top executives of a less effective company, and hold onto the status, perks, and privileges of being the big dog, than let power settle where it can be used to best effect and relinquish some of their supremacy.

Take the Internet companies that sucked in billions of what was effectively free money from gullible investors. Most of the people who started these companies were intelligent human beings with superior talents and skills in their areas of expertise. Had they taken the time and trouble to think about what they were going to do with the money, had they studied the lessons of the past and figured out what they didn't know and found ways of compensating for their shortcomings, and had they spent investors' money cautiously, many of them might have made their glittering dreams come true. *If they had worked at using the money well instead of just going along for the ride, they might have succeeded!* Failure is easy. Success is hard. The difference is whether you're lazy or not.

Let me tell you about the experiences of one of my clients, because what happened in that case clarified the issue for me. There were two men—call them Daniel and John—who started a chain of Canadian health and personal fitness clubs in the 1970s. When they started, most clubs were pretty shady operations and the industry had a decidedly gamy reputation. Companies were formed, collected multi-year membership fees up front, and then vanished, leaving investors and members with nothing but bitterness and disillusionment. Or individuals bought memberships, used them for a couple of weeks, lost interest, and didn't come back.

Daniel and John entered this unsavoury industry with a vision of creating clubs that would give people full value for their money by treating them well and helping them succeed with their fitness resolutions. The two partners studied what members wanted: clean facilities, modern equipment, and friendly employees who would help them set and meet reasonable goals. Daniel and John also studied the specific needs of the local neighbourhoods where their clubs were being established and provided for those needs, whether they had an interest in tennis and swimming or a need for daycare or sports medicine.

But more than anything else, Daniel and John focused on the employees who made the clubs pleasant places to work out. They studied how successful companies coached and supported their employees and how they built customer loyalty and satisfaction. They brought in management trainers for their supervisors and held seminars on every conceivable subject that could help their people give superb service to their customers. They gave recognition awards and banquets for their employees and listened to their suggestions about how to improve the clubs. The two men were brilliant leaders, but they always said that the strength of their organization was the culture of excellence that they and their people created.

They were approached several times by large organizations that wanted to acquire their chain of clubs, and always turned such offers down. In particular, they were approached by a large, publicly traded company with a questionable reputation. The first time, they turned the approach down flat. Later, in the mid-1990s, there was a change in ownership and management of this large company, and the new CEO approached them again, this time telling them that it wasn't just the chain of clubs the company wanted to buy. The company wanted Daniel and John to do for this North American giant what they had done for their small Canadian chain. The CEO was dead earnest and offered them the one thing they had never had before: scope. Daniel and John had always struggled with a lack of investment capital and had never been able to extend their vision into a large organization. This was their opportunity to try their ideas out on a large scale. The temptations, both financial and professional, were irresistible.

Five years later both men left the firm, disillusioned. Both are financially secure and will never have to work another day in their lives, but their bigger dreams remain unfulfilled. The large company paid lip service to the desire to change, but wasn't willing to do the work necessary to make it happen. Senior management always said the right things, and encouraged Daniel and John to work with other people in the company, but those at the top weren't willing to change their attitudes, trust the judgment of their employees, or learn new, more team-oriented behaviour.

The key principle that top management didn't grasp was that you have to treat your people fairly and well, and as peers, not peons, because employees are the ones who deliver results. Management produced all the trappings of caring: the contests, the recognition ceremonies, the seminars, and so on. But they didn't listen to their employees; they didn't return phone calls from them; and they didn't look for opportunities to encourage, support, and recognize excellence. They viewed it all as rah-rah sales propaganda, good for revving up the troops but not something they needed to bestir themselves about.

In short, they paid good money to acquire the two best team coaches in their industry and then were too complacent to be part of the team themselves. It didn't matter that Daniel and John were able to produce a member renewal rate of close to 65 percent in their original Canadian operations compared with an industry average of about 30 percent, keep their employees more interested and engaged, and produce higher profit margins than the larger company. Although the senior executives worked long hours, they were mentally and emotionally flabby and as a result they lost both men after Daniel and John's initial contracts were up. Along with the pair, they lost the chance to dominate a fragmented industry with enormous potential at a time when the baby boomers were beating a path to the health and fitness market. Their laziness probably cost them billions of dollars in profits and stock value.

This story is repeated every day in contemporary businesses. We're all fundamentally lazy because it's easier to keep doing things the way we've done them in the past than to take the time and effort to learn or invent new ways. Deep down, managers usually know what needs to be done, but it's easier and serves our vanity better to just slide along doing things the same old way than reinvent the company.

We're all fundamentally lazy because it's easier to keep doing things the way we've done them in the past than to take the time and effort to learn or invent new ways.

A smart company, therefore, is one that does everything it can to maximize its most important assets, the brains and abilities of its people, as described earlier. Smart companies hire differently, are organized differently, have different reporting lines, and treat people differently than the average company in today's marketplace, precisely to maximize their employees' contributions. Since every company is different, you can't do this by applying someone else's blueprint. Instead, like Ralph Stayer of Johnsonville Foods, you'll have to invent a structure and a worker–management style that works for your people, your vision, your shared values, and your company.

So for you to take ownership of the future, you could start by demolishing the status quo of your management structure. In too many cases it's an obsolete system—the Prussian General Staff model—that's more than a century old and is keeping you chained to the past. To cling to this model because it's familiar and comfortable is to waste at least part of your organization's most important resource, and to give up a crucial competitive advantage in a business world that is unforgiving.

The opposite of "smart" is "lazy," because laziness causes companies to minimize their intelligence. Lazy companies *choose* to be dumb, and in today's world that's dangerous. In tomorrow's world it will be fatal.

That's only part of the status quo that needs to be changed. Beyond the way that companies are organized and managed, the way that they identify and interact with their prospects and clients is changing radically as well. The status quo of marketing and sales operations is changing, and you can choose to lead or fall behind.

4

Assassin Marketing and Jigsaw Sales

My left foot is slightly longer than my right, which means that I sometimes find that one shoe of a new pair doesn't fit properly. I can't get the 0.5-percent low-fat milk here in Canada that I prefer and sometimes get in the States. The last VCR I bought for my family was vastly more complicated to program than the one it replaced, which drove us all crazy. When I go into a store to look for something, I'm approached by a clerk who says "May I help you?" but really means "Of the things we have in stock, what can I sell you?" When I call technical support for my Internet service provider, I usually wind up listening to a recording telling me that "Your call is very important to us" when I know that's a lie.

All of us go through life without thinking twice about buying and using products and services that don't quite fit or aren't quite what we want. We've been conditioned by a lifetime of mass production to accept things that are almost right or to settle for what's available. We literally can't buy anything that's exactly what we want because it's not there on the shelf, so we take what we can get.

Before mass production, when we bought something it was probably made specifically for us. We were served by the owner of the local store, who knew us by name, knew our parents and children and their likes and dislikes, knew what we'd bought in the past, and ordered in something that he knew we'd like.

The reason why we came to accept mass-produced, take-it-or-leave-it goods instead of things made specifically for us, of course, is that they were much cheaper and generally of much higher quality. And mass production changed the entire structure and approach of business. The uniformity of mass-produced goods led to the creation of brands and brand names. After all, part of the appeal of a brand was its guarantee of consistent quality and price. We built our marketing around this uniformity, using broadcast advertising to convince people that what we made was what they wanted. And factories churned out products to feed the inventories of the stores and merchants who sold their goods, with no idea about the identity of the final purchasers of their products. There was a complete divorce between producer and consumer. They never encountered each other except through the one-way messages of advertising.

But the era of accepting not-quite-right goods and services and all that goes with them is coming to an end. Mass production, the creation of identical goods and services through the 18th-century technology of the Industrial Revolution, is gradually being replaced by mass customization, the creation of individually tailored offerings at a price competitive with or even lower than that of mass-produced goods. Mass customization is being fostered by the enormous flexibility that computers and modern manufacturing are creating.

In 2002, Procter & Gamble, one of the acknowledged masters of mass-market consumer goods, created a new brand for mass-customized beauty products sold exclusively over the Internet. Whereas a well-stocked department store carries perhaps 15 items from a particular supplier, the Reflect.com website

The era of accepting not-quite-right goods and services and all that goes with them is coming to an end.

allows the customer to specify thousands of individual choices in skin care, shampoo, cosmetic products, and related goods; P&G manufactures the items to order. "One-of-a-kind products for a one-of-a-kind you," croons the website.[1]

Lands' End, a catalogue retailer, now offers a "virtual model" on its very successful website. You specify the size of various parts of your body (after measuring them), and the company's computer creates a male or female image of a body shaped like yours, then displays the items of clothing you are interested in on that model so you can see what they would look like on you. Furthermore, Lands' End now sells custom-tailored slacks and jeans, cut and sewn to your measurements, so that you don't have to settle for pants that are almost right.

All of the major automobile manufacturers have build-to-order (BTO) projects under way. The tide of BTO cars is rising, and the time lapse from order to delivery is falling. Although fewer than 7 percent of North American cars are built to order, that number rises to 19 percent for Europe, and is much higher in some individual countries. In Germany, the figure approaches 60 percent. In Britain, the number of BTO cars more than tripled from about 10 percent in 1992 to almost 32 percent in 1999.[2]

Consumers are starting to pick up on customization. In a *Toronto Star* article titled "Mine Alone," fashion editor Bernadette Morra reported: "The most compliments I've ever received on a piece of clothing have been for a Roots T-shirt airbrushed with my name across the front. . . . it continues to get more reaction than designer clothes I have that cost more than 10 times as much. . . . 'We're definitely into personalization at Roots,' [Roots Canada spokesperson Raymond] Perkins says."[3] As the market adapts to customization, consumers develop a taste for it, which will prod marketers to pursue it.

Moreover, mass customization may allow producers not only to please their customers but to save money while doing so. Toyota Motor Company invented and largely perfected the art of "just-in-time," or small-batch, manufacturing, primarily because the company couldn't afford to have large piles of inventory sitting around, eating up working capital. But in order to have a just-in-time system work properly, the company had to cut down on flaws in the manufacturing process, which meant that the quality of its cars went up. So, by having parts delivered to the assembly line at just the right time, it was able to dramatically reduce its parts inventory and decrease its cost of manufacturing while simultaneously increasing customer satisfaction.

Dell Computer Corporation is the poster child for this process, and has been the subject of intensive study and many admiring media reports. The Texas-based company sells desktop and laptop computers either over the phone (toll-free) or through the Internet. Purchasers specify exactly what they want in a computer—how big the hard drive, how much RAM, what speed processor, what kind of monitor, and so on—and then pay by credit card. Dell inserts the customized orders into its manufacturing queue and tells the customer when to expect delivery—typically a few days hence. Moreover, customers can log onto the Dell website and track where their computers are in the process, right up to the moment of delivery to their door.

Dell takes payment from retail customers when the individual computers are shipped, typically within a week after the computer parts are ordered from the company's suppliers, who are paid 45 days after the order.[4] As a result Dell actually generates working capital with each order: the more orders it gets, the more cash it has sitting in the bank earning interest, and with no inventories of parts or finished goods sitting around. This exceptionally lean manufacturing process allows the company to undercut competitors' prices and still deliver exactly what the customer wants. By comparison, Dell's competitors, notably Compaq Computer Corporation (now owned by Hewlett-Packard), have been manufacturing in the traditional way—making what seems to be selling through the stores that carry their products. This means that their customers have had to settle for what's on the shelf (although they can walk out of the store with it immediately), and Compaq has to tie up working capital financing inventories. Done properly, then, mass customization allows the producer to deliver precisely what the customer wants, and to cut costs at the same time. It's a powerful force, and one that is revolutionizing industries around the world.

Mass customization won't completely eliminate mass production. Do you really need customized salt, for instance, or care if your laundry detergent is made specifically for you? Moreover, it's going to take time to make the transition to mass customization. Nevertheless, the practice is going to invade most products and services—and, along with data mining, assassin marketing, jigsaw products, and virtual brands, it will create massive changes in the marketplace.

Data Mining and the Golden Customer

Not all customers are created equal. Salespeople have known this forever, describing it as the "80:20 rule," where 80 percent of your sales or profits come from 20 percent of your customers. Now companies are starting to track exactly which customers are buying, and how often, and they are producing ever-more precise results. Dorothy Lane, an American supermarket chain, has a frequent-buyers' club that allows it to track who purchases what and how often. The company found that 30 percent of its regular customers accounted for 82 percent of its sales. Dayton Hudson, an American department store chain, found an even more extreme relationship: an astonishingly small 2.5 percent of its customers accounted for 75 percent of its profits.[5]

When you have information like that, you start to make use of it to encourage the golden customers who are most important to you. In the case of Dayton Hudson, the company instituted a "Great Rewards" program, and lavished gifts and attention on that crucial minority in order to keep them sweet. Frequent-flyer clubs such as Aeroplan allow airlines to do the same, so that their best customers get the best perks, including free upgrades, special booking privileges, faster luggage handling, and targeted promotions through cross-referrals to other travel-related companies— Hertz and Fairmont Hotels, for example.

Eliminating unprofitable customers is traditional marketing heresy. It's also highly profitable.

Such information can also be used to discourage or eliminate those customers who cost more to serve than they produce in revenue. First Union Corp. is an American bank and financial services organization. When a customer service representative (CSR) fields a call from a client, she identifies the client on her computer system, which then produces a red, yellow, or green flag next to the client's name. This tells the CSR how to treat the client. A red flag means the client doesn't pull his financial weight, and so the CSR will likely charge him a premium for anything the bank does for him, partly in hopes that he'll leave for a competitor and take his unprofitable business with him. A yellow flag means the client is a marginally profitable customer and should be treated with respect, but probably won't get any freebies. A green flag means that this is a heavy hitter and so should be treated like visiting royalty.[6]

Eliminating unprofitable customers is traditional marketing heresy. It's also highly profitable. When U.S.-based Paging Network Inc. decided that it would be better off eliminating the heaviest users of its paging network, the company hired consultants to crunch its customer usage numbers. Once the system hogs were identified, PageNet significantly increased its prices for heavy users. Although its subscriber base shrank by almost 500,000 (to 9.8 million) in six months, PageNet found the demands on its network dropped significantly, giving it room to sell more paging service without investing another nickel on network capacity.[7]

But that's not where data mining will end. In fact, these are very crude models of the ways data will be used. Where we are headed is typified in a 2001 newspaper ad that the California-based application software company PeopleSoft placed for its customer relationship management software. The ad shows four copies of a photograph of a woman, starting with a fuzzy rendition and ending with a crisp one. Under the first, fuzzy photo is the caption "Olivia Webb—Acct# 82004162341." Under the final, crisp photo, they have a much more detailed description of hypothetical customer Olivia Webb, including her age, how long she's been a customer, her chequing account balance, to whom she's married and for how long, a description of their son, her job title, her annual salary and household income, the balances in her savings account, brokerage account, and retirement plan, how much she has invested in her sister's catering business, and how much she spent on ski lift tickets last week.[8] Clearly you would collect this kind of data only if you had a use for it—and increasingly companies are finding a use for all kinds of personal information.

Beyond the buttering up of valued clients is another, more subtle, game. Data mining also allows companies to identify customer behaviour patterns, and then to start managing their operations to optimize profits. For instance, Thomas Blischok, an American drugstore chain and pioneer in data mining, found an odd correlation between the sale of diapers and beer between the hours of 5 and 7 P.M. Once that relationship was revealed, it was easy to figure out that men would drop into a store on the way home from work to pick up diapers and grab a six-pack on the way out. Knowing this, Blischok moved the beer closer to the diapers.[9] This kind of search for patterns in massive amounts of data is going to allow companies to increase profits.

Suppose, for instance, that an individual supermarket in an affluent area, perhaps a Miracle Mart in the Montreal satellite community of Westmount, analyzes the data it collects from its involvement in the Air Miles program, and realizes that people are more likely to buy frozen meals at 5:45 P.M. on a weekday than at 9:30 A.M.—obviously buying their supper on the way home from work. It could use this information to increase the price of frozen entrees during the most active hours, and then watch to see if this affects consumer behaviour, say by causing a decline in sales. If no such decline occurs, management would conclude that people are more interested in buying something quickly than finding the lowest price, so that it can safely increase profit margins on selected items at specific periods of the day. Tesco, Britain's largest supermarket chain, already alters prices on specific food items by time of day, day of week, and day of month by analyzing point-of-sale information from its cash-register scanners.[10]

Tesco also tailors discount offers to each of the more than eight million holders of the Tesco Club Card. They each receive a monthly statement listing their current frequent-buyer points. Attached to the statement are discount coupons for various kinds of products. Each member's coupons are specially tailored, based on what the customer has bought in the past, combined with what would increase the chain's profits according to a computer analysis of what offers the customer might accept. And as each individually coded coupon is used or not used, it refines Tesco's computer profile of what motivates that individual. These kinds of specifically focused actions will become more and more prevalent as the technology becomes cheaper and marketers' experience with it expands.

Eventually data mining and analysis are going to allow companies to zero in on the exact preferences of specific clients. Companies will be able to start adjusting their offerings and prices to increase the satisfaction of their most important customers, discourage or overcharge their least profitable ones, and optimize their profits—all in real time. This is the second part of the marketing revolution, and segues naturally into the third.

Assassin Marketing

Mass marketing through the broadcast media has been compared to hunting with a shotgun, spraying your message over thousands of people in the hope of hitting at least a few of them in an effective way. Narrowcasting, which is the delivery of a focused message to a narrowly defined target group, has been described as hunting with a rifle. Here the object is to bag a specific kind of client from a particular neighbourhood, or one who subscribes to a specialty magazine, or watches a particular soap opera on weekday afternoons. Taking this to the logical extreme means identifying the precise individuals you want to sell to based on previous spending patterns, then aiming a message at them that is precisely tailored to their interests in order to maximize your chances of making a profitable sale. This kind of specific targeting of one individual at a time has variously been described as one-to-one marketing or personalized marketing, but I call it assassin marketing because you are using a sniperscope to maximize your chances of hitting a specific individual in the wallet. Regardless of what it's called, this practice is now well entrenched and spreading through the marketplace.

As assassin marketing makes its way into the real world, it's showing up first and fastest on the Internet, where information can be processed by computers to produce individualized attention and service in real time. Amazon.com is one of the most sophisticated—and certainly the most visible—practitioner of this art. If you're a regular customer of Amazon's website, the Seattle-based company knows who you are, what you like (based on what you've bought), what your credit card number is (if you've given Amazon permission to keep it), and where you've been on the web recently (again, if you've given Amazon permission to examine this information). This translates into steadily improving customer service— and a dedicated focus on offering customers things they're more likely to buy. Hence, if you bought a video of Jane Fonda's B-movie *Barbarella* from Amazon, the next time you visited it might offer you *Slave Girls from beyond Infinity*.[11] And if you were known to be influenced by special offers, it might throw in free shipping or a discount on another purchase if you bought the video then and there.

Of course, attempts to project what you might find interesting aren't always right. Indeed, sometimes they're hilariously wrong. But pioneers always make mistakes. The key is that they are more likely to learn by doing than by standing still. They experiment and keep what works, while discarding what doesn't. Through this process they gradually discover what customers actually want among the many things that are possible. This is crucially important because technology is making new choices possible that have never existed before, and with which companies and customers have no experience and no previously known preferences.

Attempts to project what a customer might like can be hilariously mistaken— pioneers always make mistakes. But they learn more by trying than by standing still.

One example of this experimentation was the flap over Amazon's "purchase circles." These were customized lists of best-sellers presented to people based on their e-mail addresses. Hence, if you had an e-mail address that indicated you worked for Ontario-based Nortel Networks Corporation, for instance, it might offer you a list of books on job-hunting that other Nortel people had bought. The implication was that if those people were buying such books, you might want to own them too. There was an uproar about purchase circles violating personal privacy, and Amazon quickly dropped them, not because customers themselves were objecting but because of the public outcry.[12]

The ability to remember things about your customers in order to deduce what else they might like, and then to offer them exactly what they want comes straight out of the past, when the local shopkeeper knew you and your likes. Now, however, this highly personal process is being done impersonally by computers, and on a massive scale. Companies that you've never heard of are gathering, trading, and selling information about you so that other companies can collect and collate this information to assemble a highly focused sniperscope, with the crosshairs centred on you and your buying habits. The result is revolutionizing marketing, merchandising, and retailing.

Imagine, for the moment, that you're a bookseller competing with Amazon for the attention and the business of a specific individual. You may send a direct-mail ad to the individual (call her Sharon) offering a best-selling book at a 10-percent discount if she brings the ad to your store or orders it by phone. You don't know if she really wants this book, but you know her name is on your mailing list, which indicates she's bought from you before. Your chances of selling the book to Sharon are so-so at best. In fact, you send the same offer to everyone on your mailing list, since you really don't know who is likely to be interested.

If Sharon is a regular Amazon customer, here's how I surmise Amazon could go about a similar campaign. First, it would know that the book is becoming a best-seller before anyone else because the company provides a real-time tally of how well every book it offers is selling. When it identifies this book as shooting up in the company's standings, it decides to bring the book to the attention of everyone on its list of people who have an interest in similar books. Amazon combs through its database of customers and pulls out all those who have shown a reasonable interest in this kind of book before. Those who have given Amazon permission to e-mail them get an immediate message about this great, new best-seller, probably before they or their local best-seller lists have heard of it. Those who have not given permission for such e-mail alerts will see a pop-up or banner ad about the book next time they visit the Amazon site. Let's suppose Sharon has given her permission to be put on the list of people who will get e-mail alerts. Sharon's past buying behaviour is assessed, and it appears that she doesn't care about discounts but likes express shipping. Accordingly, Amazon offers her the book at full price with express shipping for no more than standard shipping if she buys right now. Since Amazon has made offers to Sharon before, and they've mostly turned out pretty well, Sharon responds positively and buys the book at full price. Accordingly, by the time she gets your ad in the mail, not only has she already bought the book but she's finished reading it. Your ad reaches her almost a month after the book arrived from Amazon.

Amazon doesn't do this today, but it could. This is merely an illustration of the power of assassin marketing. The result is profit optimization coupled with superior customer service—a win-win situation compared with traditional marketing.

It also allows Amazon to change the nature of its relationship with the customer. Instead of saying "Of the things we have in stock, what can I sell you?" its message is very different. Here's a summary of how Jeff Bezos, the CEO and founder of Amazon, describes it:

> Our business is not selling things. Our business is to help customers make purchase decisions. . . . By helping people sort through the infinite shelf space of the Internet, we are establishing a relationship with them. If you're a store, you have a limited amount of shelf space and you have pressure to sell what you have. But if you have infinite shelf space, you

no longer feel any pressure to sell what you have. You can try to sell the right thing to every individual customer.[13]

In short, it won't pay to fight the assassin. You will, instead, need to become one in order to keep your customers. But that's only the third factor in the marketing revolution.

Jigsaw Products and Services

If we look just a short distance into the future, we have systems that can create unique products and services for individual clients (mass customization); the ability to identify, deduce, and infer the interests and desires of those clients based on their past behaviour (data mining); and the ability to create individually tailored marketing appeals for specific products (assassin marketing). Now if you add one small, additional piece, you get something startling and new: jigsaw products and services. The one additional piece necessary would be real-time cooperation between different companies—potentially even competitors—in order to exploit opportunities as they emerge. Here's a hypothetical example of how it might work:

You log onto Amazon.ca to review books about California and the San Francisco area. While you're pursuing these, the Amazon computers look at your profile, see that you've bought travel books at this time of year in the past, that you once clicked through an ad for Travelocity from the Amazon website, and that you eventually booked a vacation, also at this time of year. From this and the timing of your current query, it looks as if you might again be planning a vacation.

Amazon's computers now suggest four different books to you, while simultaneously contacting the travel computer for the Canadian Automobile Association (CAA), with whom Amazon is developing a relationship. Amazon indicates that it has a potential

client for a trip to San Francisco and vicinity in the first half of January, and asks if the CAA has any special packages for that period. The CAA responds with an eight-day, seven-night proposal, including airfare. It also includes a self-guiding tour of the Napa and Sonoma wine regions, based on an article it published recently in its member magazine. Amazon checks its records, finds that you've bought a couple of books on wines and have also been sent one by your son with a birthday card, all ordered through Amazon. It transmits a request to the CAA to supply a teaser from the article, which Amazon then posts on the website in a sidebar on your screen. You shift your attention from the travel book reviews you've been reading and look at the teaser. Finding it of interest, you click through for more. Amazon passes the request through to the CAA, which returns the full article, including an ad for CAA membership.

As you read the article, you become intrigued by a couple of the vineyards, and click through one of them to its website. Amazon intercepts the click, and forwards a request for that information to the vineyard's website, along with a query as to whether the vineyard offers tours and accommodation. Both answers come back in the affirmative, along with a rate card for the vineyard's bed-and-breakfast. Amazon indicates that it has a potentially interested Canadian who has read about the vineyard's wines in a CAA article, and asks if there are any wine tours through the area. The vineyard comes back with a proposal for a three-day stay, including three breakfasts and dinners and the use of bicycles for getting around.

While this is going on, you finish the article and click back to the book reviews. Amazon and the CAA exchange a range of information, then Amazon contacts a few other websites and places a specific offer in the sidebar on your screen featuring two air tickets to San Francisco; three nights in the Napa Valley vineyard; a three-hour class on wine selection and tasting; one night in a B&B in Sonoma; three nights in a residential hotel in San Francisco; a rental car; a variety of discounts at various local attractions; maps and a recommended itinerary for touring the region; plus the two most popular travel books of those you have been considering as well as the current copy of *What's On in San Francisco* magazine, all for one package price. The price is lower than you would have to pay if you were to go out and buy everything piecemeal. The package also includes membership in the CAA, or a discount equivalent to the membership cost if you're already a member. Amazon also offers a loan from an online Canadian bank for the total cost of the package, subject to credit approval. Amazon places a four-day time limit on the offer.

You download the offer so that you can consider it and compare prices elsewhere. After talking it over with your spouse and doing some comparison shopping, you accept the travel package, including the CAA membership, but decline the loan. As a result of the transaction, Amazon sells two books and a magazine, gets a commission for recruiting a new member for the CAA, a commission for assisting in the sale of a vacation package, and commissions from the Napa vineyard and the wine-tasting class. The payment Amazon accepts from the CAA for the membership referral is an agreement that it will share the data it accumulates about you over the next 12 months.

A jigsaw product or service is one that is created specifically for you from pieces provided by a variety of suppliers. In fact, products become a mere vehicle for providing an overall service—in this example, a personalized travel package.

This is already starting to happen in limited ways. Home Depot, for instance, which has outlets across North America, is starting to offer matchmaking services between small contractors, who are its most important customers, and its retail consumers. In effect, it is offering to put contractors in touch with consumers who need specific work on their homes. Home Depot

These four factors—mass customization, data mining, assassin marketing, and jigsaw products—are reshaping the relationships that companies have with their clients and customers.

then supplies just-in-time materials plus subcontractors, such as electricians or plumbers, as well as expert advice on a variety of aspects of contracting, including scheduling, quantitative surveying, and billing. It doesn't charge for this service. Instead, it reaps stronger relationships with all of its clients, as well as developing much more detailed data on their needs and behaviour. As it increases the volume of this kind of service, it can start to pare down its in-store inventories to save working capital, ordering just-in-time from its suppliers to fill contractors' orders.[14]

These four factors—mass customization, data mining, assassin marketing, and jigsaw products—are reshaping the relationships that companies have with their clients and customers. The result is a decline in the traditional meaning of brands, and the emergence of a new, less stable, but more dynamic kind of brand.

The Brand Created for You

Brands are in decline. Brands were created by mass-production uniformity coupled with mass-media advertising. The problem now is that consumers are being overwhelmed with advertising and are tuning it out, making it increasingly difficult to create or sustain a brand image. "Consumers are like roaches," according to marketers Jonathan Bond and Richard Kirshenbaum. "We spray them with marketing, and for a time it works. Then, inevitably, they develop an immunity."[15]

As a result, brands have a tougher time maintaining consumer loyalty. Kellogg's, which has been one of North America's premier brands for decades, and was rated the number 2 brand in 1991, dropped to number 39 just 10 years later. Only 79 brands appeared in the top 100 in both 2000 and 2001, and the estimated market value of those 79 brands dropped by more than 5 percent—a loss of some US$49 billion in market value in a single year.[16]

Yet, in a world where we are overwhelmed with messages, advertisements, and choices, a brand becomes an important channel marker. I recall a friend who bought a bread-making machine that allowed her to produce fresh-baked bread overnight. After a while, she decided she wanted to try some different recipes, so went to Indigo to look for a new cookbook. She approached a clerk and asked him if he had any books with recipes for breads. He pointed to a table display, where my friend found something like 26 different cookbooks. There was no way she had time to examine that many books, so she looked for names she recognized, such as *Reader's Digest*, Julia Child, James Beard, or *Chatelaine*. This allowed her to cut through the clutter, and focus on a few books instead of 26. This is one of the great—and continuing—values of brands. But it's no longer enough.

Whereas in the past a brand stood for uniformity and quality, it now stands for something very different. In a world where products are customized, and no two are the same, what does a brand mean? If you had a customized car made by Ford, for instance, what model year would it be? In a world where the pieces of a jigsaw offering come from different suppliers, such as the vacation package in the earlier vignette, whose brand is involved?

The answer to these questions is simple: a brand is no longer a product or service. It's the customer's total experience with the supplier. That experience starts and ends when the customer believes it does, whether the supplier wants it that way or not. If you buy a Ford today, and a part manufactured by a third-party supplier is defective, do you go to the part supplier? Absolutely not. You run to the dealer that sold you the car, and expect the dealer and Ford to make it right. It's up to the seller to deal with defective parts, no matter who made them.

Consider the travel-package vignette again. If something went wrong, whom would you contact to correct it? Amazon—because that's who sold it to you, even though Amazon may not be in the travel business. Amazon might hand off the management of the problem to the CAA, or the vineyard, or whoever supplied the defective part of the package, but Amazon would, in your eyes, retain ultimate responsibility for the outcome. If it failed in that responsibility, then it would lose a customer, probably forever, and you would bad-mouth the company to others. If that happened often enough, the company would go out of business.

Of course, Amazon knows this, so it might never get into the kind of jigsaw products and services I've described. That will ultimately be a strategic decision for their management to make for precisely the reasons I've just given. But every supplier that intends to stay in business will have to stand behind what it sells, even if—perhaps especially if—it doesn't supply all the pieces.

Disney is one of the best-known brands in the world. But what is a "Disney?" Is it movies, TV programs, books, toys, Broadway plays, golf courses, cooking lessons, vacation time-share homes, cruise ships, theme parks, T-shirts, collectible china figurines, restaurants, magazines, broadcast TV, sports, or cable television? Is it these things plus the other goods and services the Walt Disney Company sells? Yes and no. It is all of these things, because Disney does sell them all, but more than this, it's the feeling you get from using or owning these things: the Disney experience. Disney's corporate objective is simple: "We make people happy." Its goal is to deliver an experience that will make you happy so that you will want to come back for more. This is the purest example I know of what a brand is becoming.

Moreover, as we move to a mass-customization/assassin-marketing world, the uniformity we have long expected from a brand-name product vanishes. There are no benchmarks any more, no "six sigma" numbers to measure. All a company has to go on is something fuzzy and indistinct: *Did the client appreciate the experience enough to want it again?* Granted, your computer models and neural networks and sophisticated computer software and client surveys will guide you as to what the client may want, like, or need. But at the end of the day, people are more complicated than models or software, and decide what they decide because they decide it. So, ultimately, you have to rely on your people to deliver the final experience.

People are more complicated than models or software, so ultimately you have to rely on your people to deliver the brand experience.

Again, Disney is famous for this. In one example—taken from the book *Inside the Magic Kingdom,* about Disney's ability to create a happy experience—a family visiting Disney World in Florida on a hot summer's day ran into a dilemma. Their young daughter was just starting an ice-cream cone when they got to the front of the line for Space Mountain, one of Disney World's premier rides. Unfortunately, food isn't allowed on this roller coaster, and their daughter started to cry. In stepped a Disney "cast member" (as Disney calls its employees), who offered to hold the ice-cream cone for the 20 minutes it would take them to be loaded onto the ride, experience it, and exit out the other side. The little girl was elated, and quickly agreed—and when she exited from the ride, there was the Disney cast member with the ice-cream cone. Since it's impossible for ice cream to last 20 minutes on a hot, Florida summer day, what the cast member did was to dispose of the first cone, then, knowing how long the ride would take, get another one just before the family exited.[17]

There's no instruction manual to cover this kind of contingency. Your people need to be able to decide what to do and then have the willingness and authority to do it. Disney probably lost money on that ice-cream cone, but gained enormously in the family's experience of the Disney brand.

Nor is Disney the only company that does such things. Nordstrom, mentioned earlier, is famous for it. Nordstrom people are known for doing such things as ironing a dress shirt for a client who's running late for a formal dinner; refunding money to a customer for a set of tire chains when Nordstrom doesn't sell tire chains; delivering travel accessories to an airport for a client who's caught between connecting flights; and many other apparently ludicrous examples of over-the-top service, well above and beyond the call of duty. But Nordstrom is famous not just for service quality but for customer loyalty as well. The Nordstrom experience keeps customers coming back. Customers are loyal to the experience, not to the goods and services they buy there.

Not every company will choose to go to such lengths. That's a matter of deciding what your brand experience is. But your brand doesn't end when you seal the flap on the box containing your product. Making that mistake will kill your enterprise, and someone else will wind up owning your tomorrow.

Beyond the Brand: Who Are You?

The status quo—doing things the way you've done them in the past—is no longer an option. Your relationship with your clients and the way you compete for business are changing. The way you advertise and sell, the way you run your organization, and the way you go after repeat business will all be different. So, if the techniques and hallmarks of your business are losing their power, the historic brand relationship with your client is no longer effective, and the products or services you supply are now of only secondary importance, what defines your company? What defines who you are, and what does that imply about what you need to do to create tomorrow's success?

The second secret builds on the first: you are defined by the people who represent you, your ability to inspire them, and the human values you hold in common. The tools you use in the marketplace and the way you manage your employees must all change to reflect this new reality. The status quo in management, marketing, and sales is dangerous, even fatal. But how do you decide what to do, and how to do it? Where are the answers to unlock tomorrow? And what's the cost of this knowledge? That's the subject of the third secret.

Seek Clarity, Not Facts

*"Irrigators lead the water;
fletchers fashion the arrow;
carpenters carve the wood;
the wise mind disciplines itself."*

—BUDDHA, *THE DHAMMAPADA*

5

The Information
Swamp

Knowledge is power, but information is a curse.

Consider a recent comment from John Rizzo, senior counsel for the Central Intelligence Agency (CIA), concerning all the new data flooding in following passage of the U.S. Homeland Security Act: "One thing I am concerned about: What do we do with all that information?" he said. "Woe be it for us if we lose one shard of information that in retrospect would have been key if, God forbid, we had another terrorist attack."[1]

There is no shortage of information these days. We're awash in the stuff. But this makes our jobs harder, not easier, for the two reasons that Rizzo identified. First, there is so much of it that it's getting harder and harder to wade through it all. Second, we run a steadily rising risk that the very information we need, which will make a crucial difference to our lives and our decisions, is already in our possession but we don't know it's there. And when you make a wrong decision, and someone discovers that you had the key fact all along, it becomes scapegoat time. Few people understand the differences between facts, information, and knowledge, and fewer still understand what to do with these things. No one will accept as reasonable the explanation that although you had the decisive fact, you either didn't know that you had it or you didn't realize its importance. This is viewed as an admission of both guilt and incompetence.

Few people understand the differences between facts, information, and knowledge, and fewer still understand what to do with these things.

Moreover, information overload is making it harder to reach decisions, both because there is more information to consider and because decision makers are (rightly) going to be scared that they've overlooked something important. In many cases this leads to "analysis paralysis," where companies research topics to death but never actually do anything. Yet doing nothing is usually worse than making a mistake, if you're prepared to act and also correct mistakes when you make them.

So whether you're the CEO of a multinational or the owner-manager of a one-person enterprise, the likelihood of overlooking something important is increasing. And doing more and working harder isn't going to help.

Communications Clutter

A while back I did a seminar for a major software company and its clients, and noticed that all of the senior people carried a cellphone, pager, and wireless BlackBerry communicator on their belts. As more communication becomes possible, it becomes mandatory. Clearly, a lot of people are going to be at risk of having their trousers fall down unless something changes.

Meanwhile, mental clutter is invading our mind space. E-mail volume seems to be growing exponentially. Cellphone use is becoming a life-threatening danger on the highways, and producing zombies who stumble blindly down the street, clutching their hands to their ears, gesticulating and shouting to themselves. The advent of go-anywhere communications is creating a monster: you can't be off duty any more.

We are approaching the limits of what we can cope with in terms of our ability to speak, listen, read, and process volumes of communications. We are being forced to build virtual fortresses around ourselves, screening out unwanted and low-priority messages. The problem is that the tools to do this haven't yet arrived. It's not enough to screen calls, e-mails, advertisements, and information; we need it done intelligently. This will only happen once we have a computer companion that is with us constantly, that can learn what we want, and get progressively better at acting on our behalf.

But let's start with the cause of information overload. Where has it come from, and where is it taking us, this torrent of information hurtling chaotically onwards like a flash flood down a desert canyon?

Roiling Through the Data Stream

The history of humanity has largely been one of too little communication. For roughly two million years of human existence, up until the advent of the telegraph, most communication between two ordinary people (that is, not members of a ruling class, the military, or those involved in high finance) relied on one person travelling to another person, carrying a message. Eventually this evolved into postal services, but the principle remained the same: you had to physically carry a message from A to B.

The telegraph, patented by Samuel Morse in 1840, was probably the single most revolutionary invention in the history of communications. It allowed messages to travel quickly over long distances at incredibly cheap costs compared with hand-delivered messages. Today we regard Morse code as a tiny, antiquated trickle compared with the rampaging data streams we now employ, but the difference between "zero" and "some" communications is far more dramatic and important than the difference between "some" and "a lot."

Since the telegraph, successive inventions—the telephone (1876), wireless telegraph (1895), radio (1901), television (*circa* 1929), the electronic computer (*circa* 1946), fibre-optic cable (1970), the Internet (1969), and the World Wide Web (1991), which popularized the Internet— have steadily increased the quantity of communications possible and decreased the cost. This has all happened with astonishing speed on a historical time scale: 154 years from the telegraph to the World Wide Web, compared with two million years without any rapid communication. Of course, for an individual 154 years is a long time, so we often fail to appreciate just how fast this is.

When you were a child, and your grandmother called for your birthday, your parents would shout at you to "Come quick! It's Grandma—she's calling *long distance!*" Long distance was seriously expensive, and people were afraid to talk on the phone for very long. Today, long-distance telephone calls are incredibly cheap, especially in North America. My wife routinely calls friends and family members in Ireland, England, and France, and I call friends and family all over North America, yet we pay no more for such calls than the pennies per minute it costs us to phone friends just outside of our local dialling area.

So person-to-person communications has come down in price dramatically, which means that the volume of such communications has skyrocketed. The same has happened with commercial communications.

At the turn of the 20th century, most advertising was first by signs, and then by print media, as it had been since the first recorded use of movable type by Johannes Gutenberg in 1454.[2] That all changed with electronic media. Today, the rising babble of advertising has become increasingly desperate, making effective delivery of a commercial message more difficult. We're inundated with messages wherever we look: on the screens of our phones, the floors of the supermarkets, and the peel-off labels on the fruit we buy; in messages towed behind airplanes at sporting events; in washroom stalls and over urinals; on safety films on airplanes; on the back of cash-register receipts; and in pop-up ads on websites and at the bottom of e-mails we receive from family members. I once heard someone say that we are bombarded with an average of 1,500 messages of all kinds per day. I don't know how you count or measure that, but I suspect it's roughly true.

Meanwhile, communications capacity continues to expand. Most people are familiar with Moore's Law, coined (and revised several times) by

Messages and information will become more obtrusive, more shrill, and more irritating as they seek to rise above the babble of all others.

Gordon Moore, which says (approximately) that computers will double in speed and halve in price every 18 months. The effects of this have produced the tremendous changes in computers that we have witnessed over the past 50 years. It has been, quite simply, the most dramatic (and traumatic) change in tools and technology humanity has ever experienced. But the communications revolution promises to put Moore's Law and its consequences to shame. The so-called Law of Optics says that the capacity of optical fibre doubles every nine months or less. Optical fibre is not the only means of communications, and will never replace everything else since it's relatively expensive to lay and can't be used for mobile applications. But it is the high-capacity trunk from which everything else grows.

In consequence, communications capacity will explode and the price will plummet. This will have deadly consequences for many traditional communications companies, as I'll discuss later. For now, let me focus on the continuing explosion in information overload, for as the cost of communications continues to drop, the use of communications will continue to grow—and, in consequence, the desperate struggle for the attention of each individual will escalate. Messages and information will become more obtrusive, more shrill, and more irritating as they seek to rise above the babble of all others. The result will be psychologically overwhelming:

Mark pauses with his hand on the handle of his car door, taking one last, long look at the serenity of the lake before him. He sighs, then reluctantly gets into the car and starts it. Music begins blasting from the entertainment centre. He grimaces, and quickly switches it off. He'd forgotten the frenetic mood he'd been in a week ago, when he'd arrived here with his buddies for a canoeing holiday.

With the music gone, he now hears the clear, contralto voice of his car's message centre, informing him that he has mail. Mark hesitates, then tells the car to plot a course for home and show him how many

messages he has. The screen lights up, and shows that he has 97 voice-mail messages and 2,437 e-mail messages. Of the voice mail, 7 messages come from people Mark has tabbed as family and close friends, and 12 come from his boss and immediate co-workers. Voice spam accounts for 52 of the remaining messages. Of the e-mails, his computer has marked 14 as urgent and 217 as important. The majority—1,598—have been identified as junk mail.

Mark grunts in disgust, and instructs his computer to trash all the spam of both types. The computer replies that it will cost him $147.38 to avoid junk mail he has previously agreed to read or hear. Mark stops, not having realized he was so committed to so many advertisers. He changes his mind, and tells the computer to save the spam that he's committed to and trash any he's not. He tells the car to hold all messages until he's on the highway.

Once the car's computer is safely under the control of the Trans-Canada Highway traffic-control system, Mark instructs the computer to play his most urgent voice mails. After each one, he dictates a reply, but tells the computer not to send it until he reaches home because he wants to postpone plunging back into the thick of things till then. Then he views his urgent e-mails, again dictating replies for delayed transmission.

Meanwhile, the view around him has become chaotic. Images are projected onto roadside screens for the short period they are within view, as well as on the road and the hood of his car. Some of them, the ones sponsored by companies to whom Mark has given permission, are projected on the windshield and side windows of the car. They are all aimed specifically at Mark, and tailored to appeal to him.

When Mark finishes the urgent messages, he instructs the computer to play back the remaining voice and e-mails. He deals with the messages as they arise, deleting most of them immediately after hearing them. Some are personal messages, but Mark doesn't even bother to reply to any but the most important ones. Replying to all the messages people now receive is no longer practical, and very few senders actually expect a reply, even from their friends. People reply if they want to, and ignore messages otherwise. Earlier generations would have considered this rude, and Mark's mother still gets angry with him when he doesn't reply to every single message she sends, but no one else even thinks twice about it.

When he takes control of his car again from the car's computer, most (but not all) of the display ads disappear, in accordance with highway safety laws. A few ads, shown in the heads-up display on his windshield, contain valuable traffic, weather, and safety information that makes it easier for Mark to drive. The heads-up display also shows logos for several of Mark's normal suppliers featured prominently around the edges of his field of view.

Finally Mark pulls into his driveway. As he puts the parking brake on, ads pop up all over the car windows again. He hesitates before turning off the car because he knows all of his stored replies will be sent as soon as he does, letting people know he's back from his vacation. He feels weary and frazzled from the drive home, just from the sensory bombardment he's suffered over the past $2\frac{1}{2}$ hours. All of the tranquility he felt up at the lake has worn off, and it feels as if he's never left. With a final sigh, he switches off the car, pops the trunk, and gets out. As he closes the driver's side door, his cellphone starts ringing . . .

This is certainly a nightmare scenario, but it's merely an extrapolation of trends evident right now. What are the consequences of this rising clamour for our attention? And how are we likely to respond to it?

The Need for Barriers with Intelligent Gates

As mentioned earlier, information overload is pushing us to withdraw from contact with the outside world, or at least develop ways of protecting ourselves from it. The advent of answering machines and voice mail, coupled with the elimination of secretaries as corporate "overhead," has led to more and more messages going unanswered. Indeed, one of the great complaints about voice mail and e-mail is that the only way you know messages have been received is if the person at the other end deigns to reply—and people seldom do because they're so overwhelmed.

The ease of e-mail has changed the way people relate to each other, because e-mail is so quick, so convenient, and has become such an important way of sending messages. That very ease has created problems that interfere with communication. First, people will sometimes respond too quickly, not thinking through what they are saying, or how it will be received. This leads to unnecessary irritation and misunderstandings. Second, tone and subtlety are often lost in e-mails, and since "it ain't whatcha say, it's the way that you say it," this, too, tends to create friction. But perhaps the most important change is that people are erecting higher and higher barriers, such as anti-spam software, to block unwanted messages, and these barriers make it harder for legitimate messages to get through, or to be answered.

We want to communicate with people, but only those whom (a) we know and want to deal with, or (b) we don't know, but who turn out, after the fact, to have something to say that we want to hear. Suppose, for instance, that someone you've never heard of wants to hire you for a large amount of money to do really interesting work, and is e-mailing you for that purpose. Clearly you want to receive that e-mail, but you don't know you want it until after you've had a chance to read it. This kind of "unknown" message, which virtually requires foresight, is going to be the hard part.

The rising tide of messages has also changed the etiquette of communicating. It's no longer considered impolite when people fail to return phone calls or e-mails, which makes it harder for new connections to be made. When a stranger calls, and you don't know why she's calling, it's generally easier to ignore the message than return it. And the crush of everyday life, with its steady stream of daily emergencies, gives everyone a perfect excuse for not responding. The same is true in our personal lives. As the clamour for our attention rises, we become more and more efficient at screening out messages of all kinds. We tend to communicate with people we know and who are willing to return our messages, and block everyone else out.

The result, both personally and professionally, is increasing isolation in a world of rapidly rising communications capacity. More communications quantity is producing poorer communication quality.

Yet, despite our efforts, the volume of communications of all kinds continues to rise and will repeatedly slop over the information dikes we erect to protect ourselves. If we are to be neither overwhelmed by the clamour nor completely cut off from the world around us, we need new ways of filtering out the noise. This, more than anything else, will lead to the computer butler or genie I've written about before, but which I purposely left out of the vignette above. We need a semi-intelligent agent, effectively a secretary, to screen information for us, letting through those things that we want, and deflecting everything else. We need, in short, barriers with intelligent gates.

Wearable computers will eventually become the medium through which such genies serve us, but that will come about gradually, and only as wearable computers become more powerful, better designed, and generally more usable and popular than they are today. Meanwhile, today's software filters for spam e-mails fill a small part of the function of tomorrow's genies.

The same will be true of telephone messages. Not only do we need a better way of dealing with voice mail, but we are going to start experiencing voice-mail spam. If you have a voice mailbox provided by your telecom service provider, then voice mail can be slipped into your mailbox without anyone actually calling you on the phone. This implies that a message can be recorded once by a marketer, then addressed and delivered to thousands of people through the phone network without the marketer having to wait for phones to ring. I can't imagine that this will increase our happiness, no matter what it does for phone-company revenues.

If we are to be neither overwhelmed by the clamour nor completely cut off from the world around us, we need new ways of filtering out the noise.

Regardless of what happens, though, we're going to need a better way to make sure the information we want gets through our message screening systems, however they evolve.

Fragmentation of Audiences, and the Rise of Trivial Media

Another important implication of information overload is that the fragmentation of news, information, and entertainment media is making it harder to reach a large audience. When all we had was broadcast television, for instance, we had much less choice and much more in common with each other. We'd all watch the same programs and discuss what we'd seen. We had, in effect, national and regional communities, based on experiencing the same news and entertainment.

As cable television systems appeared, they offered much more choice, and the fragmentation of media began in earnest. With more and more channels, there were smaller and smaller audiences for any one channel, and fewer people watched the same things. Now we have hundreds of channels, on the way to thousands of channels, with digital technology increasing the capacity of existing delivery systems, new delivery systems threatening to add additional capacity, and video on demand (VOD) looming on the horizon. As a result, we have less and less in common with our neighbours.

Indeed, we are developing new, self-selecting "neighbourhoods" in cyberspace, global villages based in part on the media we choose to experience. And once we choose to receive our media (movies, sitcoms, music, and so on) through the Internet or equivalent, which has already started, we will be fragmented down to tiny slivers of the population who may have nothing in common (age, background, geographic region, and so on) other than what we choose to watch or listen to. The interests we hold in common with our physical neighbours will continue to decline, and our involvement with them will dwindle.

The commercial side of this is that the lower audience numbers for any one outlet mean lower revenues. You're already seeing this in television. The demand for video production personnel and onscreen talent is growing at the same time as their pay and job security are declining because media outlets can't afford to pay them more. Most of these people work on contract, or even from project to project, very much like the traditional film-production model.

Meanwhile, all of those proliferating channels need to be fed, so content is being stretched to fit. Already most of the specialty channels take each produced or purchased program and play it over and over, often repeating it several times in a single day. They can't afford 24 hours of new material a day, so they play what they have often enough to fill the space.

This is leading to the rise of what might be called trivial media. Television has been slammed since its early days for its lack of intellectual content, but when that lack of content is spread out over thousands of outlets instead of a handful, what we get is a proliferation of trivia and the celebration of the shallow: the tracking of O. J. Simpson's "getaway Bronco" instead of thoughtful commentary by Walter Cronkite, for example, or the creation of cheap "reality" programming instead of new dramatic productions. Indeed, the occasional exception—the big hit shows that still attract large audiences—merely point up the trivialization of media by contrast.

Nor is this confined to electronic media. I am regularly asked if the Internet is leading to the demise of print media and books. My answer is no, not at all. Print media and electronic media, especially through the Internet, tend to fill different but mostly complementary needs. There are several different print publications that I read regularly, for instance, because they help me keep tabs on a broad range of subjects on an ongoing basis. Books fill in the depth that print media lack. Moreover, my years of files of print clippings provided the basis for this book's structure and content. But performing research for specific chapters and on specific topics for this book was much easier and therefore more extensive online than would have been possible if I'd leafed through print publications at my local reference library, as I did for earlier books.

That doesn't contradict what I've said about the trivialization of media. For example, there are more magazines than ever before, appealing to ever-smaller specialty niches. Yet the total number of magazines sold for all titles has been pretty well constant, which means that each magazine title sells fewer copies. This means thinner magazines, less money for writers, scarcer resources for research and the development of story ideas, and shallower results.

Indeed, most newspapers are gradually being pushed into what might be described as the *USA Today* format: lots of superficial appeal packaged in short articles, most of which is content culled from other outlets rather than developed in-house. There are exceptions, but they are mainly the big-city dailies.

Customized Media, Fragmented Society

For all media, the fight for audience is ferocious now and will increase over time. Only narrowcasting, delivering the specifically targeted audiences that are highly prized by advertisers, can justify and pay for each new splintering of media. Indeed, media are now being defined by and created for niches that advertisers want to sell into, with content slipping as the primary focus.

As assassin marketing gathers force by zeroing in on larger numbers of specific individuals, it will again change the economics and content of media. Advertisers will pay anyone who can deliver particular individuals, and probably pay according to the potential commercial value of each person. This will lead media to start skewing content to the specific people who buy their products, which will lead to more modular media. Snap-together modular information or entertainment will allow media to deliver more customized results appealing to specific subscribers.

In television, for example, if a cooking channel's computers know that you're watching (and they will), they'll tailor the components of a show to your interests in order to increase their "stickiness" and keep you watching.

If they know, based on your past viewing behaviour, that you enjoy watching pastry being made but switch off when vegetarian dishes are prepared, they'll deliver more pastry recipes and eliminate vegetarian fare from the programming delivered to you. Meanwhile, another household with different preferences will see different content on the channel you are watching. This kind of modular media will be no more difficult to deliver than having a website send different pages to different people visiting the same web address at the same time.

In print media, it's theoretically possible right now to create a magazine or newspaper that has content customized to individual subscribers. It's merely an extension of the regional, demographic, and psychographic split runs that magazines and newspapers produce today. It's just not economically practical at the moment. Yet, as assassin marketing becomes more widespread and computer-layout software and computer-run presses become more flexible and more powerful, we will get nearer and nearer to individually customized publications. This doesn't mean that each magazine will be completely different from subscriber to subscriber; there will be overlap. But it will mean ads are customized to the individual, and the content skewed to your individual interests. Columnists will start to be paid according to how many editions include their writing. If you develop a large following, and are included in lots of editions, your income will go up. As interest in your writing wanes, so will your income. In effect, every columnist will be syndicated, whether he's an employee or a freelancer.

The end result—customized media—will further fragment society. We will have less and less in common intellectually or emotionally when the media we experience are tailored to our individual interests, so that you don't read, see, or hear what I read, see, or hear even though we live next door and consume the same media. Our physical proximity will become a mere coincidence. We will no longer be neighbours in a more fundamental sense, and politics and human relations will suffer as a result.

Rising Customer Rage, Shrinking Customer Satisfaction

We will have less and less in common intellectually or emotionally when the media we experience are tailored to our individual interests, so that you don't read, see, or hear what I read, see, or hear even though we live next door and consume the same media.

A tangential effect of information overload is a rising tide of dissatisfied customers. You've probably noticed that when you call someone for customer service, you're waiting on hold more now and enjoying it less. That's not an accident, and, unfortunately, there's more where that came from. Indeed, a number of "customer service" phrases are taking on the same sinister overtones that "some assembly required" has long held for many parents on Christmas Eve. These include: "For your convenience . . ." which actually means "We're making your life more difficult because it's easier for us, but we think you're too stupid to notice"; "Your call is very important to us," meaning "You're gonna wait there, sucker, until we're good and ready to talk to you"; and the ever-popular "We are experiencing a heavy volume of calls. Your call is being held in priority sequence," which means "You're in for an excruciating wait, and there's no way of avoiding it, so just sit there and shut up because, heh-heh, 'your call is very important to us.'" Why is this happening, and what are the implications for the future?

Well, technology is a large part of the problem for several reasons. First, telephones used to be expensive, and were answered by cheap human labour. That put some limits on how many calls could be left on hold, and for how long. That's no longer the case. It's now virtually impossible to speak to a human being in many so-called service organizations without going through some kind of voice-menu system first. And it appears to make good financial sense for a company to stack up the calls and make efficient use of cheap technology rather than expensive service people, but it's a false economy.

Another reason why customer service is deteriorating is that technology is pushing the rate of change so rapidly and increasing levels of competition so quickly that companies are looking for anything that can help them economize. And, to a corporate cost accountant, customer service looks like that most dreaded of all corporate entities: overhead.

Finally, many companies are often unduly influenced by technological propeller heads who speak a language that intimidates their bosses, and are long on engineering but short on human understanding. They think that producing feature-bloated new offerings is exciting and attractive. Yet U.S.-based Forrester Research surveyed 90,000 people in Canada and the United States and found that 47 percent said they were "technology pessimists" or "hostile or ambivalent" towards technology.[3] This is a direct result of propeller-head logic: more is better, whether it's useful or not.

All of these behaviours are, in fact, wonderfully efficient ways of losing customers. They're actually horribly bad management, but it's easier to do things like this than to actually think about them. They also illustrate perfectly the second secret: that the opposite of "smart" is not "dumb" but "lazy."

Now that we've explored some of the implications of information overload, let me move on to how to deal with it.

Taming the Information Torrent

If you're paid to think, plan, and prepare for a rapidly changing future, you need the time and mental energy to do so. Communications clutter threatens your ability to do this. If you're going to prosper, there must be times when you need to be out of touch. You'll need to set ground rules about when and how you're available, rather than being "always on." Constantly racing to do more will mean you actually accomplish less.

Time is your most precious and irreplaceable commodity, and considered thought and understanding your most valuable tool. More isn't always better; sometimes it's excessive or even overwhelming. So how do you cope with the torrent of information washing over you? There are two keys to doing so.

The first key I learned from my days as an institutional investor, managing a stock-market portfolio for a major financial institution. The first decision every portfolio manager, or every effective investor for that matter, must make is what investments they will exclude. No one has the capacity to consider, research, and select from all the possible investments in the world, so you need to pare the universe down to those that you might reasonably want to contemplate. This allows you to dismiss the vast majority of global investments and do serious research on those you might buy. Hence you may have decided not to buy pork bellies, or frozen orange juice futures, or Malaysian equities, or British Treasury perpetuals, or Canadian penny mines, which means you don't even have to think about them when considering what to invest in.

The same is true about information. There are millions of sources of information in the world, and you cannot consume them all. So the first step is to decide what you don't want to know about. For instance, I have no interest in, and refuse to even skim, stories about flying saucers, super-natural events, Madonna, O. J. Simpson, or the late Diana, Princess of Wales. I have little or no interest in recipes, advice columns, or professional football, except as they may reveal something about developments in society and individual behaviour. Similarly, I avoid stock-market prognostications because most are highly perishable, and of questionable value. On the other hand, an article about the stock market that offers detailed analysis may provide valuable insights and inspire additional thoughts, even if I happen to disagree with the conclusion.

These kinds of pre-decisions allow me to perform triage on news magazines, newspapers, broadcast media, online information sources, and e-mail messages, eliminating rafts of factoids that are of no interest before I ever

The first decision every portfolio manager, or every effective investor for that matter, must make is what investments they will exclude.

encounter them. And the more clearly you can define what information you don't want, the easier it will be to focus on things you find of value.

The second key is to understand the structure and hierarchy of information. I find it easiest to explain this with a diagram that I've used for years in my public presentations but never published before (see below).

Every time we encounter a new body of information, we start in a state of anxiety and confusion, surrounded by a morass of unconnected ideas and factoids that make no sense to us, but somehow seem important. The first step to making sense of this morass is to separate those bits of information that are useful from those that are irrelevant, in much the way I just described selecting your information sources. This is the foundation of the information pyramid, which can be described as "data" or "statistics." This foundation of the information pyramid is necessary, but insufficient because unconnected data points have no intrinsic value.

To make use of these disconnected facts we need to give them structure, to create a systematic framework to connect the facts together. At that stage,

The Information Pyramid

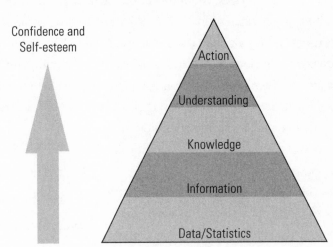

The structure of information, and the challenge of information overload.

it becomes "information" that has potential value, but is not, in itself, valuable. For instance, information in a book on your bookshelf is useless unless you know where it is and what it says. This is the transition to "knowledge." When you consume information, it belongs to you, and it becomes knowledge.

But knowledge is of marginal value. It becomes useful only when you *understand* what it means, when you place it in context, and know how it relates to other things and know how to use it. This is the most important transition in the information pyramid, because without understanding, knowledge can be misleading and harmful.

Once you achieve understanding, which is also called "wisdom," then you lose the pervading sense of anxiety and confusion that ignorance produces. Instead you become confident, and can decide intelligently how best to deal with a situation. Therefore, understanding leads to the pinnacle of the information pyramid, which is right action. I mean "right" in both meanings of the word: correct or successful, and ethical or moral.

In turn, right action leads to success, which produces self-esteem and self-confidence. This gives you the energy you need to tackle additional challenges. And, of course, every time you engage in a new activity or study a new field, you start off at the bottom of that information pyramid again, surrounded by meaningless data points, and suffering from confusion and anxiety. Now, though, you have the confidence from past successes to calm your anxiety and make it easier to move up the information pyramid anew.

The Importance of Purpose

Achieving understanding, the crucial step up the pyramid and the goal for which you should be aiming, is best approached with a purpose in mind. For instance, my job as a futurist requires me to try to make sense of everything that happens or that might happen. Clearly this is impossible, but it is the compass that gives direction to all of my research. Since it implies that I must study everything, I have to boil this down to a manageable task. I do this by dividing the information I need into about a dozen major categories, which represent the major forces at work in the world that will produce most of the changes we experience. These categories include demographics, technology, geopolitics, social trends, and so on.

For each category, I've developed a mental model of what I believe is happening and where it will lead us. Hence, in the fast-moving field of technology, for instance, I have worked out a mental blueprint of how I think computers are going to develop, how they are going to be used and by whom, how they will relate to and rely on communications, and what kinds of applications they will be used for. Then, when I'm reading, talking to people in the field, or otherwise studying computers, I look for nuggets of information that support my blueprint, contradict it, or provide a new insight that suggests new possibilities that I hadn't considered. But in every case, I'm trying to integrate the new data points or facts I'm studying into an already-existing structure. That way, achieving understanding is an ongoing process rather than having to start at the base of the information pyramid each time.

You need to translate this into your own operations. If you're selling widgets, then start by developing a blueprint or mental model for the future of your business based on achieving understanding about anything that affects widgets, breaking the business into the separate, crucial forces that affect that business. As a result, you would think through what affects the production of widgets, contemplate new technologies, and consider the factors that influence the demand for widgets, those that affect your customers' attitudes towards widgets and the purchase of widgets, and so on. Then, every time you encounter new facts on any of these things, you stop and consider how it might change, clarify, or improve that aspect of your mental model of how the future of the widget business will unfold. Every time you get a new communication or factoid from someone, ask yourself how it fits into that mental model, like a new piece of a jigsaw puzzle. This makes it easier for you to gauge the value of a fact and so decide how much time you should devote to it. Trivial facts or messages are dismissed quickly. Important ones can be given the consideration they deserve.

Planning Helps Overcome Analysis Paralysis

The world will never give you all the information you need to come to a complete assessment of any situation. As a result, you'll always have to make decisions with imperfect and incomplete understanding. This can't be helped, but it must not prevent you from acting. There comes a time when you must act, based on your best judgment, even though your understanding is incomplete. With the steadily accelerating pace of change, you'll usually find that taking no action will be more dangerous and more expensive than running the risk of making a mistake—provided you're prepared to accept new information and correct mistakes as you recognize them.

A survey published in 2002 illustrates this dilemma and its consequences, as reported in *The Globe and Mail:*

> *Fifty-four per cent of respondents [CEOs of companies with at least $1 billion in sales] reported that the volume of data is doubling or even tripling every year. As a result, the number of decisions they have to make every year is increasing proportionately . . . over the past year, the data flood has increased the number of missed business opportunities and cut their competitive position. They have less time to get products to market, make lower profits and poorer decisions. Worse, there is an erosion of employee morale.*[4]

More information means more missed opportunities and mistakes. It's also leading companies to spend more time doing research, which further slows the decision rate, leading to even more missed opportunities. Yet, if the volume of data is doubling or tripling every year, clinging to old behaviour patterns will make things progressively worse. Clearly you need to take a different approach by seeking clarity, by chancing mistakes and being prepared to correct them, and by looking further out into the future to better anticipate developments.

Someone once said that the process of preparing for the future consists of having strong opinions, weakly held. This means you must come to decisions, and have opinions about what is going to happen and what you should do about it. At the same time, you shouldn't be too attached to those opinions if it turns out you are wrong, but must be prepared to change your mind. This is the opposite of what most people do. They tend to avoid having opinions, but cling ferociously to positions, once taken, in order to avoid having to admit they were mistaken, or to try to retrieve the money they've already sunk in a mistake.

So, once it's time to make a decision, or when a fleeting opportunity arises, whether you have all the information you need or not, decide and then move on. This doesn't mean reacting on gut feel alone. Instead, you should be anticipating possible events by peering further into the future and thinking through possible actions and responses in a systematic way. And the way to prepare for the necessity of correcting mistakes is by contemplating more than one future. This leads into the area of planning, and particularly scenario planning, which I'll deal with at more length in the seventh secret. For now, keep in mind the idea of considering alternative futures as a means of preparing contingency plans.

The word "clarity" implies being able to see without interference or clutter—and chopping down clutter means being able to quickly assess what's important and what's not. Clarity comes from understanding, not from an enormous grab bag of facts. Not all facts are equally important, so spend the most time on the most important things, integrating them into what you already know, and seeking to become wise in your field. The alternative is to fall further and further behind as the muck of the information swamp rises.

6

Living Naked: The Destruction of Privacy

The destruction of privacy is the inevitable consequence of the information torrent and the rise of assassin-marketing techniques. Privacy will continue to be whittled down until we are eventually stripped naked, with all of our most private activities, foibles, and secrets available to those interested in learning about them. In many cases, this will happen with our consent. In other cases, it will happen even if it's illegal. I don't relish or approve of this prospect. It's difficult to bring home just how malignant the lack of privacy will become, even for people who think they have nothing to hide. Let's begin by considering the many different aspects of the destruction of privacy, before thinking about what it means to your organization in your dealings with the public.

Why Little Sister (and Little Brother) Is Watching You

Companies have been sued because of things their employees have done without their knowledge or approval. For example, Morgan Stanley, an

American brokerage firm, was sued for US$70 million by some of its employees over racist jokes e-mailed by other employees.[1] The company didn't sanction or condone the action, and would certainly have stopped it if management had been aware that it was happening. However, the company was deemed to be responsible for actions that its employees had committed, using its equipment, on its premises. There is a dangerous trend emerging of making companies responsible for anything that happens anywhere close to them, or that anyone employed by them does, even if it's explicitly against company policy, and sometimes even if it's done outside of a work context. The net result is that more and more companies are being forced to behave like Big Brother: monitoring what is being done with their computers, looking over the shoulders of their employees, and watching what happens in the places where they do business.

Yet, when you combine the increased monitoring of what happens in company spaces with the world's heightened concerns about terrorism and the projected rise in the use of technology to monitor, identify, and track people, you get a world very much like George Orwell's *Nineteen Eighty-Four*, where your every action is watched—at least outside of your own home. You can already see the emerging outlines of such a world:

- Credit- and debit-card transactions are routinely tracked and analyzed, as described earlier in reference to assassin marketing. And more and more companies are developing or subscribing to frequent-buyer clubs, which require you to give them explicit permission to amass and trade information about what you buy, how often, at what price, in what colours, and from whom.

- If you have life insurance, the most intimate details of your medical records—including your doctor's opinion of your health—have been shared around between suppliers, with your explicit permission. Indeed, when applying for such coverage, you sign a statement that generally allows the insurer to share such information with anyone it deems appropriate.

- Police in Britain use cameras—for the sake of public safety—to monitor activities on public streets and to keep an eye on the way drivers operate their cars on highways.
- Governments in the United States and Canada have been talking about the need to be able to pinpoint the location of a cellphone for 911 emergency calls. Once this happens, your cellphone's location (and therefore your location) will be traceable any time your phone is on, anywhere in the system.
- Penal systems in North America have started using radio-location devices fastened to the wrists or ankles of people confined to their homes or certain locales, or restrained from visiting certain places or people, in order to monitor their movements. In time, this monitoring will be by a global positioning system (GPS) that can locate someone anywhere in the world, right down to the exact floor of an office tower where a particular person is. A computer will then be able to track where that person is and trigger an alarm any time she goes somewhere she shouldn't.
- Similar tracking devices are now available for small children, either as microchip implants under the skin, or as collars or bracelets, to protect against kidnapping.[2] That, of course, raises interesting questions about when a child is entitled to privacy from his parents: Will it be when he turns 10 years old? At puberty? At 18? Will this be a matter of parental choice, parent–child negotiation, or court-approved age-of-consent decisions? This will undoubtedly become another irritant between parents and children, and will probably lead to lawsuits and legislation.
- There's been discussion about being able to track the location of paper money electronically, partly to stop money-laundering operations and to smoke out other illegal activities. But what about the vast majority of people who hold such money for perfectly legitimate reasons?
- Both the U.S. and Canadian federal governments have proposed authorization to read and, if necessary, crack any encryption on e-mail messages. In effect, this would give them access to one of the fastest-growing means of interpersonal communications.

- It's been rumoured (and I tend to believe) that the U.S. government's true cloak-and-dagger operation, the National Security Agency, has computers that listen in on phone traffic around the world and flag conversations that contain certain words, such as "heroin" or "al-Qaeda," for human attention. What is known is that intelligence services from Britain, Canada, the United States, Australia, and New Zealand have established a joint operation, called Echelon, to monitor international telecommunications traffic and pick out specific words and phrases from the trillions transmitted.[3]

- Iceland has agreed to sell the DNA database of its entire population to a medical research firm. The Icelandic population is, understandably, isolated, and hence its gene pool is about as pure as it's possible for a largish group to be, which makes it ideal for genetic research. But this move, while undoubtedly beneficial for medical research, sets a dubious precedent about the commercial ownership of DNA records.[4]

- A major force that is rapidly whittling down privacy is individuals with video cameras. Aside from ever-smaller and -cheaper video cameras themselves, digital cameras the size of a pack of cigarettes already have limited video capabilities, which will expand rapidly. And cellphones with built-in video cameras can record and post video on the Internet directly. Eventually, whenever you are outside your home (and possibly within it as well), you will run the risk of having your actions and comments recorded, and potentially used to your detriment.

- There are companies that are working on the creation of so-called smart dust. These are tiny machines about the size of dust motes that may float or even fly, and can be used to track and monitor the activities of armies or individuals. The initial applications of such technologies will be intended for the battlefield, to allow U.S. forces to monitor enemy actions.[5] But then again, the Internet was originally developed to permit U.S. government agencies to communicate with each other in the event of a nuclear attack that might take out major communications centres. Once the technology is perfected, it will be a matter of time before the price drops. It's already possible to record people without their being aware of it using tiny video cameras, such as the so-called nanny cams that parents currently use to monitor nannies, babysitters, and cleaners in their homes. However, smart dust will dramatically extend the capability for surreptitiously tracking and perhaps recording you anywhere, even in the privacy of your own home, all without your permission or knowledge.

In short, there will come a day in the not-very-distant future where it will be possible for someone to monitor your every public movement, purchase, action, uttered or e-mailed word, and almost your very thoughts. It may be possible for law-enforcement agencies, as well as people acting illegally, to easily record you in the privacy of your own home. This information may be examined and analyzed by increasingly sophisticated computer software to develop remarkably astute insights into the way your mind works, and begin to predict how you will behave in many different circumstances. And it won't be just one Big Brother that will be watching; it will also be Little Brother and Little Sister, for that matter, who want to know what makes you tick. This kind of monitoring may be done by individuals, seeking to record embarrassing situations for possible sale or display to reality shows, for instance, or by companies seeking to understand you better so they can improve their ability to either serve or use you, depending on which side of the privacy divide you are. And it's hard to tell which is worse: those situations where your privacy is invaded with your explicit or implicit permission, or those where it's invaded without your knowledge and against your will. Both will happen, and with increasing frequency.

Frightening, isn't it?

The Great Privacy Divide

If the issue of personal privacy were simple, it would already be settled. However, it's terribly intricate and complex, and will never, I suspect, be fully settled. Instead, we will likely have a progression of privacy laws that

It's intrinsic in the professional paranoia of security people to always seek more because they never have perfect information or perfect knowledge.

will be different in different jurisdictions and that partly open or close your personal life to outside scrutiny.

Take the obvious reasons for privacy invasion, starting with governments. One of the primary responsibilities of government is to provide security from external armies, and from thieves and criminals on the domestic front. And one of the primary tools of such security measures is the ability to gather and collate information about the actions of groups and individuals. There is no clear demarcation between information that is necessary to achieve security and information that is excessive. It's intrinsic in the professional paranoia of security people to always seek more because they never have perfect information or perfect knowledge. Since they are blamed by armchair second-guessers for any attacks on personal or national safety, they always want more information.

As a result, security forces often step over the rather fuzzy boundary of what's acceptable surveillance. And as technology allows for the collection and assessment of more and more information, such agencies are going to naturally tend to become more invasive. This trend has dramatically accelerated since the September 11, 2001, attacks on the United States.

So, for a voter, the question becomes: What balance do you want between personal privacy and personal security? Privacy is meaningless if you're dead, but high levels of security without privacy will—literally—drive you crazy. A balance between the two is necessary, but where that balance should be is hard to know—especially when you consider that the world keeps changing and upsetting the balance.

Now consider the commercial reasons for the invasion of privacy. When you shop, you want the best selection at the best price, and with the best service. Increasingly your suppliers are saying that they can give you better prices and better service if they know more about what you like and dislike. Taken to the extreme, this means that if they had perfect knowledge about you, they could anticipate your every want and desire—but at the price of knowing every intimate detail about you.

Suppose that you own a small business, for instance, and apply for an operating loan, which you guarantee personally. The bank offers you two rates: the standard small-business rate and a preferred rate. The preferred rate is at lower interest, and so is obviously preferable. But in order for the bank to offer this loan at a lower rate, it needs to be better able to assess your ability to repay the loan. As part of the assessment process for preferred status, you authorize the bank to keep tabs on your personal health, since you are guaranteeing the loan.

Now suppose that, independently, you apply for life insurance, and in that application you authorize the insurer to review your health. In the process, the insurer performs a new genetic test to determine if you have any known genetic faults that might affect your heart. This is the first time you've ever had such a test, and it turns out that you are at risk for heart disease, even though you have experienced no heart problems to date. The insurer rates you as a slightly above-average risk—and the next morning, your bank calls your small-business loan, right in the middle of your busiest season, seriously disrupting your operations, and potentially threatening you with bankruptcy. The bank's staff retrieved the information from a common financial database, since you authorized them to access such information. You've authorized these uses of personal information for perfectly valid business reasons, and now they've come back to haunt you. It was done with your explicit permission and it cannot be undone, but you resent it as an invasion of privacy, and it may cost you your business and your livelihood.

Questionable Invasions of Privacy

We naturally think of the media, and especially *paparazzi*, when we think of unauthorized invasions of privacy, but such invasions can go far beyond this. At the one end of the spectrum is a grey area where it's not clear whether the information (or image) involved is private or not, and at the other end is the truly criminal zone, where information about you is stolen and misused. Here are a few examples, starting with the probably legitimate, and moving further off into the questionable.

- Some rental cars have navigational GPS to help you get from A to B. Such systems can also tell how fast you've travelled in getting there. As a result, some rental car companies have taken to charging large penalties, in the hundreds of dollars, for each occurrence of speeds above the posted speed limit for more than a few minutes at a time. The rental companies claim this is to recoup the higher insurance costs that result from the increased incidence of accidents that happen at higher speeds. Critics claim this is merely to increase the companies' revenues, but the central issue here is: Have they invaded your privacy by monitoring the speed at which you drive?
- For the 2000 Super Bowl in Tampa Bay, local police employed an experimental biometric software system to scan the faces of all 72,000 fans as they entered the stadium. They ran these images through the FBI's criminal database. From these 72,000 images, they identified 19 people as criminal suspects. Although no arrests were made, many were outraged at being metaphorically fingerprinted because they had attended a sporting event.[6] Are the police allowed to photograph you in a public place without reasonable cause for doing so? If so, what are the limits on what they do with that information?
- In a somewhat more threatening example, in May of 1996 a Los Angeles television reporter bought a mailing list from R. R. Donnelley & Sons, the largest U.S. compiler and vendor of consumer data. The reporter sent in a money order for US$277, using the name of Richard Allen Davis, a convicted child killer, and received a list of 5,000 children's names, ages, addresses, and phone numbers.[7] Donnelley never asked how such information was going to be used, or by whom. The company is in the business of selling mailing lists (among other things), and this, superficially, was a legitimate order of a kind it fills

every day. Yet I'd bet that the parents of these children would regard this as a clear and dangerous violation of privacy.

- Identity theft is currently among the worst examples of illicit invasions of privacy, and one of the fastest-growing kinds of white-collar crime. It consists of someone gathering enough information about you to be able to impersonate you, and then applying for bank loans, credit cards, income-tax refunds, and the like in your name before disappearing and leaving your life and credit record in ruins. It is a relatively low-risk, high-return crime that can mostly be done over the Internet, and will spread as thieves become more proficient and as electronic signatures become legally acceptable. For example, many credit-card companies would use your mother's maiden name as a password if someone were to call in reporting your credit card had been lost or stolen and asking that it be reissued, say to a holiday address. But there is now so much genealogical information on the Internet that finding your mother's maiden name is pretty simple.

Beyond these examples, there will be deliberate violations from shock jocks, sleaze reporters, and reality programmers that skate the edge of privacy, or clearly violate it in search of ratings and notoriety. International law is still emerging, and violators will seek out the shadows: the poorly policed areas, or the jurisdictions that purposely become havens for illicit operations. As such outlaw havens become better established, they will foster the development of, among other things, people who enrich themselves by violating other people's privacy in new, unconventional ways for which we currently have no defences.

Such people may deliberately select as victims people who can't afford major legal bills to sue for violations of privacy, defamation, and so on. The perpetrators might offer them appearance contracts to make it look as if the victims were seeking notoriety, all to discourage legal retribution. All of this would be in the grand tradition of shows like *Springer* and *Geraldo,* although this is merely hypothetical supposition.

Privacy Legislation

Earlier I pointed out that traditional advertising and marketing were losing their effectiveness, and that assassin marketing was the way of the future. This is predicated on access to increasingly detailed information about clients, which assumes the ability to gather and use such information. Yet privacy legislation may prevent that from happening. The European Union (EU), for instance, has implemented legislation that allows companies to gather personal information, but then prohibits them from using it for anything other than the immediate purpose for which it is gathered. Hence, if you pay for a purchase using a Visa card, the credit-card company may use your name, address, and other relevant personal information to verify that you are the actual purchaser (in order to avoid credit-card fraud, for instance). However, they could not then use it to create a profile of the kinds of things you buy in order to try to sell you other things. Moreover, the EU wants to apply this yardstick to purchases over the Internet, even if the vendor is not resident in the EU. Whether the EU sticks with this relatively tough stand remains to be seen. There has been significant opposition to it, including resistance from external trading partners, notably the United States.

Vendors are clearly opposed to this kind of strict restraint on the use of information. Whether they've thought it through to the logical conclusion of assassin marketing and jigsaw products and services or not, they instinctively know that they will be able to do more, and make more profit, if they know more about their clients. As computers increase in power and decline in cost, and as computer software becomes progressively more sophisticated in mining the mountains of data assembled, the temptations will continue to grow and personal information will become ever more attractive, like an addictive drug.

So privacy legislation is going to be drafted in an environment where the users of personal information—companies as well as governments— are opposed to strict regulation, and the general public is uncertain. As individuals, we're ambivalent because we want the benefits of personalized service, as well as higher levels of public and individual security, but we're uneasy about having too many people know too much about us. The likely result is, initially, going to be legislation that is pretty wishy-washy, that doesn't really protect personal privacy but puts up a pretense of doing so.

Sooner or later, though, someone in government or private industry is going to go too far, exploit the wrong information for questionable purposes, and get caught with a hand in the cookie jar.

Sooner or later, though, someone in government or private industry is going to go too far, exploit the wrong information for questionable purposes, and get caught with a hand in the cookie jar. This has happened once already. DoubleClick, one of the pioneers of Internet banner ads, married the purchase records of individuals in the real world with the individuals' behaviour in cyberspace to create a database the company wanted to sell for online assassin marketing. This created such outrage that the U.S. Federal Trade Commission investigated DoubleClick and instituted regulations on the abuses of privacy—the first on the Internet.

I feel quite confident that there will be other abuses. When and where such a disaster occurs, it will create a new public uproar that will lead to tougher legislation. And if I were to be cynical about the process, I would suggest that governments will give themselves more latitude to violate your privacy, and then enact draconian legislation that applies to private industry, effectively using corporations as a scapegoat for the peccadilloes of government, much as the terrorist attacks in the United States have clearly been used as such a pretext.

But there's another dimension to the debate on privacy legislation: different generations have different attitudes about being metaphorically naked in public. Older generations—baby boomers and beyond—don't want their personal affairs aired in public. I don't sense the same kind of reluctance in today's teenagers, who have grown up with the Internet and are more used to the idea of being "out there" and open to the Netizens of cyberspace. Eventually, then, I suspect that privacy will gradually dwindle, as the benefits anesthetize us and we develop calluses over our more tender sensibilities. Over time, legislation will evolve to allow more and more information to be used for most legitimate applications, and our private lives, as we think of them now, will gradually shift as we learn to live naked in the spotlight.

What It Means for Your Organization

As described earlier, the future of most kinds of marketing will depend on knowing and personalizing the service you offer your clients and customers. The better you know them, the better you'll be able to serve them and prosper. But never forget that you are dancing in a minefield. Members of the general public are sensitive and uneasy about the use of their personal information and they know that more and more of it is finding its way into the hands of third parties. If you happen to be seen as abusing such information, or even using the services of a third party that is perceived as being predatory, then it could well destroy your entire business. At the very least, it will damage your reputation.

Accordingly, regardless of who your clients are or what kind of business you are in, if you gather and maintain almost any kind of information about your clients or prospects, you need to have a formal policy about how this information will be used. Moreover, you not only need to *be* responsible, you need to be *seen* as being responsible. As a result, your policy on personal privacy should incorporate any applicable local legislation, but it should go further than that. Among other things, you should state:

1. that your purpose in holding this information is purely to allow you to serve your clients to the best of your abilities and in their best interests;

2. that you will use such information only to the extent allowed by law, and with the permission of your clients;

3. that any person or entity contained within your database has the right to request their removal from that database;

4. that you will only trade, sell, or exchange personal data if you have obtained individuals' permission to do so, and then only because you believe that doing so will confer potential benefits on them, say by informing them of products or services that might be of interest or value to them; and

5. that you will exert your best efforts to ensure that all client data is secure from thieves, hackers, rogue employees, or anyone else who might abuse it, and that no data is used in a manner contrary to your code of privacy.

Statements aren't enough. You need to mean what you say. You need, in fact, to entrench procedures for gathering and safeguarding information, including making sure that your company attempts to secure clients' permission to use information responsibly. One such means for doing this might be through a frequent-buyers' club, which collects and trades information among the members in order to offer specific benefits to the participants.

And Information Overload Applies Here, Too

Finally, I must note that although there is a vague perception among the general public that Big Brother, Little Brother, and Little Sister are all peering over our shoulders and into our private affairs, the reality is, at least for the moment, much less dramatic. The truth is that integrating different kinds of databases and then successfully interpreting and using the results is both difficult and very much in its infancy. If you wanted to create a predatory system to abuse personal privacy, you could do so on a retail basis, one person at a time, say for the purposes of identity theft. But doing so on a systematic, wholesale basis would be much more difficult—today.

The entire field of assassin marketing and customized use of information by businesses, charities, and governments is in its infancy. Today you and I are largely protected by a general level of incompetence and incompatibility among record keepers. For instance, the greatest protection for your medical records lies in the fact that they are largely handwritten on pieces of paper held in a filing cabinet in your doctor's office. It will take many years before most people's medical histories are in electronic form, although it will eventually happen.

Those years will pass, as will the infancy of this field. And as they pass, abuses will arise, create storms of public protest, be dealt with on an ad hoc basis, and subside. But the general direction seems clear: we will eventually wind up living naked, with our most sensitive secrets known by anonymous exploiters who will use the information for varieties of purposes, only some of which we will sanction.

However, there's no action without reaction. As the world changes the context in which we live, the tools that organizations use to serve and solicit business from the general public shift and mutate. So, too, do the attitudes of that general public. These changes are significant, and are going to rock your world, as we'll see in the fourth secret.

Prepare for the New Consumer

*"Parents are trying to raise kids in a
'socially toxic environment.'"*

—ROBERT GLOSSOP, VANIER INSTITUTE OF THE FAMILY

7

Who We Are,
Who We Will Be

One of the greatest temptations, and pitfalls, in planning is to assume that tomorrow will be like today, a so-called straight-line extrapolation. This is particularly dangerous when a trend undergoes a dramatic change, which is precisely what's happening with consumer behaviour. Consumer behaviour is vastly important to the future of many organizations and the economy as a whole, and we are now starting to experience significant shifts in the way consumers think, act, and buy. In this chapter I'll deal with the underlying demographics of the population, and in the next chapter I'll describe the other, less quantifiable aspects of consumer behaviour.

Demographics are among the most dependable tools in any planner's toolbox. Over most reasonable planning periods (anything under 10 years), demographics are highly reliable, since the vast majority of the population you will deal with already exists. For the past 15 years or so we have experienced a period of relative demographic calm, when the most important demographic groups matured within well-defined stages of their life cycles. That calm is about to be shattered as key groups in the population make major lifestyle shifts. To illustrate the importance of such shifts, recall the traumatic days of the late 1960s through 1970s, when the baby boomers first made their presence felt as adults.

Before I plunge into a discussion about the upcoming changes and their importance, let's identify the different groups in the population and see where they are in their life cycles.

For the past 15 years or so we have experienced a period of relative demographic calm, when the most important demographic groups matured within well-defined stages of their life cycles. That calm is about to be shattered as key groups in the population make major lifestyle shifts.

The Generations

Different commentators have different descriptions for different demographic groups, and the precise groups they are referring to vary greatly. Hence, today there are many contradictory references to "Generation X," for instance, a term that was originally coined by Douglas Coupland in his novel of that name. Coupland's book referred to people born from about 1961 to 1972 who were well-educated, disaffected, and restless. However, the concept caught on and has become a kind of catch-all term for any adult younger than a baby boomer. That's why I dislike the term, especially since I count 1967 as the end of the baby boom and therefore include as boomers most of the people Coupland categorized as Gen-Xers. Accordingly, to be clear, let me define Canadian generational groups:

The pre-war group: Everyone born before 1938. By 2014, such people will be 77 and up.

The war babies: Those born between 1938 and 1946. By 2014 this group will range in age from 68 to 76 years of age.

The baby boom: By my reckoning, boomers were born from 1947 to 1967, which were the years when births took off, as you can see from the accompanying chart. However, not all boomers had the same kind of

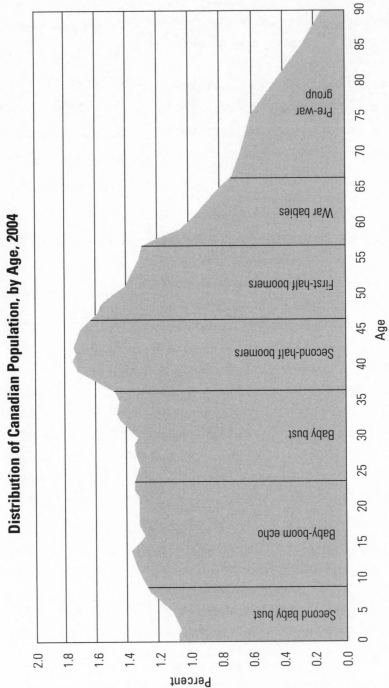

Distribution of Canadian Population, by Age, 2004

Second baby bust

Baby-boom echo

Baby bust

Second-half boomers

First-half boomers

War babies

Pre-war group

Percent

Age

Data source: Statistics Canada

experiences as they were growing up. Those who were born in the second half of this period had a markedly harder time slogging behind the first half, who surfed on the crest of the age wave. As a result, I sometimes break the baby boom into two halves.

> **First-half boomers:** Those born from 1947 to 1957. They will range in age from 57 to 67 in 2014.

> **Second-half boomers:** Those born from 1958 to 1967. They will be between 47 and 56 in 2014.

The baby bust: Those born from 1968 to 1979. They will be 35 to 46 in 2014. These folks struggled behind the first-half boomers too. When they were in school, governments were closing schools and firing teachers. When the baby busters looked for work, the boomers were hogging all the jobs. They've lived in the shadow of the boomers all their lives.

The baby-boom echo: The children of the baby boom, born from 1980 to 1994. They will be 20 to 34 in 2014. These kids are currently clogging the school system, and have forced many school districts around the country to resort to temporary classrooms.

The second baby bust: As the baby boomers move out of their childbearing years, the birth rate is dropping, resulting in a "baby bust echo," so that school enrolments at the lowest grades are dropping right now, and will continue to do so for some time. This group is, or will be, born from 1995 to 2006, and will be 8 to 19 years of age in 2014.

The second echo boom: These kids aren't even with us at the time of writing, but they will constitute another, much smaller, population boom, being the children of the baby-boom echo and the grandchildren of the baby boomers. It's hard to be precise about people who don't exist, but I believe this will be a short-lived boom and that it will run from roughly 2007 to 2017, possibly petering out earlier.

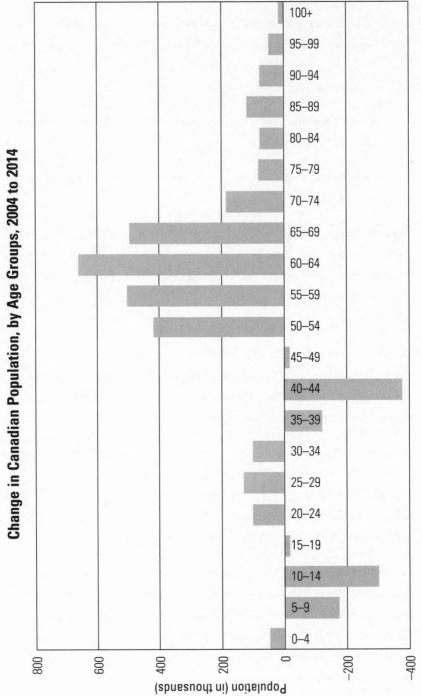

Change in Canadian Population, by Age Groups, 2004 to 2014

Age Groups

Population (in thousands)

Data source: Statistics Canada

Running through all of these groups, starting with the boomers, is a rich vein of immigrants. Starting in the mid-1980s, the government of Canada recognized the problems of an aging population without enough young people filling in the demographic gaps. Accordingly, it started increasing the levels of immigration. The current, stated policy is to allow 225,000 people a year into Canada. Immigration levels this high happened very rarely prior to the late 1980s, but I expect that the federal government will increase this quota as labour shortages appear, and as the tax base starts to suffer. Eventually the federal government will aim for immigration levels roughly equal to 1 percent of total population, or more than 300,000 people a year. The population projections I'm using from Statistics Canada assume the current, lower immigration quotas.

Transitions in the Three Key Generations

Of the seven groups I've identified (counting the boomers as a single group), three are just edging into significant life-cycle—and therefore lifestyle—changes: the pre-war group, the boomers, and the echo boomers (essentially, the boomers plus their parents and children). These changes will have significant ramifications for the economy, shattering the demographic calm.

The "Oldest Old" (Pre-War Group) Will Need Increasing Help

People are living longer and healthier lives, staying active and vigorous well into their 70s and 80s, and occasionally beyond. This trend will continue, and even accelerate, as the biosciences revolution continues to lengthen life expectancy and to improve the quality of life for what used to be considered "old people"—traditionally people in their 60s and up.

However, despite these advances, and to a certain degree because of them, the number of what Statistics Canada calls the "oldest old"—being people in their 80s, 90s, and over 100—is going to blossom in the future. In fact, the growth rate in the number of people over 80 is greater than for any other group.[1] Some of the pre-war group fall into this category today, and the rest will do so within the next 10 years or so. Even with medical improvements, eventually the machinery of the body and mind begin to break down, so that an increasing percentage of people in this category will move from being fully independent to being partly or even fully dependent for the management of their daily affairs. This will apply across the spectrum of human activities, including shopping and getting around as well as balancing chequebooks, managing finances in general, and caring for personal physical needs.

Few people live in a vacuum, which means that the more dependent people there are, the more it affects the friends and relatives who care for and assist them. In particular, the children of the oldest old are typically 20 to 30 years younger than these people, which makes them first-half boomers in their 50s and 60s. They may still be working, thinking about retirement, or even fully retired. Regardless of their own situations, their lives will be affected by the needs of their parents.

The transition of this rapidly growing group of people from independence to dependence will place novel strains on society. Up until now, relatively few people have fallen into this category, and so society has been able to manage their demands on the social safety net either with a small allocation of resources, or by ignoring them entirely. In the future, though, the growth in the numbers of such people will be so rapid that it will outpace not only the ability of existing resources to provide the necessary support, but also our political will to devote resources to the needs of this group.

This is inexcusable, because it is simple to document the rising need, and Statistics Canada has done an outstanding job of providing the necessary data from which we should draw the obvious conclusions. However, the same could be said of the needs of the Canada Pension Plan (CPP) back in the 1970s, or the demands that would be placed on the Canadian health-care system. I (and others) researched and wrote position papers on both the CPP and health care for the media and for political parties, both in power and in opposition, back in the mid-1970s. The result was the usual one-day wonder: a few headlines, some chatter in the relevant legislative assemblies, and then nothing. Since there were no immediate crises, and no votes to be gained by planning so far ahead, these issues received little attention. In consequence, we now pay up to 10 percent of our earned incomes in CPP "premiums" instead of less than 4 percent, and we now see our health-care system as being "in crisis."

Well, a crisis that is foreseen but ignored is better described as incompetence and neglect. The same will be true of the inevitable future needs of the oldest old. We will ignore these rising needs until we can postpone action no further. Then, when the problems finally make newspaper headlines, we will declare a crisis and rush to implement band-aid solutions instead of well-thought-out and carefully prepared ones.

However, public inaction doesn't mean we can't prepare as private citizens and as private-sector organizations. As individuals, especially members of the so-called sandwich generation (meaning people who have both dependent children and dependent parents), we should be thinking about what resources our parents will need when they can no longer handle everything themselves. The list might range from help with their financial affairs to housing that affords them as much independence or support as they want.

For private-sector charities it means preparing to meet the needs of a steadily rising number of elderly people for such services as Meals on Wheels, religious worship for shut-ins, and nursing and housekeeping help. In turn, this implies planning and preparation that would involve financing, relations with government agencies, the recruiting of volunteers, and so on. You should also be looking at where these services are going to be needed. Some of the oldest old will stay in their family homes as long as they can, but many will move to assisted housing, supported-living facilities, and retirement communities. For financial reasons, many of these will be outside of the urban centres, where costs and taxes are lower, and in the smaller communities that surround the major cities. For climate reasons, many older Canadians will settle either in British Columbia—in the Lower Mainland and Vancouver Island—or in the more temperate areas of the Maritimes. This will affect the political and economic affairs of these regions, both positively and negatively, and the results are highly predictable.

For private corporations, there is real opportunity in many different areas, starting with housing. The rising demand for assisted-living developments is going to make this one of the hottest areas of real estate. Real-estate companies, contractors, and developers who identify the right locations, develop the right financial structures, and provide well-planned and well-thought-out developments are going to make fortunes.

The financial services industry can also profit, and in a number of different ways. The oldest old are not technologically adept, and so are much less likely to want to transact business over the Internet, even though logically it would make the most sense for them to do so in the convenience of their own homes. Finding a way of allowing them the ease of access to the financial services they need, without the technological sophistication currently necessary to do so, will produce significant market share. Tailoring services to the needs of this group will likewise become a successful way of building business, particularly if a way can be found to deliver it in person rather than forcing the elderly to venture out to the dwindling number of bank branches. The elderly are also notoriously the targets of sophisticated frauds. Providing ways for the elderly to safeguard their finances while allowing them, their children, and their assistants access to the finances will not only win friends but provide an opportunity to gain business through referrals.

Indeed, working with the elderly should become a major source of referrals to financial planners, financial advisers, and financial institutions, because it will bring them into contact with the children of such people. These "children," aged anywhere from 50 to 70, are generally the clients most prized by people in the financial industry. They are either nearing or at the end of their working careers, and therefore have the richest portfolios of just about any age group in the population. So financial groups should be targeting the oldest old as an emerging group that not only needs different kinds of financial services but also offers a variety of rewards for providing them.

Retail groups should also be thinking about the needs of the elderly. There is going to be an explosion in demand for all kinds of devices for assisting people, both physically and mentally. These will include walkers, powered scooters, bedroom and washroom fixtures that support the physically infirm, as well as computer resources. The high-tech side is a new category, and potentially a very rich one. Increasingly sophisticated computers will be able to do a wide range of tasks: read to those who have a hard time seeing; watch over those whose health is failing and call for help if trouble arises; identify visitors through biometrics for the elderly who have trouble remembering people and faces; remind them when to take pills and keep appointments; help them to find their way from home to a doctor's office; and so on. Computers may, in fact, provide the most dramatic improvement in assistance for the oldest old in the history of humanity—yet few companies are thinking about such applications.

In all, there is a lot to be done for this group, for their own good and for the benefit of both society and the corporate income statement.

Baby Boomers Gradually Shift from Work to Retirement

Through most of their lives, members of the baby boom have dominated society. Their entry into schools resulted in overcrowding and the need to spend a lot of money on school buildings. Their entry into the labour force prompted *Time* magazine to name the then under-25 generation its "Man of the Year" in 1966. Boomers' influence on politics—from the flower-power 1960s and 1970s to the neo-con 1990s and 2000s—has been profound, and created tidal waves where other groups have created ripples. Their influence on financial and economic matters has, in my view, been largely underestimated, from the rampant inflation of their household-formation years in the 1970s to the stock-market boom of the late 1990s.

Their transition from work to retirement is going to have dramatic effects in many different areas.

Historically, people start fading out of the workforce in their mid-50s, either because their health starts to suffer and they have to cut back on their working hours, or because they've amassed enough capital that they can start having more fun and working less. The traditional "goal line" for retirement—65 years of age—is based more on history than on medical necessity because, as noted earlier, we are living longer, healthier lives. Yet the concept persists that retirement comes somewhere in the 60s, plus or minus, depending on what you can afford, and people continue to act that way. Moreover, rich-country governments, including the government of Canada, have gradually made it easier for people to retire at earlier ages and collect benefits, with the result that the effective retirement age has been consistently edging downwards.[2]

This is a mistake. Not only do we, as a country, not have the resources to finance the baby boom into retirement, but as discussed earlier in Chapter 1, we're going to need many of the skills that they take from the workforce. This is, again, an obvious fact we're studiously ignoring, and for which we will all pay later.

Meanwhile, boomers as a group are feeling uneasy about leaving the workforce entirely. They suspect that health care is going to continue to extend life expectancy, but are concerned about its cost. They further suspect that it will be easier to stay at least partly employed than it will be to find employment when they're in their 80s and their money's running out.

As a result, retirement is changing, and fewer people are going "cold turkey," quitting the workforce entirely. Many boomers are "taking the package" from their employers, who are foolishly offering incentives to get rid of expensive (and well-trained, highly skilled) employees. These people are then turning around and finding new work, often as a contract worker or consultant for their former employer, but at a higher daily rate. Other boomers are easing into retirement by working part-time, cutting back on days and hours, choosing to work on contract instead of as full-time employees, or otherwise keeping one foot in the workforce. And some are leaving employment, then setting up their own businesses.

A crucial ingredient of our future is that for the boomers themselves, the next 10 years or so represent their last, best chance of preparing financially for their approaching retirement.

A crucial ingredient of our future is that for the boomers themselves, the next 10 years or so represent their last, best chance of preparing financially for their approaching retirement. Many have left this awfully late, and will have difficulty saving and investing enough to build up the capital they need. This is particularly true of the large number of self-employed, who don't have a company pension plan. Moreover, many companies in recent years have switched from defined-benefit pensions to defined-contribution plans, which place more of a burden on the pension recipient and let the company sponsor largely off the hook for the final result.

In consequence, most boomers are going to feel at least a little panicky about fast-approaching retirement. As one woman told me, "My retirement plan is to buy lottery tickets." She was dead serious, and she's not alone. In consequence, we're going to witness a number of ripples in the financial services field that reflect this suppressed panic. Some will respond by saving more, cutting back on consumption (and worrying governments and retailers as they do). This should lead to a variety of new financial planning products and services tailored to leading-edge boomers and pandering to their sense of urgency.

Some will plunge into high-risk ventures, hoping to do with spectacular investments in a few years what they neglected to do in the previous decades of working and saving. This will include those who bet heavily on tech stocks in the late 1990s, expecting to get rich quick. Many have sworn off stocks as being "too risky," but they could turn around and fall for fast-talking con-artists, real-estate schemers, and inventors with venture-capital plans that have hockey-stick forecasts on the upside (and final returns of zero on the downside). Financial market regulators will have to work overtime to cope with all the slick and sleazy stuff that comes out of the woodwork.

Many boomers will surreptitiously glance at their parents' portfolios, look at their aging parents, and while they don't actually want them to die, hope that when they do, they'll do it quickly rather than linger and drain off their assets. Indeed, money is going to split many families apart. Lawsuits over estates will rival divorce proceedings among family-practice lawyers, and all kinds of poorly thought-out legislation will be introduced, both to protect parents from rapacious children and to prevent parents from "wasting" their own assets.

And some boomers will smile, shrug, and continue to spend to the limits of their credit cards, expecting that something will turn up. Moreover, they'll expect governments to ride to their rescue with hefty pensions, even though they've been bad-mouthing the Canada Pension Plan for years. What's more, they'll start demanding, through CARP (the Canadian Association of Retired Persons) and other lobby groups, that tax rates on retirement income be lowered. Boomers are used to being catered to, and they believe they have the political clout to force the issue. What this means, of course, is that they will be asking governments to saddle younger generations, including their own children, with unreasonably high tax rates. Since there are limits to how far this can go, we are going to experience a rising drumbeat of intergenerational conflicts. And since money will be the issue, the conflicts are going to be pitched battles, and no one will take any prisoners.

While all of this is going on, the boomers are going to discover that they're not invulnerable. They started to get hints of this in their 40s and 50s, but as leading-edge boomers enter their 60s, they will find that their bodies start to betray them. They will, as they always have, turn to quick fixes and untraditional ("alternative") answers when their ever-younger-looking physicians, already harried with impossible work schedules, shrug and tell them it comes with getting older and they should get used to it. The boomers don't take this kind of dismissal well, and will look for other, happier answers. Not surprisingly, given how much they'll be willing to spend on happy answers, they'll find lots of people waiting to tell them what they want to hear, producing a further boom in the already thriving businesses that surround aging and physical problems: vitamins, supplements, herbal remedies, yoga, chiropractic treatments, massage therapies of many different flavours, spas, machines, fitness clubs, diets, and every other possible fad or fashion that promises to restore youthful vigour.

Regulators are already starting to edge into this area, because this much attention (and the money that goes with it) always attracts fast-buck artists and charlatans, as well as genuine practitioners. Restrictions on the claims of food supplements and nutriceuticals will become more stringent. Statistical testing will establish and give credibility to some of the treatments that are currently regarded as alternative in North America— chiropractic, yoga, tai chi, and properly tailored fitness regimes, for example—while exposing others as useless or even harmful.

Mechanical devices of ever-greater complexity and sophistication will emerge to support and assist the boomers' bodies. Many of these will include computers. Hence, a boomer with knee problems may buy and wear a brace that monitors the stresses placed on the knee. If it detects a lateral stress that is harmful, it will cause the brace to stiffen, protecting the knee from harm, while remaining supple and flexible otherwise. Eventually, partial or complete exoskeletons will emerge that look, at first, like bulky body stockings. These will augment the wearer's own muscles and provide assistance, taking the strain off tender parts of the body. And from such computer-assisted devices will emerge the constant monitoring of health by personal genies that I've described elsewhere.

Consequently, just as the boomers revolutionized obstetrics by insisting that fathers (and eventually many others) be allowed to be present at the birth of their kids, so, too, are boomers going to revolutionize the process of aging. And because of their wish to deny aging, they are going to spend billions of dollars on it. This is an opportunity waiting to happen for any organization that can cut through the rising clamour of competing claims and offerings.

Another area that will prosper is travel, as boomers fancy themselves the first true citizens of the world. Those who can afford it in retirement will make travel a centrepiece of their activities, planning trips and gathering in groups. In particular, two kinds of travel will receive a great deal of attention: adventure travel and "edutainment." Adventure travel is already a rising category for those tired of just holding down a patch of sand on a sunny beach. They want to "boldly go" to lots of places, preferably where there aren't a lot of other tourists. Appealing trips will include ecotourism in the Costa Rican rain forest, dogsledding in Yukon, trekking to the South Pole using the same kind of equipment that the early explorers used (and having to be rescued at great expense when they get into trouble), and as much more as the fevered imaginations of eager travel packagers can dream up.

Edutainment packages will take travellers up Machu Picchu in Peru in the company of archaeologists who will explain what these people were thinking; recreate Darwin's voyage to the Galapagos in the company of biologists; take tourists to Olduvai Gorge in Tanzania, to perform light excavation for pre-human remnants; or join a crew working on a rumoured new site in the Valley of the Kings in Egypt. No place on Earth (save, possibly, outright war zones) will be safe from tourists. They will be welcomed, fleeced, and urged to tell their family and friends what a wonderful time they had.

Competition for these dollars will be fierce, so that even though the total number of passenger air miles travelled will rise, airlines, for instance, will continue to suffer from low margins and profits. Much of the travel industry will remain a commodity, and it will only be enterprising people who can invent new categories or come up with imaginative, proprietary twists who will make money.

Meanwhile, as entertainment moves to increasingly high-tech methods of delivery, boomers are going to lag behind the bleeding edge of the market, waiting for trends to be well established by younger generations before edging into them. They're going to become trend followers because (and this is a broad generalization) boomers use newer technologies but they aren't particularly comfortable with them. Eventually, their buying power means that new equipment will be easier to set up, and easier to integrate.

For instance, Wi-Fi—a wireless protocol that allows mobile computing devices to share high-speed Internet connections within a short distance (approximately 30 metres) of a base station—is currently changing the way we attach equipment for web surfing. Eventually, the home entertainment system will have a central processing unit (CPU), the purpose of which will be to monitor the activity of, and manage the connections to, outlying devices such as personal video recorders, televisions, and music centres. The cables that snake around the back

There will be conflicts during public performances as more and more people feel free to chat back and forth, even as it intrudes on others.

of such devices will vanish, replaced by built-in or plug-in wireless devices that automatically connect to the central controller. As a result, eventually, the only wires coming out of such devices will be electric cords. There's money to be made here for companies that do this right.

Simultaneously, the content of entertainment will shift, mostly because of younger generations. Boomers will keep to traditional forms of music, movies, and video, but will gradually adopt new forms pioneered by multi-tasking youngsters. This will include interactive programming, a cross between computer games and television programs. It will lead to multiple experiences: listening to, watching, and participating in different things at the same time. The boomers will find this tough sledding, because their minds usually work more linearly, but as they are exposed to more and more of it, they will gradually and grudgingly adapt.

Just as an aside, this will probably also lead to audience conflicts during public performances, as more and more people feel free to chat back and forth during movies, plays, ballets, and opera performances, because this is integral to their experience, even as it intrudes on the experiences of others.

In the non-profit sector, the approaching retirement of the boomer should be seen as a major opportunity to recruit volunteers. As boomers scale back on their paid working hours, they will seek other activities. And retired people, along with housewives, have traditionally been the backbone of most volunteer organizations. Since housewives are rare today, this leaves retirees.

Yet boomers feel that their time is valuable and the majority won't want to waste time on trivial matters such as tutoring just one individual in reading skills or doing administrative paperwork. They want to use their existing skills and networks to good effect. It helps them keep their hand in and their networks alive, and allows them to maintain a sense of their pre-retirement status. The number and dedication of recruited boomer volunteers may make the difference between survival and failure for many charitable and non-profit organizations, and the way you organize and pander to boomers will be crucial to your recruiting success and survival.

The Echo Boomers Reach Adulthood

The third major demographic shift will come from the children of the baby boomers—the echo boomers, or "echoes"—as they reach legal maturity, finish their formal schooling at whatever level, and edge into the workforce. Over the next 10 years they will take entry-level jobs and begin to move up. Consequently, they will become the focus of a large segment of consumer companies, even more than they are already. They will provide almost all of the labour-force growth (with immigrants providing the rest), and will move away from their parents' homes and their parents' values, creating their own lives and assuming their place as a major new force in the economy. By 2014 they will range in age from 20 to 34, and they will change many things about tomorrow's world, starting with politics.

There's a quote, attributed variously to Shaw, Churchill, Disraeli, and others, that goes: "Anyone who is not a socialist at 20 has no heart. Anyone who remains a socialist at 40 has no head." It is generally true that the young are more idealistic than their elders. I suspect that, pragmatic and greedy though the echo boomers may be, just like their parents, they will start out as idealists. Indeed, the anti-globalization movement has young people as its foot soldiers, even as trade unions and protectionists try to harness their youthful enthusiasm for their own purposes.

This idealism will lead to some form of "New Left" to oppose the "neo-conservative" leanings of many boomers. The trend will be furthered and supported by the taxes that the aging boomers want to settle on the working young, arousing the intergenerational conflict described earlier. Because of this conflict, echo boomers are likely to espouse politics that are opposed to those of the boomers, even in cases where they might otherwise actually agree, much as pro-life and pro-choice activists will tend to automatically oppose each other in everything.

This will, of course, enrage the boomers, who are not used to having their wishes opposed. And their rage will tend to throw fuel on the dispute. This will lead to "generational politicians," whose natural power groups fall along generational as well as ideological lines.

It will, indeed, be an uncomfortable time to be a politician, and will create opportunities for a so-called great leader to arise. Times of emotional crusades are times that give rabble-rousers great scope, for the public tends to narrow its focus to single issues to the detriment of other equally important, but less sexy, ones.

Next, even though the economy is going to be searching for skilled people in a wide range of fields, many echo boomers are going to find it difficult to settle into careers. Not only are they less loyal to potential employers than earlier generations, and not only do they have shorter attention spans, but work is being transformed. Companies now develop needs for particular kinds of workers, then toss the workers overboard when they no longer need them. Lack of loyalty works in both directions.

Moreover, as routine work disappears, as discussed earlier, it's going to be tougher for anyone, immigrant and Canadian-born alike, to find entry-level jobs. With the greater pressures of a faster-moving marketplace, employers will want workers who can hit the ground running and be immediately productive, instead of hiring young or inexperienced workers and nurturing them. This, plus the rising instability of jobs, works against young people looking to put their feet on the first rungs of the job ladder.

The best strategies for individuals will be to focus on occupations that don't change rapidly, and where skilled labourers will remain in demand. This kind of work will encompass everything from furniture installation and repair to nursing and carpentry. Those who have an entrepreneurial bent should study up on how to succeed as an entrepreneur, plan their moves carefully into low-risk areas, and create their own businesses and their own jobs.

Meanwhile, smart employers will find ways to hire young people as an investment in the future, whether as interns, apprentices, or junior management. Businesses of all kinds are going to need these people—it's just that they will need them later on, when they have more skills and are better seasoned in the ways of work. But the only way for the economy to "manufacture" people of that kind is to put them into a position where they can gain the knowledge, skills, contacts, and experience necessary to become the productive workers that will be needed tomorrow. This is the other side of the problem that young adults are facing: they need experience to get hired, but they can only get experience once they're hired. Likewise, companies need experienced workers, but they will only find them by giving them experience. Managements will need to look beyond the next quarter's results and think strategically.

Meanwhile, the social and consumption implications of all this are significant. Adult echo boomers, finished with their schooling but unable to find decent jobs, will linger around their parents' homes. The echoes won't enjoy this, because they will want their own lives, their own privacy, and money for fun and goodies. Their parents won't like it either. They'll be unhappy because their children are unhappy. They'll be disappointed because they find it inconvenient to have adult children knocking around the family home in rooms that are too small for adults. And it will interfere with the parents' need to save for their looming retirement.

Likewise, the consumption of these young adults will disappoint consumer companies that were hoping for big things—but where there's no discretionary income, there's no demand. And governments that need the tax revenues to pay for ever-rising health-care and pension costs for the boomers are going to be hard-pressed to manage their finances without the added worry of a large group of underemployed 20-somethings. The days of surplus financing will be remembered with nostalgia.

The results will include such developments as a rise in the underground economy, an increase in entrepreneurial businesses, a rash of government jobs programs (most of which won't work), and a growing mismatch between the people who need jobs and the companies that need workers. These issues will eventually resolve, but they will bring a stormy decade of disappointment and discomfort as the echo boomers move through their 20s.

The fashion industries will likewise be roiled. Every group and every generation has its own "in crowd" signals, from clothes to greetings to behaviour. For instance, consider the air kisses of the boomers versus the "'sup?" greeting of their kids. Echo boomers are even more fickle when it comes to fashion than earlier generations, and more idiosyncratic as well. Fashion trends, carried on the pulses of the Internet, change rapidly and globally, but individuals also carve out their own places within those trends, sometimes following them by opposing them. This will be emphasized by the move towards mass customization, with the result that the "look" of the echoes will often be wild diversity. Indeed, many times the only thing a group of echo friends will have in common is their ages.

This will drive fashion suppliers wild. Not only will fashion needs be unpredictable, making it difficult to create strong brand identities, but fashion suppliers will find it difficult, even financially dangerous, to inventory goods. In turn, this will further accentuate the need for mass customization, assassin marketing, and jigsaw products.

Finally, people who feel beset or even persecuted tend to band together, identifying with each other. The echo boomers will tend to commiserate with each other, share many of the same interests, and have a greater technological sophistication than their parents. The result will be the emergence of a new culture, distinct from that of older generations and emphasizing those differences. Multi-tasking, multi-sensory entertainment, and running multiple conversations—online, in person, and by phone, all simultaneously—will bewilder the boomers but identify the echoes. Bitterness about the financial mess left to them by their parents' generation, plus the lack of opportunities in businesses run by older

The result will be the emergence of a new culture, distinct from that of older generations and emphasizing those differences.

people, especially boomer executives, will accentuate the desire to be different. There will be a greater inclusion of global influences, and a fusion of foods, arts, ethics, music, and ideas from different cultures will flow freely among the echoes.

The precise form and fabric of this culture is beyond me. For one thing, I'm a boomer. But more importantly, the behaviour of individuals is, at present, largely unpredictable, and fashion and cultural trends are the summations of the unpredictable natures of millions of individuals.

It's going to be a heady, worrisome, frothy, stressful, weird, and wonderful period.

Generational Cross-Currents

These demographic events, when combined with some of the other factors at work, create interesting ripple effects, some of them seemingly contradictory. My earlier discussion of the growing shortage of skilled workers, combined with the inability of echo boomers to find work, is one example of such a ripple.

Another strange development is that the boomers, although still very much in evidence, seem to be disappearing as far as marketers are concerned. Marketers, and therefore advertisers, have a fixation on consumers in the 18- to 39-year-old range, and only the very youngest of the boomers fall within that category. As a result the biggest age group, which has the most (collective) money and the greatest economic and political clout in our society, is being labelled as irrelevant. I suspect that this represents enormous opportunity for smart companies that know a good arbitrage situation when they see it.

Companies that sell things that boomers buy—cars, clothes, foods, travel, books, magazines, and just about any other consumer good—will be able to market to people over 39 at near-bargain prices. Advertising rates for these groups, especially for the over-49 crowd, are cheaper, and television programs that target boomers are fewer, which means boomers' viewing choices are limited. Eventually, some smart ad agency is going to specialize in these "over the hill" consumers, go out and collect smart consumer-product companies—even if they aren't national but regional— and work this unwanted sector of the market. And some smart media-content company is going to figure out that people who are over 39 but still breathing constitute a worthwhile market, and is going to specialize in programming for that group. Older people were originally supposed to be the market for CanWest Global's Prime TV cable station, but somehow they got sidetracked into sitcom reruns. But sooner or later someone will realize that where there are consumers with money to spend, there's money to be made, and will capitalize on this sector.

Politics, as mentioned, is going to be much less settled than in the past decade or so. Politics never feels settled, because opposition parties always cry about how terrible things are. However, we are about to embark on a period when there are two major power groups: the boomers and their echo children. We'll have an interesting situation where the boomers and the war and pre-war babies are going to line up on one side, and the baby busters and echo boomers are going to line up on the other in a tug-of-war to see who is going to pay the most taxes. The numbers are with the boomers, which would argue that older voters are going to impose their wills on the younger, creating a gerontocracy in all developed countries, including Canada.

On the other hand, the younger generations are going to grow into more and more of the positions of power, giving them more influence. Then, too, the mortality rates of the baby boomers are going to rise as they get older, even with all the advances in medical research. Over time, this is a match the boomers can't win so that the echoes will eventually have their way, as the Young Turks always eventually overthrow the tyranny of the old guard.

And there's one final demographic factor to consider. Canada's population is expected to peak somewhere around 2040 because our birth rate of 1.5 children per woman is below the 2.1 needed to replace our existing population. This means that our entire society is going to be experiencing things that have never happened before, such as having fewer schoolchildren than old folks and having dramatically fewer people working to support a much larger proportion of retirees. There's lots of savings in aggregate, but not as many people creating current economic value, which argues for a rapid increase in imports.

We don't know how such an elderly society behaves because we've never had one before. We're about to start finding out, and I suspect there are going to be great problems as well as great opportunities along the way. And for those who wish to get an advance peek at this future, watch closely to what happens in Italy and Japan, the countries with the world's largest proportion of elderly inhabitants.

This chapter has been about numbers: how many people there are in each age group. The dramatic changes in consumer behaviour, though, are about much more than numbers, because attitudes, and the social structures that go with them, are shifting—and not in a positive way.

8

The Gathering Storm

If the potential for intergenerational conflict is high, then the emerging attitude changes of consumers and society as a whole are even more explosive. I see storm clouds gathering, for we are in the middle of a long-term shift in what people believe and how they behave, which will have significant implications for how your organization operates. This is happening for two major reasons. Let's deal with global awareness first.

Increasing Global Awareness Is Changing Demand and Behaviour

This is the less explosive of the two factors affecting behaviour, and the changes due to greater awareness are easy to identify. Take fashion and food, for instance. Greater awareness of different ethnic groups and customs is creating a fusion culture that opens new panoramas of taste and interest. Three generations ago, people largely ate what was grown nearby, exchanged recipes within their own communities, and, with few exceptions, wore what everyone around them wore. Today's horizons are much

People will pick and choose which fashions to follow and which to ignore based on personal preferences, peer-group pressure, and their ability to afford rapid change.

broader. Nor is this fusion culture exclusively American. True, American brands like Coke, McDonalds, and Levi's have global clout and influence. Yet consumers' increasing cynicism about brands, coupled with a desire for novelty and exposure to new alternatives, is creating a much deeper awareness of possibilities than just the shallow consumer culture that many in the West love to hate. In particular, the Internet has become the carrier of culture and fashion among the young.

This means that what's hot this morning in Japan can become hot this afternoon in Saint John and Victoria. Computer games, music, and buzz go global instantaneously. Comments on movies (and sometimes pirated versions of new releases) follow shortly after. Global groups for peace, for gays and lesbians, to combat AIDS, or to oppose oppressive regimes exchange information, tactics, and ideas in time periods measured in days or weeks. Fashions and food take a little bit longer, because people take time to experiment with them and see others pick them up. But the old, slower trend patterns are breaking down under the influence of broadband communications.

Companies are, both deliberately and inadvertently, encouraging this faster rate of contagion in new fads. When you combine the marketer's natural desire to sell what is "new" with the move towards assassin marketing, you get strong forces both pushing and pulling the marketplace in two major directions: fleeting fads and fashions that change with increasing speed; and personal eccentricities that slavishly ignore fads and fashions. Although it sounds as if these are contradictory, they are, in fact, both logical outcomes of these trends. In fact, people will pick and choose which fashions to follow and which to ignore based on personal preferences, peer-group pressure, and their ability to afford rapid change.

The Rise of Personal Environmentalism

Meanwhile, a separate information factor is going to impose a different kind of change on the marketplace. As we develop more and more knowledge about subtle genetic differences between one person and another, we will start to become aware of how our immediate environment affects our health. Hence, you might discover that you have allergies to particular kinds of building materials, such as insulation or adhesives, that don't affect me or most other people at all. This kind of awareness is just starting to emerge. As we learn more about these subtle genetic differences and become aware of how they affect our bodies' reaction to a wide range of materials—food packaging, pharmaceuticals, clothing, building materials, and more—a rising number of companies and industries will start labelling the contents of their products, much as today's food products show lists of their contents in North America. Already, California supermarkets are required to post warnings to the public about compounds used in their buildings, refrigeration equipment, and so on, that might be harmful to the health of selected individuals. This trend will spread, and will force companies to know what's in everything they sell as well as the offices where their employees work.

Likewise, greater awareness of how our bodies work, and how they differ from other people's bodies, will lead to customized diets, tailored dietary supplements, and even, potentially, the colours of the clothes we wear and the colours we paint our homes. We are finding already, for example, that diet makes a big difference to the cholesterol levels of some people, but has almost no effect on the cholesterol levels of others. Hence, while one person may successfully combat elevated cholesterol levels in the blood through diet, others may adhere to draconian food regimes and yet show no improvement in blood cholesterol, possibly needing drugs to do the job. Likewise, some people may benefit greatly from vegetarian diets, whereas others may do poorly on them.

This is a radical change from our past, where we talked about the "goodness of whole wheat" or the superiority of natural fibres.

Organizations will be faced with a future where what works for one customer or one employee may be harmful to another. This is going to make life much more complicated—but the nature of increased awareness is that it imposes increased responsibility.

Society's Core Values Are Changing

If greater awareness is the first factor producing culture change, then a shift in the core values of our society is the second. And while changes emerging from increasing awareness will complicate our lives, they are nowhere near as explosive as the changes in core values. There is no single cause for these shifts; they are happening because of combinations of factors. Moreover, they are complicated, controversial, and some of them are subtle and open to interpretation. I could be wrong about any or all of them, but they concern me greatly.

Tit-for-Tat Is Hard-wired

The biological underpinning of our society is the principle of tit-for-tat. Recent studies of higher mammals, such as those by Leda Cosmides and John Tooby of the University of California at Santa Barbara, indicate that the brains of higher mammals—including ours—are wired so that we do favours in the expectation that such favours will be returned.[1] Moreover, our brains are very good at identifying cheats—people who accept favours but don't repay them. Human societies have, historically, been based on the premise that cheats are ostracized. Contrary to the golden rule, we expect to be treated as we treat others.

Yet, this hard-wiring of our brains and behaviours happened in a prehistoric society where our ancestors saw and interacted with everyone who was important to them on a daily basis. In modern society, people we have never met may be crucially important to our daily lives. We no longer live in a "touchable" society, where tit-for-tat can be enforced, and where those who cheat by not repaying favours can be punished. Instead, modern society includes a great deal of anonymity. We can treat people as objects to be used and discarded, often without fear of reprisal. Think, for instance, of the behaviour of drivers on the 401 superhighway around Toronto.

The Erosion of Ethics

In place of the principle of tit-for-tat in a touchable society, humans developed codes of ethics and morality to help their societies function. These codes were based on common beliefs, shared religions, and communities that tended to enforce adherence to these codes with punishments ranging from shunning and censure to torture and execution. In today's multi-ethnic, multicultural societies, these common codes of behaviour are evaporating. In the words of Canadian sociologist Reginald Bibby:

> *Children who attended Sunday schools, for example, were exposed to the importance of such characteristics of honesty and kindness, politeness and generosity. . . . Some say that schools should pick up the slack: but our Canadian schools operate in a milieu that is highly conscious of cultural diversity, where people are extremely suspicious of anyone who wants to postulate values. "Whose values?" is the predictable objection.*[2]

Or, as American commentator Christopher Lasch put it: "To say that all beliefs are equally deserving of tolerance is to admit that they are all equally unimportant."[3]

Similarly, the radical Catholic theologian Hans Kung noted in 1991 that leaders such as the Ayatollah Khomeini and Pope John Paul II, plus religious fundamentalists of several faiths, seek a return to an earlier century with a stricter morality. But Kung noted that this cannot work for an emerging global culture because the vast majority will reject such a retreat from modernity. He then goes on to comment on the problem of discarding the absolute moralities of the past:

> *For the most part, the alternative [to a return to the past] has been to float uncommitted amidst an ultra-modern potpourri of beliefs, content*

with radical pluralism or relativism, the anarchy of trends, the method-
ological "anything goes" and the indifferent attitude that "all is per-
missible." . . . The mechanisms of modernity can displace a past ethic,
but they cannot themselves produce a new ethic or, in an age "beyond
good and evil" as Nietzsche properly called our modern times, even
provide a justification for ethical behavior.[4]

In other words, we no longer agree on the ethical systems of the past,
but can find no way of creating a new, consensual ethic for the future.

Without an ethical yardstick that most people are willing to accept, we
are rudderless. There's no effective way to encourage behaviour that
supports the functioning of society, and no way, short of the law, to
discourage those who undermine it. In 1994, Laval University professor and
anthropologist Bernard Arcand was quoted as saying that the
fragmentation of modern society and the extreme tolerance of different
lifestyles were new in human history, and not necessarily good.
"Traditionally, censure is essential to human society," he said. "Without it,
there's not much left."[5]

This trend towards a lack of ethics and an accepted code of behaviour
has been emerging for several centuries, in part because of the growth of
science and the erosion of superstition, compounded by increases in
communications and travel that have brought disparate groups into
contact with each other. However, it accelerated significantly in the
developed world with the emergence of the self-indulgent baby-boom
generation.

In 1998, PBS television interviewed the pioneering American pollster
Daniel Yankelovich and asked him, among other things, how he assessed
the changes in social attitudes since the 1960s. He replied that the affluence
of the 1960s and 1970s caused baby boomers to first question, and then
discard, the idea that they needed to sacrifice their own personal desires in
favour of the economic needs of their spouses and families. As a result,
there was a widespread movement to embrace self-expression and
fulfillment, and to avoid self-sacrifice for family or society. This produced

both good and bad consequences. On the positive side, Yankelovich said, it dramatically increased our level of tolerance for people of different races, religions, sexes, and sexual preferences. But this tolerance came at a cost: "There was a kind of narcissism, preoccupation with self, a loss of moral centered-ness, and this hubris and egoism."[6]

The hallmark of our society is becoming the avoidance of responsibility. Individuals do everything they can to evade responsibility, to the refrain of "it's not my fault!"

We have become self-absorbed narcissists, to the detriment of our society. Indeed, someone who talks about making sacrifices for the social good is often looked at as odd, a "real Boy Scout," as if being a Boy Scout was, itself, a weird and inexplicable thing. And the result is that many of us behave as if we really don't care what happens to other people as the result of our actions. This leads to people talking on cellphones during theatrical performances; parents bringing small children to fancy restaurants, then letting them roam freely, causing havoc and annoying other diners; pet owners failing to police their pets; drivers cutting each other off, and having virtual battles on the highways; grown-ups dumping litter on public streets; corporations dumping poisons in the local water supply in the expectation they won't get caught; and governments scrapping emission controls to encourage investment by polluters. The functioning concept of "society" is being replaced by collections of selfish individuals and organizations that behave like spoiled children instead of responsible citizens.

Indeed, the hallmark of our society is becoming the avoidance of responsibility. Individuals do everything they can to evade responsibility, to the refrain of "it's not my fault!" *The Economist,* in a rare fit of editorial pique, described the development of this attitude in the trend-setting United States as the emergence of "decadent puritanism."[7] Decadent puritans demand that everyone else be held to account for any real or perceived misdeed, but they themselves rigorously deny any restraint on their behaviour, loudly demanding their "rights." This ranges from the character assassination of public figures to lawsuits against companies for any problems—spilling hot coffee on their laps, perhaps, or becoming obese from overeating. It means that if a university student flunks an exam, she sues the university, or accuses the professor of racism, sexism, or some other form of discrimination. It means if someone in a competition loses, he claims the rules are unfair, or the start was flawed, or the other competitors cheated, or the judges were biased, and demands that the competition be done over until he gets the result he wants. This is the behaviour of infants, yet a small but rising proportion of our society acts this way.

On a political level this has consequences as well. First, fewer people bother to vote, partly because they feel that they are powerless, and their votes have no effect, and partly because they feel disconnected from the officials elected. "They're all crooks anyways," is the common theme, "I wouldn't vote for any of 'em."

Moreover, this indifference to equity and fairness has led to a dramatic rise in the demands for special treatment. Every self-defined group that can find an excuse for using the label "victim" seeks special privileges from government, or exemption from rules or taxes that the group finds onerous or inconvenient. This includes corporations and organizations, some of which have no rationale for special treatment other than their ability to get it. After all, if it's passed into law or regulation, then it's legal. Who cares if it's ethical?

The United States, typically ahead of Canada in social trends, shows us where this is leading. When enough people join "special-interest groups," they cease being special and become the norm. Journalist Jonathan Rauch noted in 1994 that 7 out of 10 Americans belonged to at least one politically oriented group, and one-quarter of Americans belonged to four such groups or more. "Thanks to interest-group politics, any policy that confers advantage on a group tends to become permanent, however ineffective it may be at achieving its original purpose."[8] Our politics are quickly becoming a matter of "What can we get away with?"

We are becoming an amoral society, and the people it hurts most are our children.

The Rise of "Divorce Culture"

Everyone agrees that children thrive best in a stable home environment. Yet the environment in which our children are being raised is increasingly unstable. This doesn't apply to all children, or even a majority, but a steadily rising percentage are raised in divorced, re-formed, or single-parent families that offer less support than the classic nuclear families of an earlier generation.

This is not always a bad thing. It's undoubtedly worse for children to grow up in an abusive family situation, and divorce is in many cases the only escape from such relationships. But even when divorce happens for good reasons, it has consequences. Anne-Marie Ambert, a professor of sociology at York University, says the consequences of divorce include:[9]

- Poverty, especially for ex-wives. When figures are adjusted for family size, an ex-wife's income drops by 40 percent while an ex-husband's increases slightly. Meanwhile, 16 percent of married women lived below the poverty line before divorce, 43 percent after divorce. In 1994, 21 percent of all Canadian children lived in poverty but an astounding 65.8 percent of children of single-mother families did, and single parents who are poor have incomes that, on average, are 40 percent below the poverty line. Poverty has obvious harmful effects on children.

- Most children of divorced couples grow up much like their peers. However, statistically, children of a divorce are more likely than their peers to suffer from depression and other emotional disorders; exhibit higher levels of hyperactivity, aggressiveness, and hostility; become young offenders; drop out of school earlier and do less well while in school; have problems with relationships with their peers; have children out of wedlock; be unemployed and do more poorly as adults; and have more marital problems of their own.

Moreover, divorces don't always happen for good reasons. As columnist Michael Valpy commented: "We are creating a lot of dysfunctional kids because adult Canadians to a distressing degree have been treating the family as an institution whose form and durability is a matter of personal convenience rather than the enduring and protective cradle of child development."[10]

Nor is it just the children of such families that feel the effects. Robert Glossop, executive director of programs at the Vanier Institute in Ottawa, told me in a personal interview that "increasingly unstable family environments create an awareness of instability even among children who grow up in stable families. This is part of the 'divorce culture' in which we now live, where all personal commitments and promises are seen as being temporary."[11]

So divorce happens and it sometimes harms children. There is, however, something worse going on.

The Betrayal of Our Children

Almost all the books on childrearing emphasize the need for consistency in setting and maintaining boundaries for children. After raising two children of my own (with my wife), and having been a Scout leader for more than a dozen years, I believe that the primary reason children push against such boundaries is so that they know where they're safe. But for this message of safety to be received and believed by children, the answers have to be consistent. If an adult says it's bad to stay up late and watch television one school night but it's okay the next school night, then the message is confusing and the anxiety of the child rises because it's no longer clear what works and what doesn't. When this happens, the child will push harder against whatever boundaries there are, wanting the reassurance of knowing when and where and how they will be okay. If the parent continues to send conflicting signals, the child will push harder still. Moreover, there are rewards for successfully getting around some of the boundaries: you get to stay up late, eat food that may be inappropriate but tastes good, play the games you want, get the toys you want, and avoid doing your homework. This further reinforces the natural tendency to test boundaries.

Now, however, parents are ignoring these psychological needs in their children. Not all parents, and not all the time, but an increasing minority are, and it is producing two major problems. First, it is creating a generation of children who are even more self-indulgent than their parents. They are becoming the spoiled children of spoiled children. And second, it is creating a climate of anxiety for children unfortunate enough to have parents who are so self-absorbed that they can't be bothered to be consistent in their discipline, and so are unpredictably harsh or lenient, as the mood takes them.

When combined with a society that increasingly sends the message that personal expression, rights, and freedoms are all important, and responsibility is for chumps, what emerges is a society that encourages permissiveness, discourages civic responsibility, and instills anxiety in all children.

But the problems don't stop with the children of such parents. When combined with a society that increasingly sends the message that personal expression, rights, and freedoms are all important, and responsibility is for chumps, what emerges is a society that encourages permissiveness, discourages civic responsibility, and instills anxiety in all children. And as this message becomes pervasive, it creates a climate of confusion about right and wrong for diligent parents as well.

U.S. author and educator Sal Severe was quoted in a recent *Toronto Star* article as saying that our society has become very pluralistic in its value system. "When I was a kid," he recalled, "no matter where I went to play, the rules were pretty much the same. That made it easy for me to learn right from wrong." Now, he said, some households are allowing even 10-year-olds to watch R-rated movies. A lot of permissiveness happens today, he said, because parents "don't want their kids to not like them, they think they've got to be their kids' friends. Those are mistakes, in my opinion. You are an authority figure."[12]

Meanwhile, our commercial culture—the marketing efforts of corporations—undermines the efforts of the majority of parents who try to

give their children a secure home environment. Robert Glossop of the
Vanier Institute commented on just this point in a speech he gave in 2002:

> *I have heard this suggestion that it is [parents'] duty and [parents'] obli-*
> *gation to guide their children expressed by the music producers of*
> *"Gangsta Rap." It has been used as a defense by a British company that*
> *now designs, produces and promotes sexy lingerie to 9-year-old girls. It is*
> *articulated by those who would have us believe that Britney Spears suc-*
> *ceeds on the basis of her musical talent alone. And, even more self-*
> *servingly, those who entice our children into pornographic web sites or*
> *online gambling would have us believe that it is up to parents to better*
> *instruct, monitor, control and, if necessary, punish their children if they*
> *visit the wrong addresses in cyber space.*
>
> *. . . Until recently, parents were largely supported in their efforts to*
> *instill in their children certain "traditional" civic virtues of duty, honour,*
> *honesty, contribution, temperance, dignity, conscience and sacrifice. Yet,*
> *today, these words that were once reinforced by neighbours, teachers,*
> *community groups, faiths, employers, and politicians all sound just a*
> *little too quaint. And, especially so when so few of us adults have chosen*
> *to live our lives in accordance with these values. Ask yourself how many*
> *of our success stories (other than Mother Teresa) in business, sports,*
> *entertainment and politics have achieved their success because of*
> *their sense of duty to others, their honesty, their contributions, their*
> *temperance, dignity and sacrifice.*
>
> *. . . My point is that it is neither fair nor realistic to blame parents for*
> *failing in their responsibilities when most of the commercial interests that*
> *drive popular culture, the mass media, the clothing industry are dead set*
> *on systematically undermining the good work that most parents try to do*
> *in raising their children. Those who produce and sell violent video games*
> *are not in the business of child development; they are in the business of*
> *making money. And, in too many ways, peer culture too is working*
> *against the goals of parents. I think [Cornell University Professor] Jim*
> *Garbarino is right when he says that parents are trying to raise kids in*
> *a "socially toxic environment."*[13]

The classic example of this is the video game that was all the rage for Christmas of 2002: "Grand Theft Auto: Vice City." In this R-rated game, the player fills the role of a car thief and general low-life who can pick up prostitutes, steal cars, rub out competitors, and generally behave in a way that would get you locked up or killed in real life. It was widely acclaimed by critics as the greatest, most realistic, most addictive game of the year. My concern with this game was not the game itself—let those adults who like such things play them. I'm concerned about the reports of adults who bought this game for children, either their own or someone else's. They did this because it was a really cool game, and they thought the kids would like it, or because their kids nagged, pleaded, whined, and wheedled until the parents gave in. As Robert Glossop commented, commercial interests view this kind of thing as a private matter between parents and children, even as they hope the adults cave in.

It's not just a private matter between parents and children, for it affects us all and our society. John Colwell, a lecturer at Middlesex University in England, completed a study in 2000 on the effects of violent computer games on boys, and concluded that such games incited them to violence. He found that children became more aggressive the longer they played violent computer games. Those who played such computer games the most shouted, pushed, and hit other children, and had the fewest friends. Indeed, such children reported that they saw the computer as their friend, sometimes their only friend. Colwell's report tallies with another British study, by Mark Griffiths, a psychologist at Nottingham Trent University, who found that boys between the ages of four and eight who were allowed to play mildly violent games showed dramatically higher levels of aggression.[14]

It's Not *All* Bad

Before you take a razor to your wrists because of all this bad news, it's important to note that there are good things happening as well. First, most people still behave morally. It's a minority—albeit a steadily increasing minority—of people who behave amorally. You know this from personal experience when you run into people who don't care what problems they cause for others or for their society. Second, the rise of tolerance for people of other belief structures and styles of living, as Yankelovich pointed out, and the rise of travel and immigration are creating a diverse, exciting, and vibrant new culture. Even without a formal new set of ethics, certain things are coming to be accepted as globally right, such as the education and emancipation of women, and wrong, such as the exploitation of children for cheap labour. These are all outgrowths of these same forces, and they will eventually evolve into a global sense of right and wrong. But for the moment, I want to focus on the role of business in what's happening, and the actions you need to take to defend yourself.

The Implications for Business

My point in criticizing commercial culture is not that business people are profiteering scum, because I don't believe that. My point is that in pursuit of profit, we in the private sector frequently don't think about the downstream consequences of what we do. But for the moment, let me sidestep the philosophical and social consequences of short-sightedness, and focus specifically on the practical, immediate steps you need to take to secure the future of your organization. These rules apply no matter what kind of organization yours is, private-sector or public, profit-oriented or non-profit.

Guard Yourself

In an increasingly amoral society, don't automatically expect fair play or honesty from your customers, clients, or employees. You will most often be pleasantly surprised, because most people try to behave ethically. But when people don't behave ethically, they won't announce themselves beforehand. They'll look and act just the way everyone else does—until they attempt to savage you. Consider one possible scenario from the near future:

Toby is ambling through the West Edmonton Mall, people-watching, when he spies two men arguing over something at the top of an escalator. He casually yawns and stretches, then leans on the railing overlooking the floor below and idly glances in their general direction, apparently looking at the display in a store window, but choosing a window that allows him to keep the pair in view. He mumbles an instruction to his computer genie, and hears the conversation amplified in his earpiece.

As he listens, it becomes apparent to him that they're planning an "accident" on the escalator. Abruptly, the younger one chops off the conversation and moves into the line on the escalator, making sure that the two or three steps in front of him are clear. Toby turns to watch the descent, and—sure enough—as he reaches the bottom, the first man apparently catches a shoe on the grille at the bottom of the escalator and collapses in a heap, rolling in apparent agony, clutching his back, and howling in pain. The second man quickly crouches down beside him, apparently offering assistance.

Security guards quickly arrive on the scene, and help the pair out of the public eye and into the security offices of the mall. Toby casually follows, and waits outside the office for a couple of minutes before going in. As he enters, the receptionist looks up, asking if she can help. Toby says, "Perhaps I can help you. I watched the two people who were just brought in here plan the accident that just happened." The receptionist looks startled, then asks him to have a seat and goes off to get the head of security. She arrives, looking harried, and abruptly asks Toby what's up, clearly feeling the pressure. When Toby describes what he witnessed, the security chief's face smooths out, and she asks Toby to step into another office, cautioning him to be silent. As he enters, he sees why—it's a room with one-way glass, and the two men are seated in the office next door. The head of security whispers to him to wait there, then returns to the office that is visible through the one-way glass.

It quickly becomes apparent that the man who's acting hurt is working up to threats of a lawsuit, because he's complaining more and more loudly about the negligence of the mall. When the men finally make it plain what they're after, the head of security frowns, then excuses herself for a second. She returns to the room where Toby has been watching and listening, and asks him if he can help the mall at this point.

This is what Toby has been waiting for. He smiles, and says that not only did he see the encounter happen but he has it all on video, including part of the discussion before the fact. He's more than willing to help the mall—for a price. The head of security looks sour, then asks what he wants. "One-quarter of whatever they sue you for," he replies. The security head stares at him for a moment, then sighs and says she'll have to check with her superiors, but tentatively agrees.

Accordingly, when a suit is filed against the mall, the mall counters with a suit against the complainant, using Toby's recording. The suit is quickly quashed, and Toby begins to think about how he's going to spend his new-found money.

The next day, both he and the mall receive notices of a lawsuit for violation of copyright by the videotaping of the "performance art" of the two men; violation of personal privacy; conspiracy to entrap; and defamation of character. With punitive damages, the two men are asking for $240 million—about 10 times the amount sought in the original suit.

You will need to make sure you prepare your defences against people inside and outside your organization who will attempt to exploit you any way they can. You only have to look at the latest rounds of asbestos-related lawsuits in the United States. Companies are being included as defendants in lawsuits, even though they have never been involved in producing or using asbestos, simply because they have a lot of insurance. The point of the suits is to provoke a settlement, gambling that the companies, even though innocent, won't want the expense of an extended legal battle.

The Canadian legal system is nowhere near as litigious as its U.S. counterpart, but we are heading in that direction. My point is simply that you need to protect yourself, because the incidence of people who are going to try to take advantage of you is rising.

> *One of the problems of a society with a rising tide of selfish people is that they don't make good team players.*

Create a Corporate Culture that Rewards Team-Building

One of the problems of a society with a rising tide of selfish people is that they don't make good team players. This comes at a time when companies need people with complementary talents to work together for the common (organizational) good. Typifying this attitude is the apocryphal story of the new MBA who's being interviewed for an entry-level management position. When asked if he considers himself a team player, he says, "Absolutely—as long as I'm the captain."

Accordingly, you will need to create a corporate culture that encourages and rewards team-building, and explicitly teaches people how to be team players and how to work effectively within a team. Failing to do so will result in people going through the motions of teamwork, but finally either doing nothing they don't get direct credit for, or actively sabotaging the efforts of others.

Build a "Good Guy" Organization

I'll discuss this in more length in Chapter 10. For the moment, let me just point out that "decadent puritans" hypocritically hold everyone else to standards of artificial perfection, and organizations are targets for such people. If you are seen as being neighbourhood good guys, it will be harder for such charges to stick than if you are interested only in your own bottom line.

Develop a Strong Sense of Enlightened Self-Interest

You can't find and retain good people if good people don't flourish in the society in which you operate. Accordingly, you need to be looking at the communities in which you work as the field that you cultivate for your workers, and act as if you care what happens there. This means being involved in community efforts and encouraging your employees to do the same. It means sometimes digging into your pocket for the common good when there's no direct benefit to you. It means supporting a local school, college, or university that produces the kinds of workers you'll need in the future, even though you may not be hiring just at the moment. It means looking beyond immediate profit and planning intelligently for a future of enlightened self-interest.

Be Aware of the Effects of Your Business on Your Community

Suppose you sold syringes and found out that your sales were rising because heroin use among the young was going up. You might see an increase in revenues because of such sales, and it might imply that these kids were going to become heavy customers later on—but I doubt that you'd be pleased it was happening. So how is selling adult computer games, and encouraging parents to buy them for their children, different? Just because you can make money doing something doesn't mean that it's advantageous for you to do it. And if you decide to ignore this warning and screw society to gain short-term profits, make sure you pile up big reserves for the lawsuits that will come flocking in later on.

Know and Work at Instilling Your Corporate Values

In Chapter 3 I talked about why some companies survive over the long haul when most companies don't last 30 years. One of the key points that comes through loud and clear when you examine the work of people like Arie de Geus or James Collins and Jerry Porras is that companies that survive have a strong sense of identity. This includes a vibrant corporate culture that embodies what the company believes in and encourages employees to believe and behave according to the corporate ethos, plus a solid involvement in the communities in which the company operates. All of these are transmitted by the attitudes and actions of management.

Yet the development of a constructive corporate culture is one of the most important and also one of the most difficult things to do. It takes complete commitment by management to walk the talk. It's crucial to the success of your company that everyone knows what values you think are important, and that all of your recruiting, employment policies, and behaviour support and embody these values. Most companies don't know what they stand for, beyond higher profits next quarter, which is a disastrous strategy. Know where you stand, then make sure your company's actions support that stand.

As the Storm Breaks

I know many will dislike my comments in this chapter, but we are experiencing dramatic qualitative changes in the assumptions and beliefs that underlie and drive our society. If you fail to prepare for these changes, whether you agree with the tone of my comments or not, your organization will suffer.

The old tools of demographics and psychographics are losing their power. Age, social position, income, and occupation no longer have the same predictive punch that they had before, and marketers are going to have to think more deeply to succeed. Consumers are becoming more erratic and less predictable.

If I had to sum up the fourth secret in a phrase, it would be "to cultivate a greater sensitivity to the changes stirring in our society." I'm going to develop this idea further in the fifth secret by suggesting that you dive beneath the surface of economic activity, for there are changes coming there as well. For now, let me close this section by urging you to prepare for the gathering storm. Watch the horizon and think about what you are witnessing, and what it means for your organization. You may not be able to prevent the storm, but you will be better off if you prepare for it than if you wait until it catches you by surprise.

5th Secret

Listen to the Money

*"The love of money as a possession—
as distinguished from love of money
as a means to the enjoyments
and realities of life—will be recognized
for what it is, a somewhat disgusting
morbidity."*

—JOHN MAYNARD KEYNES

9

The Economy's Wellspring

One of the most powerful forces in the world is also the economy's most important wellspring. It's one of those things that's out in plain sight all the time yet is hardly ever noticed, despite its importance. When individuals die, the houses they owned and lived in, the money they had saved up, and their personal belongings don't die off with them, but are passed on to the next generation. When a CEO retires, the company doesn't vanish, but endures. Each new generation builds on the accomplishments of the ones before it. This is the foundation of economic growth, and in economic terms it's described as the compounding of wealth.

Wealth is not money. Money is a symbol that represents the fruits of human time, effort, and skill. Wealth is not a symbol, but the thing itself. And the compounding of wealth—the building on the accomplishments of the past—is the foundation of every civilization and every society.

Yet, when considering the future, we have become so blasé about the compounding of wealth that we fail to take it into account. We talk about "economic growth" or "GNP growth" or some similar term, and forget, at least momentarily, how significant it is that there is growth. Moreover, we hardly ever ask why there is growth, or, more importantly, where there will be growth. Someone once said, "It has long been known that one horse can run faster than another—but

In planning for the future, knowing where wealth will compound is crucial.

which one? Differences are crucial."[1] In planning for the future, knowing where wealth will compound is crucial. You might almost say that knowing this is a primary purpose of planning, so let's look at the future of wealth.

The Past and Future of Wealth

It's part of the way our brains work that we want to accomplish things. We see this in a young child playing with blocks, and in CEOs of major corporations. It's innate and universal. And most of us want things to get better, whether for ourselves and our families or for the starving poor abroad. Even those devoted to spiritual matters want to improve their own purity and help those around them. On a material plane, having things get better is the result of the work we do, which produces the wealth necessary to help the poor, feed the hungry, or buy the shiny new Bimmer with the CD changer and the heated leather seats. So wealth comes from the human desire to have things get better.

But another name for having things get better economically is "growth," and there's a long tradition of people who believe that growth is an unhealthy, even evil thing. The anti-globalization movement falls into this category, as do the more extreme environmentalists. However, they're only following in well-established footsteps. In 1972, the so-called Club of Rome issued a report, *The Limits of Growth,* which predicted widespread economic doom. The global think-tank said we would run out of natural resources, especially oil, and that our farmers would be unable to feed the exploding global population, all before the end of the 20th century.

Nor was the Club of Rome even close to being the first to espouse the view that growth would lead to disaster. Thomas Malthus, the English economist who wrote "Essay on the Principle of Population" in 1798, suggested that population grows faster than food production, so that wide-scale death is inevitable through famine, pestilence, or war. But Malthus has been largely proven wrong: food production is winning the race with population growth, and the finish line—a levelling off and subsequent decline in human population sometime later this century—is now in sight. Indeed, by the end of the 20th century, for the first time in history, the amount of food being produced was enough that no one needed to go hungry—although many did. In fact, farmers in developed countries are often at each other's throats, through their governments, because there aren't enough places to sell or give surpluses away. (Unfortunately, in the developing world, starvation is often used as a means of manipulating elections, or gaining or exercising power.)

What makes this miracle of perpetual growth possible? Is Nature's bounty endless, or is there something else at work?

Well, first, Nature's bounty, so to speak, is just about endless—at a price. Proven reserves of oil are greater today than there were in 1972, but oil can't be brought out of the ground for the same price as in the 1970s. Oil may need to sell at US$30 a barrel, or $40, or $100. But the higher the price of oil, the more oil is found, whether from the Alberta tar sands or the bottom of the ocean trenches. Moreover, we have literally just scratched the surface of the Earth for resources. The deepest wells we've ever drilled, the most extensive mines we've ever dug, go down through only a fraction of the Earth's crust, which is up to 30 kilometres thick compared with the planet's 12,000-kilometre diameter.

And if we should, somehow, manage to deplete the Earth's resources, there's almost certainly more to be found in outer space. By the end of this century we will be mining the moon, the asteroid belt, and possibly Mars and Jupiter as well—if we need to. The universe, even that minuscule part that is within our grasp without *Star Trek*'s warp drive, is much greater than contemplated in the philosophies of the scarcity crowd and the doomsayers.

Yet the bounty of Nature is really of less importance than the inventiveness of humanity, which is the second part of the miracle, and the crucial part of the future of wealth. As one example, Jesse Ausubel of

Rockefeller University calculates that if the world's farmers can maintain merely the 2-percent-a-year gain in productivity that has been the norm since 1960, then we will be able to feed a global population of 10 billion people while using only half of the arable land currently under cultivation.[2]

You can see evidence of this for yourself. A couple of years back, my family and I drove to the Maritimes for our summer holiday, and drove back through Maine, Vermont, and New Hampshire. We were all struck by the immense, pristine forests through that part of our journey, but thought little about it until, some months later, I read that most of the land we had been driving through had been farmland, cleared and under cultivation, in the 19th century. In roughly 100 years all of those farms had gone back to forests, because the food they produced was no longer needed, and no longer competitive.

It may be that large stretches of the Prairies in Canada and the Great Plains in the United States will revert to wild grassland as the cost-efficient surviving farms produce more and more food on less and less land. And that's without considering the revolutions yet to come out of genetics and the biosciences. This, of course, will be a financial disaster for many Prairie farmers, and it will produce a quandary for some environmentalists: Do they decry the advance of science that allows much of the Earth to return towards its natural state? Or do they complain about all the farmland that is being laid fallow?

It doesn't really matter. One hundred years from now, the Earth will look very different from today. There will be more forests again, more swamps (or "wetlands"), and more wild grasslands as humanity pensions off large parts of the Earth that have fed, housed, and sheltered us for so long, and as we replace practices that are millennia old with more efficient ones that produce more with less. As the following vignette from beyond the year 2100 indicates, our descendants (and possibly we ourselves) might experience that world of plenty in ways that would surprise us now:

Charlie looked out over the vastness of the Alberta prairie and marvelled. As far as his eye could see, there was nothing but grass.

The sun had just appeared over the horizon, and the waving grasslands created ripples of light and darkness that somehow produced a sense of harmony, soothing him.

On the trail out from the bunkhouse, he and the other riders had seen the foundations of an old farmhouse and a crumbling old highway, reminders that humans had once lived here and grown crops. The physical remainders of farms in most of the Prairies were slowly disappearing into the mists of 21st-century history.

Charlie shifted in the saddle. He was more accustomed to riding a horse than he had been six days earlier, when he'd arrived at the ranch for his vacation, but his thighs still ached. Charlie remembered his dad telling him about farming in his youth, early in the 2000s, when farms spread over many hectares of land and farmers lived poor but died rich. His dad had talked about farms with a nostalgia that, Charlie knew from his reading of the times, existed mostly in the minds of city dwellers. It sounded like hard work to Charlie, all that plowing and planting and harvesting. Nowadays, at the dawn of the 22nd century, food came from a vat in Phoenix or Philadelphia, where genetic engineering turned sunlight and raw materials directly into the nutrients the human body needed. Foods were still cooked and prepared into the familiar forms, but they were healthier now that scientists knew what was truly safe and for whom.

Farmers had gradually gone bankrupt through the first half of the 21st century, continuing the trend from the 20th, until finally the government had paid the few remaining family farms to become living museums, such as Tucker's Ranch, where Charlie was staying. Charlie was unusual among his peers. He loved history, and earned a living by lecturing on it, from earliest recorded time on to the near past, and he was struck by how much things had changed. In the 18th and 19th centuries, people had cleared forests, drained swamps, and plowed the land under. Today they were carefully redesigning wetlands and encouraging the Prairies to return to their original state, even reintroducing plants and animals that had largely been displaced by humans. Two days earlier, Charlie had seen a herd of bison grazing, and the bulletin board at the ranch carried warnings about cougars.

The human population had peaked at just over 9.5 billion late in the 21st century, and was now trending down. Almost all disease had been defeated, even the diseases of poor countries, as the tools of biological research became more powerful and easier to use, forcing drug companies to go after less and less profitable bugs as the lucrative ones were taken care of. Food prices were negligible for staples, and the only food companies that survived were the most cost-effective producers, plus those fashion houses that could continue to titillate the taste buds of jaded consumers. There were still poor people, especially a number who were homeless, and there were still loud debates about how best to help them. But the state would provide the basics of life to anyone who wanted them. Most people tried to make a living by handicraft and art, and amateur performances were universal, and poorly attended. Tourism was the largest industry today, and most people could afford some travel as it had become so inexpensive. As for wealth, anyone who was talented enough to create a well-paying job and continually build it up could afford to live more opulently than princes and kings of old.

But there was a restlessness for something more than sitting at home, experiencing the news, and waiting for your latest government paycheque. That was why the space program had literally taken off with a vengeance in the second half of the 21st century, especially after the first beanstalk—as the space elevators were called—went up, making the departure from Earth's gravity so cheap. Even though large swaths of the media and many people in the general population still decried the money spent on the exploitation of space, it was almost as if humanity needed a challenge great enough to demand the risking of lives. Colonies on Luna and Mars and the mining of asteroids weren't enough any more. Now the Deep Space Institute was designing a probe to send to

Alpha Centauri, the closest neighbouring star system, with rumblings about a human mission to follow. It was a challenging time to be alive, and Charlie wondered what would happen next.

It's hard to know whether this kind of scenario is idyllic or horrifying. When the economy can produce enough material goods to feed, clothe, and house everyone without effort, how will the goodies be distributed? Will socialism finally triumph because of capitalism's success? And what will the purpose of life be if your labour is no longer needed? These are the big questions for future decades.

Economic Magic

Inventiveness—innovation, creativity, new discoveries, and all—is the real magic of the future, and indeed, of the past. And inventiveness itself is subject to the compounding of wealth: we build on the discoveries and hard-earned insights of the generations that came before us. It can most easily be seen in the telecommunications industry. The information that used to be carried by tonnes of copper cable can now be carried by a single strand of optical fibre—which will still have room to spare for many millions of additional conversations. We are doing more with less, and doing it more efficiently, more effectively, and more cheaply. And doing things more cheaply means we can do more things with the same money, which means our standard of living goes up. But that leads to a more contentious question.

The compounding of wealth means that, short of a global disaster comparable to the dinosaur-killing asteroid of 65 million years ago, or a worldwide nuclear or trade war, the global economy and hence the world's people are going to get richer over the next 100 years, the next 20 years, the next 10 years. But, as with wealth throughout history, we are not all going to get equally wealthy.

I remember, early on in my career in the investment business, having lunch with a director of the firm I was working for. He had been an airman in the Second World War, had been shot down early in the war, and spent years in a prisoner-of-war camp. He said that everyone arrived equally poor, with only the clothes on their backs, many of them in rags. Possibly one person might have had a spoon, or a pen, but nothing more. By the end of the war, there were dramatic differences in the wealth of different prisoners. Some scraped by on prison food, or picked up table scraps by running errands for other prisoners. Others, like my friend, created works of art that they traded for extra food or clothing or blankets. And some, the aristocrats of the camp, created large trading empires, in which they traded what one person found useless to someone who wanted it. Since trading was technically forbidden, such people often risked severe punishment, including execution, in order to run their businesses. These princes of the camp slept in soft beds, and had plenty of hot food cooked and served to them by prisoners who acted as servants.

Inventiveness itself is subject to the compounding of wealth: we build on the discoveries and hard-earned insights of the generations that came before us.

There will be those who respond to this story by saying that it's not fair for some to prosper and not share their gains. To them I ask: Would it be better if all the prisoners remained equally destitute? The wealthy ones did share their wealth, by hiring servants, and by buying things that other prisoners made. They created wealth—they didn't inherit it—by risking their lives, by pitting their skills against the skills of others, and by bringing resources in from outside the camp that improved the lives of many prisoners. But, at root, those who dislike unequal results are right: open markets are never fair. People may start equal, but they won't stay that way. Those who take risks and succeed and those who can size up a need and find a way to fill it will prosper beyond those who won't risk, or won't try, or who are plain unlucky.

So we know that while wealth will inevitably grow in the future, we also know that some will prosper and some won't. Social commentators often worry that the rich get richer and the poor get poorer. But they've only got it half right. In general, the rich get richer and the poor get richer, but the rich get richer faster. To see this, consider the poor of North America, even the homeless of our big cities. I was a shift captain with Out of the Cold in Toronto, a charitable movement operated by churches, synagogues, and temples that feeds and offers shelter to the homeless. I've met and chatted with a number of homeless people, and they are, indeed, destitute. They are badly dressed, have no regular shelter, and live uncomfortable, precarious lives. Yet, at that, they are better off, on the whole, than their counterparts in parts of Africa, say, or Bangladesh. They have access to medical care, hit-or-miss though it is, that is far superior to their counterparts in the developing world. They can find shelter if they choose, and will receive food and clothing from charitable agencies. They often have substance addictions that are unthinkable in poor countries because the cost would be prohibitive. That the homeless in our society are forced to resort to live as they do is unfortunate, and a source of great shame, but they are far better off than their counterparts in poorer countries.

Or consider those who live below the poverty line but are not homeless. They typically struggle with money, and their children are poorly fed and clothed. But those children go to school, and the families have medical care and often own a television set—sometimes a car—all unimaginable luxuries for their counterparts in poor countries.

So as an illustration of the difference between rich and poor, it's quite clear: as the rich get richer in an open economy, generally speaking the poor get richer too.

You can argue that the rich are too rich, that it's obscene that a small group of people should have so much wealth, yet even here you would have a hard time making a case when compared with recent history, never mind the princes and aristocrats of more distant times. Bill Gates, the wealthiest person today, is a comparative pauper next to John D. Rockefeller or Andrew Carnegie in terms of purchasing power. Gates's much-derided mansion in Washington State is a 2-hectare spread with a 1,035-square-metre main house. This is almost a cottage compared to the San Simeon estate of William Randolph Hearst, who between 1919 and 1947 built a palace with 165 rooms on 51 landscaped hectares within a larger estate of 100,000 hectares adjacent to the California Big Sur coast.

So it's absolutely true that the rich have more than the poor, and it's not fair. But let's put this aside, because it's not going to change. Instead, let's focus on where wealth will be puddling up in the future.

Tomorrow's Wealth

If wealth compounds, then the first and most obvious place to look for tomorrow's wealth is today's pools of wealth. As someone once remarked, when you start with nothing, making a million is a miracle; when you start with $100 million, making a million is inevitable. So start by looking at individuals and families that have money, for today's wealthy families will mostly maintain their wealth and own significant corporations. Yet that's not typically where most future growth will emerge.

The next place to look for tomorrow's wealth is wealthy companies. Like rich families, they start out with a head start. However, most companies have their wealth tied up in their operations. Operating companies do not keep their assets in bonds and clip coupons. As a result, wealthy companies literally bet the farm on their ability to continue to make money. That is their *raison d'être*. But as we saw earlier in the book, the lifespan of companies—even big, successful companies—is getting progressively shorter as the level of competition continues to rise. Having the dominant market position along with a solid, internationally known brand name and lots of muscle is not enough to ensure survival, let alone continuing wealth. And, as discussed earlier, the ability of companies to survive and prosper lies in their ability to optimize the value of the only remaining asset that counts in the long run: the brains of their people. This argues forcefully that most companies, regardless of their present stature, will eventually fall by the wayside. So, for currently wealthy companies, the wealth of the future lies squarely in the way they treat their people.

What is left as the most important source of future wealth is the money invested in the stock market, particularly when it's invested with individuals and groups that create a more competitive tomorrow. Emerging winners will do this by offering better products or services, or better support, or by finding a way of tickling the customers' fancy better than more established firms. But the net result is that new winners appear with great regularity, even as older companies decay and fall away. The overall pool of investment capital continues to grow, even as some individual investments fail.

Of course, when investment markets go down, as markets will, it's for two primary reasons. First, markets correct for prior excesses, "irrational exuberance" to borrow a phrase from Alan Greenspan, chair of the U.S. Federal Reserve Bank. Almost any investment medium—stocks and currencies included—will correct when it gets overpriced, and usually overcorrect, since investments are driven by psychology in the short run. Second, and of greater long-term importance, stocks grow by being tied to underlying economic growth—to the compounding of wealth.

As I write this, the markets are down in the dumps, the Dow Jones Industrials are jittering above and below the 8,000 mark, and the Toronto Stock Exchange is stalled near 6,500. The North American economy is slow, war with Iraq is imminent, and the psychology of the market is lousy, like a dog that's been kicked too often. Yet, short of some unforeseen disaster, such as a global war, it's certain that the economy will rev up again, companies will make money again, and stocks will rise again. The forces of demographics, corporate economics, and the substantial boost resulting from the integration of the global economy dictate that good times will roll once more. Several years ago, in 1996, I stated that the TSE 300 would easily break through 36,000 by 2020. I see no reason to change my mind, unless I were to revise my target upwards.

The global economy will continue to grow for several reasons. The first is globalization. The integration of individual national economies into a single, worldwide marketplace is boosting the potential growth of all economies. This is happening because global competition means greater competition. In turn this means more innovation, which leads to higher productivity, which leads to cheaper products and services, which lead to higher standards of living. Higher standards of living mean consumers buy more. The net result is that all economies wind up better off.

Of course, that's not true for every company or individual. Among companies, greater competition means a faster rate at which some companies will win, and others will lose. It means that most workers will improve their lives, and some will lose their jobs. But for consumers and the economy overall, it means the large majority of people will be better off.

The next reason why the global economy will continue to grow is that technology will continue to expand. We will be able to do more with less, as with optical fibre versus copper cable, and the savings will allow us to spend more in other parts of our lives. And we will be able to do new things, whatever those new things are, whether it's chatting face to face with people halfway around the world or performing telesurgery from downtown Toronto on a patient in a developing-world country.

Finally, the global economy will continue to grow because of the growing global population. Later in this century this growth will cease, as I said before. However, for someone planning for the next decade, population growth is still a factor.

A Crucial Corollary

From an organizational planning point of view, though, there is a crucial corollary to the fact of continuing growth. Innovation will create new ways of doing things, whether we're talking about a stunning new technology or merely a new insight into what fashion consumers want right now. And the growth in the pools of investment capital, coupled with the increasing speed with which established companies are pushed aside, means that investment managers are going to be hungry to fund brash, successful new companies. This funding will, from time to time, allow a newcomer to leapfrog established market leaders with a new technology, or a new technique, that will put the established company at a distinct disadvantage in cost, the ability to offer a new product, or both.

For example, the transmission of breaking news stories from one end of the country to another has, until very recently, been by satellite. Until the late 1990s, a television producer sitting in a studio in Vancouver would look at a breaking story, consider who in her system said they had video of the story, and then call an affiliate at the location where the story was breaking and ask them to transmit their video. The producer would then book time on a satellite, have the video uploaded, then downloaded to where she was working, and finally view it. This involved not only quite a bit of time and money, but the efforts of as many as 20 people to effect the transfer.

Today, with the enormous glut of optical-fibre cable in the market, television networks lease capacity on fibre networks. Someone in an outlying area who has video of an event can put a low-resolution version on the fibre network for everyone in the organization to see. If the producer in Vancouver decides she wants to see what the footage looks like, she drags the icon from her menu to her electronic in-basket and the video plays on her monitor. Meanwhile, as it's playing, the high-resolution, broadcast-quality version is spooling over the optical-fibre network to her computer, so that if she decides to use it, she can start editing it immediately. Not only does the TV network save all of the satellite transmission fees, but it eliminates the work of the 20-odd people who were involved in booking and managing the video feed by satellite as well.

This is great for the television network—but not so hot for Telesat Canada, whose business in this area is rapidly shrinking. The enormous overcapacity of optical fibre that has damaged the telecommunications industry and companies such as Canadian-based Nortel Networks and U.S.-based Lucent Technologies is a windfall for those companies that can find inventive ways of using it. And companies such as Telesat must either find new ways of retaining and enlarging their markets or watch helplessly as their clients move onto something better.

So, although everyone says "When money talks, everybody listens," it's not true. We get so caught up in the routine of daily life that we fail to pay attention to the way innovation and the compounding of wealth are changing all the rules. And when that happens, we wind up selling buttonhooks and buggy whips.

How to Listen

From a planning point of view, the crux of this issue is that you can't just keep doing what you've been doing, because sooner or later someone's going to come along with a better way and put you out of business. You must, instead, be constantly reassessing what you are doing, and, if necessary, change your business, or, better yet, become your own fiercest competitor. Market leaders who constantly challenge their own products and services with new, better offerings will usually leave competitors gasping behind, lacking the resources or the market smarts necessary to catch up. But challenging yourself seems like a bad idea to conservatives and bean-counters. Not only are you cannibalizing your own products, usually with something better and cheaper, and hence cutting into your own revenues, but you are not getting all of the milk in one cash cow before moving on to a new one. However, companies that milk cash cows are widely known as being the ones that have decided to go out of business.

Let me give you an example of a company that did listen to the money, and prospered. In the mid-1990s, Microsoft pooh-poohed the Internet as a flash in the pan and maintained that it was the desktop computer that was the future of IT. Of course, this was a very comfortable view for Microsoft to hold because it owned the desktop of the vast majority of personal computers. The Internet, on the other hand, was new, and risky, and offered no clear way for Microsoft to make use of its best assets—its market clout with Windows and Office software. So Microsoft was, effectively, taking a pass on the Internet.

Then one day Bill Gates woke up and realized that the Internet was going to be crucial to the future of IT, and decided that Microsoft had to be in it, one way or another. Accordingly, he told everyone in Microsoft to focus on the Internet, and unleashed some really talented people. They created Internet Explorer to compete with Netscape, which owned the web-browser market. This reversal of corporate policy was so successful that it eventually led to the U.S. Justice Department's anti-trust suit against Microsoft. And today Microsoft dominates the browser market, and Netscape has been sold off to a third party, AOL Time Warner.

Microsoft could have stuck to its knitting and found in the late 1990s that its grasp on the desktop was gradually being pried lose. But it listened to the money, and did a corporate 180-degree turn. I saw the results of this personally because, when Internet Explorer was first released, I had just finished doing some work for Microsoft and got three calls from three different people in different divisions of the company, all wanting to make sure I knew about Explorer, and anxious to make sure I had a free copy. The entire company dedicated itself to this strategic move, even though no one knew how it would make money for the company in the short run.

My point is this: the marketplace talks, and success will flow to those companies that listen, that are better prepared for the future, and that move aggressively to own tomorrow. And when they do, those who did not listen or were unable to respond, such as Telesat, will watch helplessly as their clients leave.

How Do You Invest in the Future?

You aren't going to see the future if you aren't looking. You won't hear the money if you aren't listening. If anticipating and planning are activities you dabble in only once in a while, when there's nothing more important to do, or only when you've finished fighting fires, or as a corporate vacation for executives on retreat, you aren't going to survive. You need to have a coherent, consistent program of seeking out tomorrow and preparing for it. I'll come back to this in the seventh secret.

Beyond this, think carefully about how you invest in the future. The safest investment you can make, bar none, is in the people who work for you. Learn how to help your people be better, then do it. Find tools that will make it easy for them to be heroes to their (your) clients, then get those tools and help them learn how to use them. And put money into training. If the only real asset you have is the collective brains of your people, you want those brains to be as sharp and as well-equipped as possible.

> *The only real asset you have is the collective brains of your people, so think long and hard before you invest in real assets and infrastructure.*

Beyond this, think long and hard before you invest in real assets and infrastructure. There's no single, simple rule that will tell you when you should invest or not, but as a general rule, in today's rapidly changing world, unless it's something that you have to have, that you can't get any other way, and that changes rapidly, you are probably better off leasing infrastructure than buying it. Most buildings are low-return investments, for instance, so unless there's a compelling reason to own one, such as a really tight real-estate market, don't buy. Lease.

In 1996 I spoke to a group of senior people for a major telecommunications company. They had invited me to give them an outside view of what was happening in the telecommunications field. Thinking back on what I said, I can see why they weren't thrilled with my message. I told them that long-distance rates were going to drop by a factor of 10,000 over the next 20 years, changing long-distance from a cash cow into a losing proposition. I told them that they might have made a mistake cutting 10,000 people from their payroll, as they recently had, because if they were going to continue to use their current business model, they should have kept 10,000 people and let the rest go. I warned them that there was too much optical fibre being built, that I didn't know what was going to fill it, and that it was going to erode their revenues.

I'd like to say I warned them about the coming tech-stock boom and bust, or that convergence was going to happen but that owning it didn't make sense, but I didn't. I didn't see the boom coming, although I knew it was unsustainable when it happened. And I knew when this company started buying up all kinds of unrelated media companies that it was a mistake, but by that time the company was no longer a client and its management wasn't interested in listening to me.

Clearly, today the mistakes of that time are obvious—as they always are to Monday-morning quarterbacks. But prospective decisions are never as easy, so here are some rules of thumb to help you decide when to buy, and when to lease, rent, or outsource:

1. Does the state of this art change rapidly? If so, then ownership may mean sinking a lot of money into something that will quickly become obsolete.

2. Will ownership be a crucial strategic weapon to use against your competitors and confer an advantage that leasing or outsourcing will not?

3. Will ownership confer an economic or marketing advantage on you that leasing or outsourcing would not, allowing you to cut costs and prices, or deliver more rapidly, or respond to market changes more rapidly than your competition?

4. What percentage of your organization's assets will be tied up in this investment? The larger the percentage, the more wary you should be about owning rather than leasing, because the more damage you'll do if you're wrong.

5. Does ownership commit you to a single course of action and significantly reduce your options and flexibility? If so, then think long and hard about whether to do it or not.

6. Are you investing in infrastructure because you don't want to have too much in cash and investments? Having too much cash is a sign to some people that executives don't know how to employ their assets. It can also be an invitation to raiders to mount a hostile takeover. But while both of these are important considerations, they do not justify making investments in the wrong technologies or assets for the wrong reasons.

7. And finally, what are your competitors doing? As General George Patton, the American tank commander, once said, "When everyone's thinking alike, no one's thinking at all." If there's a gold rush to build optical fibre, then not enough people may be thinking about what they're doing. But if your toughest competitor is making significant

investments in something that no one else is thinking about, then maybe you need to find out what that company is thinking that you aren't.

I'm also assuming that you do all the conventional things such as comparing projected rates of return with what you could get by buying bonds and clipping coupons, for example; considering the pay-back period; how you plan to finance the investment; and so on. My suggestions should be considered in addition to such conventional considerations, not instead of them.

So the first part of listening to the money is knowing that wealth compounds, the world changes, and you innovate or die, then acting accordingly. But there's another part to it as well.

10

You Need to Be Good

If you listen to what the public expects of organizations, you'll get an earful, most of it rather muddled. But it's crucial that you listen to what's expected of you today, and what will be expected tomorrow. Listening reveals two major themes, so let's start with the thorniest first: social responsibility.

The website for the anti-consumerist magazine *Adbusters* features many "anti-ads" that satirize the behaviour of major multinationals. One of them shows a blurred picture of a running mother, dragging her child. Superimposed on the photo, in colourful lettering that mimics Nike ads, are the words:

> *You're running because you want that raise, to be all you can be. But it's not easy when you work sixty hours a week making sneakers in an Indonesian factory and your friends disappear when they ask for a raise. So think globally before you decide it's so cool to wear—Nike.*[1]

Of course, Nike disputes the contention that it exploits workers in developing countries—but such comments clearly hurt, accurate or not. The public-relations problems of Nike, McDonald's, Disney, and others are well known at this point, and companies go out of their way to avoid being caught in the spotlight on the wrong side of a social issue. In fact, they may be going too far. The U.S.-based Reebok company, which has worked hard to appear on the right side of social issues, recently withdrew its orders from a factory in Thailand that was operated by one of Reebok's suppliers when it found that the factory's 400 employees were working 72 hours a week.[2]

Being a good guy means more than just slick public relations. It means deciding what the right— ethically right—thing to do is, then finding a way to do it.

At first blush, this might seem like the right thing to do. In fact, it probably wasn't. Certainly it would deflect possible criticism of Reebok for supporting sweatshop operations, but it also put those 400 people out of work. Being a good guy means more than just slick public relations. It means deciding what the right—ethically right—thing to do is, then finding a way to do it. As one magazine commented on Reebok's move: "Astonishingly, [Reebok] . . . does no research to correlate social responsibility with sales or shareholder value. . . . Since the most ethical way to do business is to attract investment and offer more people a way out of peasant labour, perhaps this practice should be relabeled corporate social irresponsibility."[3] In other words, Reebok put 400 people out of work, yet has no idea whether this move benefited either its shareholders or those 400 workers. This is where "corporate responsibility" is trending: public relations gestures that may actually be harmful. So if all you're concerned about is looking good, then the rest of this chapter will hold no interest for you: just make sure you toe every line laid down by any social critic anywhere in the world. But that's a pretty vague way to do business in a world that requires crisp, decisive actions.

A company that intends to do anything needs to survive, which means it must make profits. Attempting to behave as if your organization's first responsibility is to pursue goals of social justice will probably impair your profitability, and may lead to your demise, helping no one. David Henderson, a New Zealand economist, wrote an essay titled "Misguided

Virtue: False Notions of Corporate Social Responsibility," which was published by the New Zealand Business Roundtable and London's Institute of Economic Affairs in June of 2001. In this essay, he argues:

> When as is probable the adoption of CSR [corporate social responsibility] impairs enterprise performance, the businesses that have taken this course have a strong interest in having their rivals follow suit. They can try to mobilise public opinion in this cause, or lobby for government regulations to be imposed on all: both courses are open. In either case, the effect is to limit competition and hence to weaken the performance of the economy as a whole. The system effects of CSR, as well as the enterprise effects, will tend to make people in general worse off.[4]

Skewing a company's priorities away from competitive practice makes the company less profitable, and less efficient. It makes the company's products more expensive and reduces its market share, thereby reducing the number of people who will be employed, and reduces the pay of those remaining. If enough companies adopt such policies, the economy as a whole suffers. Goods and services are more expensive, the standard of living goes down, and people have less money to spend, with the result that fewer people are employed. The quest for social responsibility, perversely, can produce precisely the opposite effect its advocates intend—unless they want people to be poorer.

Yet, doing the ethical thing can mean doing the profitable thing as well. Ed Freeman teaches ethics at the Darden Business School of the University of Virginia. He told *The Economist* how one big chemical company found that doing well and doing good could go together when one of the company's senior executives decided that he wanted to reduce pollution to zero. Horrified, his engineers said it wasn't possible, but came back, embarrassed, three weeks later to say that they could not only reduce pollution to zero, but could save money in the bargain. "The conflict between ethics and business may be a lot less than we think," Freeman said.[5]

What, then, is a proper response to social criticism? The simple answer is that your company should behave according to the considered thoughts and ethics of its people, both employees and management. In Chapter 1, I talked about how companies need to recruit people who have similar values, so that everyone in the company will support the organization's actions. In Chapter 1, I also said that values are the compass that help an organization keep all of its people going in one direction. Common values create harmony and a sense of purpose, and one of the great benefits of having an organization with people who share values is that they will tend to respond in similar ways to new, ethical challenges.

Royal Dutch/Shell Group ran into such challenges, first in its attempt to dispose of its Brent Spar oil rig in the North Sea, and then in its relationship with a Nigerian government that executed a human-rights activist. In both cases, the company backed off from the issue at hand, invited its critics in to discuss the situation so that company officials were sure they understood them, then changed the corporate policy to accord with the internal discussions. In fact, Shell rewrote its statement of business principles, partly in response to these issues.

Sometimes this means you accede to the demands of activists, and sometimes you don't. Dusty Kidd is the director of labour practices for Nike, which has manufacturing facilities in many different developing countries. He notes that the obvious answer isn't always the right one: "In Vietnam, our workers are paid more than doctors. What's the social cost if a doctor leaves his practice and goes to work for us?"[6]

So what happens if you are good guys, but you wind up being embarrassed by publicity critical of your pursuit of profit? First, you need to consider the issue seriously. You may choose to meet the critics and ask them to explain their position in more detail. Next, you need to think through whether they have a point, and clarify what you and your people really believe. Then you need to choose how to act. If you believe you're right, and the critics are wrong, then go public and explain why. Mostly, if your actions are rooted in your beliefs, that will get across, and you may carry the day.

If you've done this and are still getting creamed, you may have to cave in for the purposes of public relations. I don't like that, but it's reality.

Remember in Chapter 8 I talked about "decadent puritans"? Many people today want to hold others, especially corporations, to a higher standard than they are willing to accept for themselves. Sometimes you just lose.

And what if you're not good guys, but are, instead, the greedy, money-grubbing robber baron-wannabes that the anti-business crowd believes every business person to be? Frankly, that's your business, but I believe that sooner or later either you'll run smack into the wall of public opinion and your sales will plummet, or you'll be chopped off at the knees by government regulation introduced in response to public outcry. And the odds are that it's going to be sooner.

In the wake of the Enron, WorldCom, and Arthur Andersen scandals, not only are there people out there gunning for companies, but the Internet is making it easy for companies to be fingered, and for tales of their misdoings to be spread across the globe. Anti-websites, devoted to showcasing your dirty linen and attracting the attention of anyone who does a web-based search, will make sure that your sharp practices are widely known. Remember that diminished privacy is a reality for not only individuals but corporations and organizations as well. Profiteering and unethical shortcuts are short-term tactics, and organizations that are survivors don't behave that way.

On the other hand, are there any benefits, other than a nice corporate public image, to being good guys? Well, much as it's nice to have the general public think well of you, the real benefit is with your people. If you do, indeed, have people who hold similar values, and your company behaves according to your common ethics, then your people will hold your organization in greater esteem and be happier working there. As Robert Solomon of the University of Texas says, the best corporate codes are the ones "that describe the way everybody in the company already behaves and feels. The worst are those where senior executives mandate a list of principles—especially if they then fail to 'walk the talk' themselves."[7] Thinking things through is harder than just reacting to public criticism, but remember that the opposite of "smart" isn't "dumb"—it's "lazy."

What Are the Expectations of Your Customers?

The final aspect of the need to be good is that you need to truly listen to your clients. What they want and what they expect have changed, and will continue to change. Anyone who has taken sales training knows that what customers buy is value. Specifically, sales trainers talk about how "prospects" won't buy until they're convinced that the value they will receive is worth more than the amount of money they have to give up. If they're convinced that the value is greater, they're eager to buy. If they're convinced they're giving up more than they're getting, it doesn't matter how skillfully you try to close, all you're going to get is "no" for an answer. Which shifts the question to: what is value? I would suggest that:

$$Value = Quality - Price$$

If you have high quality, and a low price, you've got great value. If you have low quality and a high price, not only do you have no value, but you may actually be trying to subtract value from your prospect.

Most people know how to increase customer value by cutting price, so there's no point in talking about that part of the equation. However, what constitutes quality is not only important, but it's become rather foggy over the past few years, in part because of the Total Quality Management crusade. This was a fad in the corporate world for a while, and many people became zealots for quality without ever quite focusing on what it was. So let's go back to basics.

The best traditional definition of "quality" that I've ever seen comes from Peter Drucker's 1964 book, *Managing for Results:* "What a producer thinks of as 'quality' is likely to be what is hard, difficult, and expensive to produce. But the customer is uninterested in the manufacturer's troubles. His only question is—and should be—'What does this do for me?'"[8] What Drucker is saying is that it's not how hard you work, or how smart you are relative to your competition, that matters, but rather what the customer thinks. Quality resides in the mind of the customer, and nowhere else.

Your customer judges you based on his experience with everything you do for him, and every interaction he has with any part of your organization, and, indeed, any part of the process, whether you control it or not.

That's the traditional definition of quality, and I've never heard it expressed better. But it's no longer enough, because the market has moved on. In particular, the rising levels of competition have pushed levels of quality up to the point where product differences are getting hard to notice. J. M. Juran, one of the grandfathers of total quality, remarked in a 1991 *Business Week* interview that "When 30 percent of U.S. products were failures, vs. 3 percent for Japan, that was an enormous difference. But at failures of 0.3 percent and 0.03 percent, it'll be difficult for anyone to tell."[9] Juran happened to be talking about manufacturing defects in cars, but his comment holds true for any product or service: when competition pushes quality high enough, the differences between the best producer and a mediocre producer become so subtle as to be invisible to the customer. In turn, this implies that a quality product or service is no longer enough to win in today's marketplace. Quality is the ante, the table stake that lets you play the hand, but it's not enough to win the game. Today's customer expects more.

What more does he expect? As I described earlier, a brand is no longer a product or a service, it's an experience. Your customer judges you based on his experience with everything you do for him, and every interaction he has with any part of your organization, and, indeed, any part of the process, whether you control it or not. And this implies that your competition is not who you think it is.

A while back I came across the book *Inside the Magic Kingdom: Seven Keys to Disney's Success,* and in it the author, Tom Connellan, puts forth a very different view of who your competitors are. Distilling what he said over most of a chapter, I'd put it this way: if a brand is an experience, and customers judge you on their experience with you, then *your competition is anyone who raises the expectations of your customer. Your customers compare you, transaction by transaction, with Disney, FedEx, and L. L. Bean, not just to the company across the street that happens to be in the same industry.*[10]

If the brand experience you provide doesn't measure up to the best in the world, then your customers will have a vague sense of dissatisfaction in dealing with you, even if you have a monopoly in your industry. This vague dissatisfaction is dangerous, because it means that they will be receptive to a better alternative, which is not at all what you want. In fact, most people, most of the time, won't bother to look for a better alternative to what you offer unless they're dissatisfied. Their inertia will tend to keep them doing business with you. But if they get it into their heads that they're not happy with what you do, then they will be interested if someone else comes along. And if they're really unhappy, they'll actively look for other alternatives. That's how you lose customers.

So the customers of the future expect their experience to be satisfactory from start to finish, and they're the ones who decide what "satisfactory" means. Which leads back to our starting point: if they think you're good guys, they're much more likely to stay. Being a good guy means doing the right thing. It means knowing how your clients feel, following their experience—from ethics through customer support—and having what they want, when they want it.

This doesn't mean that there's only one way to do business. Quite the contrary. Wal-Mart does discount better than just about anyone, but its stores are bare bones, and the service, while friendly, is nothing special. Despite this, the company has become the world's biggest retailer, bar none, and it's done so by managing customer expectations. Wal-Mart customers come away pleased with the experience of shopping at a discount store. Toronto-based retailer Holt Renfrew, on the other hand, aims at a much higher price point, and nails it by providing outstanding customer service. So it's not a matter of how you meet your customers' expectations. It's knowing what those expectations are, managing them, and then meeting or exceeding them throughout the customers' experience of your brand.

This applies to your behaviour on ethical issues as well as in your marketing and the way you interact with your clients. The way of tomorrow demands the ability to listen; to be sensitive to changes in the marketplace, the feelings and the desires of your clients and the community around you; and to respond to these things in a way that flows naturally from the ethics and beliefs of you and your people.

So far I've talked about management, employees, marketing, technology, society, and the economy. Now, in the sixth secret, we're going to step back and take a bigger view by looking at governments at home and around the world.

Watch for Falling Governments

"A government that is big enough to give you all you want is big enough to take it all away."

—U.S. SENATOR BARRY GOLDWATER, 1964

11

Governments Become Dangerous

Are you pleased with your government? With any of the governments that supposedly serve you, whether federal, provincial, or local? I didn't think so. Dissatisfaction with government is obvious in casual discussions, and evident from apathetic voter turnout for Canadian elections at every level. People feel that they are disconnected from their governments, that governments are irrelevant, or that governments ignore what's important to us and act according to some hidden agenda.

Of course, dissatisfaction with government is a fine tradition with a long history. But public apathy and even hostility to governments in the present day is not just more of the same. It is, in fact, quite appropriate, because governments at all levels are no longer working effectively and are, at times, even harmful. Moreover, the power of governments, particularly at the national level, is being leached away by external forces and events. But to begin, let's look at how governments are being weakened from within.

Government of the Bureaucrats, by the Politicians, for the Special Interests

Abraham Lincoln's extraordinary poetry from his 1863 Gettysburg address—"government of the people, by the people, for the people"—is becoming a hollow mockery of what we experience. It's true that if the general public gets really angry about some issue and threatens to smite any politician that gets in its way, then government does respond to the so-called will of the people. However, most of the time most people are more concerned about their own problems and issues, about picking the kids up from soccer, paying the bills, preparing for that presentation at work tomorrow, and all the other pressures of daily life, that they ignore what's going on in government. And it is that stress-induced neglect that is enabling the perversion of democratic government, not just in Canada, but throughout the developed world.

It's an obvious truism that people will work for their own self-interest. So when the owners—the general public—stop paying attention to what's going on with their governments, then the selfish interests of civil servants, elected officials, and the groups that lobby for special treatment have free rein. Few people set out to do evil things. Most people believe that they are doing what's best. Yet, inevitably, without effective and continuous oversight, all three groups tend towards perverting government to serve their needs first, and the needs of the public afterwards.

This sounds like mere cynicism, and a rehash of neo-conservative, government-bashing rhetoric, but look at the results. The share of gross domestic product, or economic output, consumed by governments has risen steadily and more or less consistently in virtually every industrialized country in the world since the beginning of the 20th century. Even governments that are notorious right-wing, slash-and-burn tax cutters have generally seen their share of income rise. As *The Economist* noted of perhaps the most aggressive government slasher of the post-war era: "In 1980, when Margaret Thatcher began wielding her Conservative ax, public spending accounted for 43% of the [British] economy. After nearly 20 years of ruthless cuts, radical dismantling of the welfare state and hard-faced suppression of public-sector unions, the state's share has shriveled to just 42%."[1] All of this radical-right axe swinging produced a total decline of 1 percent in government share of GDP after 20 years—and even then the amount actually spent by government rose dramatically.

Or consider the Mike Harris government in Ontario, famous for its "damn the consequences, slash spending anyway" attitude. This Conservative government was elected in 1995 with a mandate to cut government. Yet the number of telephone listings in the Government of Ontario phone directory for the Ministry of Health, one of its principal targets for spending restraint, grew from 2,382 in the 1995–96 edition to 3,841 in the 2003 edition. Assuming that the number of telephone listings is a reasonable indicator of the number of people employed by the ministry, this represents an increase of more than 60 percent, while over the same period the population of Ontario grew by 8 percent and the number of family doctors grew by just 1.5 percent.[2]

Even hard-core budget slashers tend towards self-aggrandizement, and the reasons are obvious. Elected officials, as individuals, prefer higher pay and better perks, nicer offices and flashy limousines, and—worst of all—tampering with the electoral system to make it easier for them to get re-elected and harder for voters to get rid of them. Meanwhile, civil servants naturally tend towards empire-building because it increases their (apparent) importance and justifies their need for higher pay.

And groups of citizens approach elected officials with a steady barrage of irresistible propositions: give us special treatment, and we'll help you get re-elected. Fail to support us, and we'll work for your opponents. It'll cost each taxpayer only a few extra bucks, and it will do so much for us—which, remember, will help us create jobs. So dairy farmers get production quotas that protect them from competition, and the general public pays significantly more for milk and butter. Automobile companies, with the support of auto workers' unions, get generous subsidies from governments to keep building cars in Ontario or Quebec, and taxpayers foot the bill.

Communications companies get competitors blocked out of new markets with arcane regulations and legislation that no one understands, and the general public has fewer service choices. The list is long and keeps growing, because it's an unbeatable proposition: you scratch our backs, and, come election time, we'll scratch yours.

Very few voters are going to care enough about any given special deal to disrupt their lives to go out in protest over higher milk prices or legislation that blocks greater competition in communications. Moreover, the more it happens, the larger the number of groups that jump in to sample the cream. In the words of cartoonist Walt Kelly's character Pogo: "We have met the enemy, and he is us!"

Moreover, voters tend to support elected officials who can distort the system in their favour. This is called electoral pork—goodies that elected officials hand out, at the public's expense, to people who support them—and pork works. In 1995, economist Steven Levitt, who works for the U.S. National Bureau of Economic Research, was able to quantify whether politicians could win support in U.S. congressional districts by distributing pork to their voters. What he found was that for every additional US$100 per person spent by the U.S. federal government in a district, the elected official reaped 2 percent more votes in the following election.[3] This is an expensive way to win an election—but if it's not your money, do you care? I haven't found any comparable studies done in Canada, but there's no reason to believe that spending public money in Shawinigan, say, or Baie-Comeau, is any different than spending public money in Texas or Arkansas.

Instinctively, the general public knows that it isn't being well served by government, which is why voter turnout has been steadily dropping. What difference does it make who you vote for if government is going to take a rising share of your wallet, feather its own nest, and do favours for people in the shadows, no matter who's elected? And when electoral districts are drawn to represent groups, rather than people, so that it takes three or four voters in Toronto or Vancouver to equal the power of one voter in Prince Edward Island, the principle of one citizen, one vote disappears, and equity under the law shrinks.

The result is that democracy is being cut out from under us, one thin salami slice at a time. And when power is increasingly gathered into fewer and fewer hands, whether it's an imperial president, a more presidential prime minister, or a provincial government that invokes closure on parliamentary debate to ram through legislation, the public good suffers and democracy is debased. This is the very clear trend ahead of us, and a troubling one, for there is no logical place for it to stop. The only solution is an electoral revolution, for voters to get so sick of being served last that they rise up and toss out all the rascals, scaring officials into probity again. This has happened many times in the past, and I suspect we're getting near time for it to happen again.

Until it does, though, the result is that governments are less stable, less predictable, and behave less rationally, all of which is bad for business and the quality of life. Governments are becoming more erratic—and this trend is being accentuated by the speed of change and the complexity of today's decisions. It's just plain harder to be right, as I observed earlier in connection with corporate decision-making, and governments are going to make more mistakes. But whereas the mistakes of a corporation affect its shareholders, customers, and employees, the mistakes of governments affect everyone.

For corporations, the solution is to think ahead and prepare for a range of eventualities. Having a long-term planning structure makes it easier to respond to short-term crises. But elected officials, by the nature of their three- to five-year election cycle, can't think long term, so long-term planning generally doesn't happen. The immediate is too urgent, and the long term too hypothetical. So unless the civil service performs long-term planning that politicians heed, the result is bad, costly policy. This is how, for example, Ontario wound up alienating doctors, thus creating a crisis in family medicine, which I'll describe in more detail a little later on. Yet the fact that governments are functioning more poorly and accomplishing less of value isn't the only problem we face.

The External Power Leak

Today, there are two sets of forces at work that are undermining the modern concept of the nation-state, and hence the power and effectiveness of governments.

The true hallmark of the modern nation-state is the rule of law. In a kingdom ruled by an absolute monarch, the law applies to everyone except the monarch. This means that subjects live or die and may hold property solely at the whim of the monarch, and have no final security they can depend on. Likewise, in a country with an absolute dictator, the despot is above the law, and there is no protection from him. Hence, for example, Saddam Hussein's decree, and the act of the Iraqi parliament in February of 2003, that no one in Iraq was to have or make weapons of mass destruction was a farce because no one internally could force Hussein to comply.

Today, there are two sets of forces at work that are undermining the modern concept of the nation-state, and hence the power and effectiveness of governments. First, more and more of the events and decisions that affect the lives of the citizens of Canada are happening outside of Canada, and Canadian governments have only limited ability to influence them. Second, these extra-national events are both undermining the traditional rule of law within the country and simultaneously moving towards the creation of a more widespread, global rule of law.

Examples of these extra-national events are widespread. Even the United States, with a reputation of being both isolationist and interventionist, is reluctant to enter into military action without some kind of international cover, whether from the United Nations (as in the 1991 Gulf War), North Atlantic Treaty Organization (as in Kosovo), or from an "alliance of the willing" (as in Iraq in 2003). Today, unilateral military action smacks of aggression, and is condemned as a criminal act—a concept that was never applied to nations and sovereign governments until after the Second World War.

Matters of trade used to be mainly negotiated country to country. Since the 1944 Bretton Woods Agreement, they have increasingly been handled on a multinational and even a global level. Although bilateral agreements are still negotiated—the original Canada–U.S. Free Trade Agreement, for example—more and more of the important bits are being managed under the auspices of the World Trade Organization, which has some of the characteristics of a world government.

Until the 1980s, a nation's finances were almost exclusively the realm of the national government. But as more and more government financing was raised on the international bond markets for national, provincial, and even municipal governments and their Crown corporations, such as the former Ontario Hydro, governments became accountable to the international financial markets. Any jurisdiction, such as New Zealand in 1984, that the financial markets deemed to be mismanaging its affairs was unceremoniously cut off from credit, which had enormous financial and economic consequences for that government and its constituents.

Likewise, the currency markets now dominate trading, and no central bank, or group of central banks, can stand against the markets when they are determined to bid a currency up or down. When Bill Clinton came to the rescue of Mexico in the peso crisis of the early 1990s, he created a US$30-billion fund to help. But at that time, the currency markets were trading more than $1 trillion a day. In that context, $30 billion was a nice vote of confidence, but otherwise just spitting into the wind.

Communications are now global, with people able to access almost any major news outlet over the Internet. Accordingly, news management by governments is reduced to so-called spin control rather than muzzling the press. Even when Canadian courts issue gag orders on court proceedings, or prevent national election results from being released in western provinces if polls are still open, Canadians can go online and find out what's happening from sources beyond the reach of such courts.

In-demand professionals in numerous fields—those in software and high tech, for example, as well as physicians, nurses, and teachers—can now move where they are wanted and well paid, and countries are being forced to take this into account. Aware that their economies are dependent on knowledge workers for their economic prosperity, nations have to consider the tax rates and working conditions of professionals in other nations rather than arbitrarily making decisions as their domestic policies would dictate, for fear of precipitating a brain drain. This trend will particularly affect medical practitioners, teachers, and professors in the next decade or so in Canada, strongly influencing national and provincial policies.

Environmental issues are no longer national, regional, or local, but global. Canada has several times been on the receiving end of negative publicity and economic boycotts in Europe and elsewhere—for clear-cutting forestry practices, for example, and seal harvesting in Newfoundland. Malaysia and Brazil have been slammed for allowing lumbering in their rain forests, and found that they couldn't merely ignore the critics because boycotts harmed their exports.

The conflicts in what was formerly Yugoslavia forced governments to get involved in civil conflicts outside their jurisdictions rather than allow acts of genocide or ethnic cleansing. When Canadian jurist Louise Arbour, acting as chief prosecutor of the war crimes tribunal in The Hague, brought an indictment against Slobodan Milosevic, she was asserting, as a *Wall Street Journal* writer put it, "that the president of a sovereign state can be hauled in to an international court of law and tried for crimes against humanity committed, *in his official capacity,* within his own state."[4] In other words, the rule of law now extends across national boundaries, and sovereignty is no longer a defence.

Indeed, the complaints of the anti-globalists—which cover a multitude of issues, such as the environment, animal rights, human rights, the status of women, social justice, and the use of military force—are now global issues, receive global attention, and force governments to take account of the opinions of people they've never heard of before. You could argue that the anti-globalization crowd represents the first coherent "will of the people" on a global level. To the extent that the anti-globalists can mobilize public opinion and sway consumer purchases or national politics, they are now a factor in shaping government policies.

The power of governments at all levels is being sapped by all of these developments—and more.

Is the Nation-State Dead?

Yet, despite the fact that governments are weakening, the nation-state is not dead, nor is it dying. It is losing autonomy, and its ability to intervene on behalf of its citizens is being curtailed, but it will survive for one simple reason: there's nothing to take its place.

The needs for security and trade management, the two primary responsibilities of national governments, are as strong as ever, perhaps even greater, due to the so-called global clash of cultures and the number of fanatical nutbars running around. Recall that increased productivity also applies to the ability to be more destructive. So the needs for external security are greater than ever—and can no longer be guaranteed by any nation, even the United States. And trade matters are becoming more important, and more difficult to manage, as trade comprises a steadily rising share of gross world product.

The needs for security and trade management, the two primary responsibilities of national governments, are as strong as ever, perhaps even greater, due to the so-called global clash of cultures and the number of fanatical nutbars running around.

But if national sovereignty is declining, then the ability of individuals to influence what happens in their lives is also waning. If voters are disenchanted with their ability to influence the policies of the governments for which they vote, how much more alienated will we feel from decisions taken by the United Nations, by the deliberations of the World Trade Organization (WTO), or, in Europe, the actions of the European Parliament?

Marshall McLuhan described the society of the future as a "global village." Unfortunately, being one voice in six billion means we feel powerless and anxious. In consequence, we demand and expect our elected officials to do more to protect us at precisely the time, and for precisely the reasons, that they are able to do less. The result is that governments are caught: they have to appear to be taking bold initiatives, but their actions will mostly be ineffective. This will contribute to the feelings of alienation, to the instability of elected governments, and to government by spin control rather than by effective policy.

It doesn't mean that effective policy is impossible, merely more difficult. To govern effectively in tomorrow's world, governments, too, will have to think further ahead, plan beyond the next election, and coordinate with other governments, even when they are in disagreement over matters such as who pays the bills for health care. The alternative will be irrelevancy, policy drift, and a short stay in office.

Where Is the Rule of Law?

But if the actions of the international bond and currency markets can cause my taxes to rise, even though I and my fellow citizens vote against tax hikes, where is the rule of law? Clearly, my sovereignty as a citizen has been compromised by global events—which is one of the arguments the anti-globalists make. (Of course, they then turn around and demand that national sovereignty be compromised through international rules on workers' rights or the environment. Clearly neither consistency nor rationality is a prerequisite for being a critic.) So what is the future of the rule of law, the basis for modern government?

Well, as I mentioned earlier, the international community of nations is struggling to produce a proto-typical international rule of law, which will largely be made up of rules that national governments accept as superseding their own authority. These can and eventually will cover almost every aspect of human life, from the environment (for example, the 1989 Montreal accord on CFCs and the 1997 Kyoto accord on greenhouse gases), to workers' rights (relating to health and safety issues, but not pay scales), to trade matters (based increasingly on the WTO), to military intervention, to crimes against humanity.

And, of course, when you look through this list, what jumps out at you is that the United States seems to be the primary holdout in many of these areas. There's a good reason for that. Historically, probably the biggest conflict in the emergence of the nation-state, a state governed by a central rule of law, was wresting the king's sovereignty from him and making him subject to the same laws as everyone else. It was only then that citizens or subjects were subject to the rule of law rather than the rule of man, and it was only then that their rights could be guaranteed (at least in theory).

Today, in the global community, the United States is the power at the top of the pile. It's the only superpower, and without it, no international agreement can be truly effective. But understandably, Americans see no reason to give up their ability to choose. They see themselves, not unreasonably, as being the good guys of the 20th century, who rode to the rescue of almost everyone. They also, rightly, see themselves as the target of envy, even among their friends, and enmity among those who want a different world order. They are concerned that if they give up their power to some international bureaucracy, they give up the ability to protect themselves.

This is not a problem that will be solved quickly, or with some magic formula thought up by a modern-day John Maynard Keynes (who had a big hand in the creation of the global economy in the post-war world). Instead, it will happen gradually, as solutions are found that offer better results and more security that everyone can live with. It may start with the United States having an effective veto over global actions that it deems to be contrary to its, or the world's, best interests. But gradually the U.S. economy will become less dominant as other nations, especially China, grow more rapidly, moving the U.S. towards more negotiation and less to unilateral action. Military issues involving mutual security will move towards a *modus vivendi* with peacemaking forces supplied by member states (of the UN, NATO, or some other body), and paid for by all members. And human rights will gradually become an internationally accepted code.

This will not happen decisively or suddenly. Globalization is not going to go away. Unless the community of nations gets involved in a mutually destructive trade war, or a for-real global shootin' war, the forces of global unification, or at least agreement to move towards what amounts to an international rule of law, are inevitable.

So let's talk about what it means to you in planning the next few years.

Preparing for an Era of Weak Governments

If you consider the constant barrage of pressures that elected officials are under within their own country to distort policy for selfish interests, then add in the external pressures of diplomacy and trade, you get a picture of officials being pulled, pushed, tugged, and bullyragged incessantly to do something more, something different, something else. In this kind of environment, you can expect governments to behave erratically, for their policies to lurch from place to place. If they have an overall philosophy, or if their electoral opposition is particularly weak or divided, then these zigzags may move in a more directed way, but at the end of the day governments are like weather. People try to predict them, and are often confounded. And people get caught in a downpour without an umbrella.

So, as with the weather, watch the forecasts and be prepared for sudden changes. And don't assume that just because you have no interest in government, government has no interest in you. Here's an example of what could happen to almost any group, no matter how favoured, from a self-professed spin doctor, Stephen Skyvington, in a recent speech to Ontario family doctors:

Up until 1985 life was pretty good for doctors here in Ontario. But then . . . [Premier Bill] Davis decided he'd had enough, and called on his party to hold a leadership convention.

After a hotly contested and highly divisive battle, Frank Miller took over from Davis as Ontario Premier. An election was soon called. After the smoke had cleared, the Tories' 42-year reign was over—and so was, for doctors, the Golden Age. . . . The Liberals and the NDP joined forces to form a coalition government. In exchange for the NDP's support, the Peterson Liberals agreed to bring about an end to extra-billing. And the anti-doctor era was born. . . .

The Ontario Medical Association, not used to dealing with a government that didn't want to be their friend, soon found themselves adrift at sea. With no public relations savvy—indeed, with no public relations department at all—the OMA was easily outmanoeuvred at every turn. So much so that doctors soon found themselves taking part in a job action—actually, a half-assed strike—that could only be described as "a public relations disaster." In 1987, having dealt the medical profession a humiliating defeat, the Peterson government went to the polls and won a massive majority.

The message was crystal clear—at least to the three political parties here in Ontario. Bashing doctors was a great way to get votes and win elections. Suddenly, doctors were fair game, as one politician after another took great delight in knocking you and your colleagues off your so-called "pedestals."

. . . By the time the 1995 election came along, doctors—and just about everyone else—were looking for a change. That change, of course, came in the form of Mike Harris and the Common Sense Revolution. When the Tories won the election and Harris became Premier there was a great sense of relief amongst doctors. Finally, the party that had proven itself to be a good friend to doctors was back in power and ready to right the wrongs of the past decade. How shocking it must've been, then, to wake up on November 30, 1995 to discover that instead of a handshake the Tories had decided to greet the medical profession with a punch in the face.[5]

What happened to the doctors in Ontario is not an isolated incident. Ironically, there is another group that is currently being exploited for political gain in Canada: public school teachers.

If government decides that there's more value, politically, in crucifying you, your company, your profession, or a group or organization to which you belong, it can happen. Not only were the doctors treated in a manner that was inherently unfair, but the general public ate it up rather than rushing to their defence.

If it seems unlikely that this would happen to you, think about the public's reaction to the accounting scandals in the United States in 2000 and 2001. Because so many people had lost so much money in the stock markets, accounting fraud became not just a legal issue, but a political lightning rod. Public opinion of the business sector, always somewhat fragile, shattered, and a business person was deemed to be guilty until proven innocent.

You can't counter that kind of political thunderstorm. The best you can do is to ride it out. Fortunately, these kinds of deluges don't happen very often. But the principle is still true: you need to watch what governments are doing, because they can and will affect your business. And you need to be involved in the political system, know your elected officials, and make sure they know you. You want to be forewarned about pending changes that might affect you. It's substantially easier to derail prospective legislation or regulations than it is to have laws repealed. You need to be proactive and try to anticipate where government is going.

Part of this can be done by belonging to an industry association, because a good association keeps its members apprised of actions by government that may be harmful, and rallies opposition to proposed changes. Such associations can also work with public-relations firms, something that only major corporations do otherwise, and be useful in helping you plan strategy to defeat or modify government actions. Here's an example of what your future might hold:

Diva Jones is a freelance animator, currently working on contract for an upcoming animated feature. Her work is interrupted one morning by a call from a friend at the production company that's hired her for

this gig. Diva glances at the call display and wonders why her friend is phoning from her home during working hours.

"Hi, Jane, what's up?"

"You're not going to believe this, but the Government of Canada's about to screw you out of your contract."

There's silence on both ends of the line, then Diva recovers and says, "What are you talking about? What has the government got to do with our contract? And why would they try to screw me out of any contract? That doesn't make any sense, Jane."

"Doesn't make any sense to me, either, but we got a quiet word this morning that funding for Canadian content in animated films is about to be cut substantially. It was also hinted very broadly that we might want to get a Chinese animation group involved in this flick. Don't ask me why—but something's happening in Ottawa and it ain't good. Look, I've got other calls to make—I'm supposedly out of the office for a dentist appointment—but I wanted to give you a head's up. See if you can find out what's going on, then DO something, for God's sake!" And with that, Jane hangs up.

Diva sits there, looking at the phone, stunned. Then she calls the Canadian Association of Animators and Illustrators (CAAI), and, through sheer persistence and belligerence, winds up talking to the executive director. She tells him what Jane told her, without naming names, and asks him if he has any idea what's going on. She watches his eyes widen on her videophone's screen when she tells him, but he says he knows nothing about it. He looks thoughtful, then says he'll get back to her.

Meanwhile, Diva calls her MP, on whose last three campaigns she had worked. She gets his executive assistant, David, whom she knows, and describes the morning's goings-on. David says he'll see what he can find out, right away.

Then Diva sits back and jitters. She knows she should be working towards her looming deadline, but somehow concentrating on her work seems impossible with this kind of sword hanging over her head. She spends the next hour surfing the Net, trying to find any mention of anything relating to Canadian animation, without success.

Then David calls back. "Bad news," he tells her. "I called a friend of mine who works for the parliamentary assistant to the Minister of Agriculture. Apparently, there are some closed-door negotiations with the Chinese government over a wheat contract. The Chinese want to break into the global film market, and they figure that animation is a good place to start, so they're willing to increase the amount of wheat they buy from us, as opposed to the Australians or Americans, in exchange for the Canadian government opening some doors for them. The feds are apparently going to announce a 'cross-cultural development fund,' only it's nothing of the sort. It's really a Canadian subsidy to Chinese animators, along with a promise from the Canadian government to have the National Film Board and Telefilm Canada provide introductions and cooperative working opportunities to Chinese animation companies. But the PMO's going to take the money from the Telefilm Canada budget for Canadian animations. In other words, they're planning to sacrifice your career to sell a few more tonnes of wheat that we might have sold anyway."

Diva's completely confused by this. "But why would they do that? Canada produces some of the best animators in the world. Why would our own government help a potential competitor put us out of business?"

David's face shows a sour smile. "It's pure politics, Diva. You're getting screwed so Ottawa can lock down the farm vote, 'cause farmers have more votes than city dwellers. That's why they get more subsidies, and why farm bills occupy much more of Parliament's time than the Canadian cities. Look, I've gotta run. You need to leak this to the press—but keep my name out of it. Okay?"

Diva agrees, then calls the executive director of the CAAI and briefs him on what she's just been told. He nods, and says, "I suspect you're right. My sources haven't gotten back to me yet, but now I know where to look it won't take long to confirm this. I've spoken to our PR firm, and they're standing by. I think your friend's right about going to the press with this. If we need to, can we suggest the press call you for an interview as a typical Canadian animator?" Diva agrees.

The next morning, there are small items in both *The Globe and Mail* and the *National Post. The Toronto Star,* though, has put the story on its front page, below the fold, under a headline that screams "Cabinet Sells out Filmmakers for Wheat Deal" and a picture of Diva at her drawing tablet. That morning, the minister of culture makes an unannounced guest appearance on CBC Radio, where she denounces the "irresponsible rumours" and chastises the *Star* for "yellow journalism." The interviewer gives the minister lots of rope, and then hauls her up short by asking, "If this is just an unsubstantiated rumour, why did your office call and ask to have you appear on such short notice?" The minister flounders through an answer, but the damage is done.

The executive director calls Diva back that afternoon and reports that the PM's pissed that someone leaked the deal before it was done, but has told his underlings to find another way to do the deal, leaving the Telefilm fund alone. Diva's contract is safe—for now.

So, easy as it is to just sit back and assume that nothing's going to happen to you, the truth is that governments are dangerous, especially because they're becoming weaker and their choice of actions is narrowing.

So, easy as it is to just sit back and assume that nothing's going to happen to you, the truth is that governments are dangerous, especially because they're becoming weaker and their choice of actions is narrowing. When governments can't solve a problem directly, they will often dump it on the private sector, as may happen, for instance, with the costs of the Kyoto accord. Sometimes such so-called solutions are impossible or place a crushing burden on a small group of people or organizations.

Moreover, you need to think globally because you live and work in a global marketplace. A court in France, say, may take offence at something you have on your website and allow plaintiffs to sue you, as happened to Yahoo! in 2000. A French court held that Nazi memorabilia being auctioned through Yahoo! should not be accessible to French citizens through Yahoo!'s Internet site and threatened the company with fines in excess of 100,000 francs (about Cdn$20,000) per day. The court ignored the fact that both the vendor and Yahoo! were outside of the court's jurisdiction.

Or you could get booby-trapped by differences in rules, as happened to U.S.-based General Electric. In 2001 the company made a takeover bid for U.S.-headquartered Honeywell International that sailed past the U.S. Justice Department's anti-trust people, and GE thought it was home free. Then in June of 2001, the European Union deemed that the takeover was not in the best interests of European consumers—and killed the deal. The EU was hardly on GE management's radar when the company started the acquisition process, and yet it cost GE an enormous amount of money and the potential for a very successful acquisition.

You can ignore governments, both at home and abroad, but weak governments are dangerous, and ignoring them may snuff your bright hopes for tomorrow. Meanwhile, working in a global economy implies that you must also be increasingly aware of global politics and international issues. And that's the subject of the next chapter.

12

The Rising Importance of Geopolitics

Geopolitics seems like a strange subject for a book on the future of business. Yet the terrorist attacks of September 11, 2001, and the war on Iraq in 2003 made it clear that not paying enough attention to geopolitics and its consequences is like ignoring a looming freight train in a tunnel. Awareness of geopolitical events and their consequences must now be a part of every organization's thinking and an integral part of your planning. But how do you assess the world stage? Geopolitical developments are as diverse and as gradual as demographic shifts, as relevant as new anti-dumping penalties, and as unexpected as terrorist attacks.

Predicting the future of the world is impossible, but assessing the major forces at work is intensely useful. Not only does it allow you to anticipate what might happen, but when the unexpected does occur, knowing what underlies the events will help you decide what you should do next. So let me start by identifying those forces that I believe are going to produce the greatest changes in geopolitics, then move on to the major players. This is not an exhaustive list in either case, but highlights events and nations that I think have the most potential to create abrupt or unexpected change. I should warn you that my review of these factors will sound largely negative, with my conclusions tending towards the pessimistic. This is because it's easier to foresee problems than opportunities. I'll end the chapter with a counterbalance. Don't lose hope.

Awareness of geopolitical events and their consequences must now be a part of every organization's thinking and an integral part of your planning.

I'm also going to look at a longer time frame, not the typically shorter corporate planning period. Moreover, except for assessing the United States' position in tomorrow's world because of its importance in the future of geopolitics, I'm going to focus on the primary sources of change, not the status quo.

The Major Forces at Work

Trade

Global prosperity—measured by GDP per person, average life expectancy, child mortality, or any of several other yardsticks—has expanded significantly because of the emergence of globalization, and international trade is important to every major economy in the world, including the massive U.S. economy. Indeed, the emergence of the global economy is giving a boost to economic activity everywhere in the world, something that will happen only once in history. This one-time boost to overall activity stems from the increased efficiencies and higher levels of competition that come from integrating so many global players, compared with competing only on a national or regional level.

As I mentioned earlier on, globalization almost happened in the 1920s. Then, as now, global trade liberalization led to a substantial increase in economic activity, producing a rising level of wealth in every country that participated. As is the case today, this wealth was not evenly divided. Moreover, these gains snowballed into unrealistic expectations that everyone could, and should, get rich—irrational exuberance, if you will—that produced asset price bubbles in investment securities and real estate.

When reality set in, these price bubbles burst, causing angst and financial suffering. In response, national governments sought to help their citizens and industries by trying to cheat on their trade agreements, instituting beggar-thy-neighbour policies that tried to protect domestic industries at the expense of their trading partners. But trade protectionism can only work when partners don't retaliate. Since every nation attempted the same protectionist policies, the result was that the protectionist attempts not only failed but also unwound the benefits produced by trade liberalization in the first place, causing international trade to contract like a snapped rubber band. World trade, measured in millions of U.S. gold dollars of the time, went from the several-billion-dollar range ($2,998 million) in January 1929 to under a billion ($992 million) in January 1933—a decline of two-thirds in a four-year period.[1] This, combined with wrong-headed fiscal and monetary policies, produced the Great Depression.

If this sounds eerily familiar, it should because there are many parallels today to the 1920s. In the 1980s and 1990s, we witnessed a major liberalization of international trade that produced a boost to the activity of all participating economies. By the end of the 1990s, wealth creation, which was unevenly distributed, had produced unrealistic expectations that led to bubbles in the price of assets such as stocks and real estate. The stock-price bubble has now famously burst, and, at time of writing, real-estate prices are teetering in most Western countries. Meanwhile, trade negotiations through the World Trade Organization (WTO) are in trouble, with fundamental disagreements over such issues as agriculture and cultural industries, as well as widespread cheating, notably—but not exclusively—by rich countries protecting their industries against cheap imports from poor countries. A clear-cut example of cheating close to home is the United States' duties on softwood-lumber imports from Canada, motivated by political lobbying from the American forest industry. Whether these kinds of irritants escalate into a trade war remains to be seen.

Ironically, if the anti-globalists get the rollback of globalization they say they want, it would precipitate a rerun of the Great Depression. However, it is not clear that this will happen. National governments, for all they are bullied by domestic lobby groups, know quite clearly the risks of a trade war, and will try hard to avoid that path. It's only if the voters of the United States or Europe elect brain-dead protectionist governments that the risks increase significantly. If trade liberalization continues, as everyone says they want it to, then trade will continue to expand and the economic benefits of globalization will continue to raise the worldwide level of wealth. But keep a sharp watch on the Doha Development Agenda round of WTO negotiations, scheduled to end by 2005, as well as the major trade disputes going on around the world, for signs of trouble.

Fragmenting Nation-States

The collapse of the former Yugoslavia precipitated a civil war that ultimately required international military intervention. As nation-states and national governments gradually become weaker, there will be international consequences that affect both business and individuals. Quebec is a good example. If the separatists ever succeed in taking Quebec out of Canada, it will be devastating to the economy of Quebec, very harmful to the economy of the rest of Canada, raise the anxiety level of the United States, and cause a moderate splash in international diplomatic circles. For Canadians and Canadian businesses, it would inflict major financial damage and create a generation of divisive Canadian politics.

I suspect, though, that the largest number of problems with fragmenting nation-states will occur in Africa and the Middle East, where national boundaries were arbitrarily drawn on maps by vacating colonial powers, notably England and France. As a result, there will be so-called civil wars that are actually inter-tribal wars, often leading to genocide, as happened in Rwanda, and emerging warlords, as in Somalia and Afghanistan. Fragmenting nation-states will create uncertainty, nurture the roots of terrorism, and require close attention and the ability to respond to unexpected problems.

Disease

AIDS is a lot more than a disease: it has become a geopolitical force, and a good example of how new diseases will affect geopolitics and business. AIDS emerged out of Africa, assisted by poverty, poor hygiene, and lack of contraceptives and sex education. Because travel is cheap and fast, it became a global epidemic. Because it affects rich countries as well as poor ones, unlike malaria, it has become a *cause célèbre* internationally, even though malaria kills many more people every year.

The downstream consequences of AIDS presage the kinds of problems that will occur with other diseases. AIDS has distorted the political debate in most developed countries, raising the hackles of fundamentalists in the United States, for instance, about God's vengeance on homosexuals. And AIDS has become a poster child for social activism. There's nothing inappropriate about such activism, but the politics of AIDS has skewed spending and social priorities out of proportion to its effects, stealing resources from other issues. Meanwhile, in developing nations that do not have the resources to combat the disease, AIDS is becoming an indiscriminate killer. Global population estimates for 2050 have been lowered by almost half a billion people because of AIDS alone.[2] And it has created a new precedent in business. Pharmaceutical companies are being pressured by both rich-country and poor-country governments, as well as AIDS activists, to cut prices or donate their intellectual property to people with AIDS, principally, but not exclusively, in poor countries. While humanitarian aid has been around a long time, blackmailing companies into donating for humanitarian needs is new.

We tend to think of disease largely as an inconvenience because of the major medical advances of the last century. But diseases are mostly created by life forms such as bacteria and viruses, and life is persistent. We are now seeing the emergence of new diseases, such as severe acute respiratory syndrome (SARS) and West Nile virus, and new forms of drug-resistant diseases, including antibiotic-resistant tuberculosis, as bacteria and viruses overcome our countermeasures. The net result is that disease will remain a major problem for humanity until medical technologies allow us to create miracle panaceas more rapidly than diseases can emerge or adapt. Until then, they will affect government policies, the conduct of business—as Hong Kong and Toronto found out with SARS in 2003—and international relations.

Terrorism

In the early 1990s I spoke at a conference along with Major-General Lewis Mackenzie, one of Canada's best-known, and most respected, military leaders. I asked him at the Calgary airport whether the military anticipated ABC (atomic, biological, chemical) attacks on developed countries by terrorists or rogue governments. As I recall, he said that the military felt there was a very high probability, approaching certainty, that such an attack would take place, and probably within the next 20 years.

Peter Drucker, in his incisive 1993 book *Post-Capitalist Society*, makes pointed reference to this: "One reason for the trend toward tribalism is that bigness no longer confers much advantage. In the age of nuclear war, not even the biggest country can defend its citizens. And the smallest ones . . . can build terror weapons."[3]

This thought complements those of Professor Joseph Nye, who is dean of Harvard University's Kennedy School of Government: "Technology has been diffusing power away from governments, and empowering individuals and groups to play roles in world politics—including wreaking massive destruction—which were once reserved to governments. Privatisation has been increasing and terrorism is the privatisation of war."[4]

Beyond this, terrorism has also been described as asymmetric war. Since no one can go toe to toe with the United States and win, anyone seeking to attack the country (or the Western way of life that it represents) must do so by stealth and misdirection. And as I said earlier, rising productivity also

Terrorism is loose on the world, and there will always be people who feel that their problems are our fault. means that fewer people can produce more damage. During the Second World War, some of the finest minds in physics and mathematics in the world devoted enormous amounts of time, effort, and money to create the first atomic bombs. Today you can download instructions for a nuke over the Internet, and our only security comes from trying to prevent nuclear bombers (including terrorists and aggressive governments) from obtaining some of the more delicate and difficult components.

And so, although most terrorists will be suicide bombers and hostage-takers, eventually, terrorists will succeed in obtaining—and then using—ABC weapons. I don't like this truth, but cannot deny it. Neither should you ignore it in your thinking, just because it's unpleasant. Terrorism is loose on the world, and there will always be people who feel that their problems are our fault.

Demographics

Of all the historic causes of conflict, population pressure is probably the most important. The areas most likely to be affected by population pressure are those with the highest population densities today, coupled with the highest rates of population growth in numbers. Clearly this identifies China, India, and, to a lesser extent, southern Asia, plus Africa and parts of Latin America. The real question is: Can the global economy expand fast enough to provide economic ways of ameliorating these problems?

Beyond population pressure, there are going to be economic consequences to the growing number of aging citizens in all the developed countries. According to United Nations population projections, more-developed regions will show population growth averaging around 0.25 percent through to 2050. In comparison, the populations of less-developed regions will grow by 1.46 percent, or roughly six times as fast.[5] This has several implications.

First, as the proportion of retirees in developed countries grows relative to the working population, it promises to burden workers with higher taxes to support the needs of the elderly, slowing economic growth. In Europe, for example, the 15 current member nations of the European Union average 2.6 workers for each person over 65. By 2050, that will plummet to 0.8 workers per person over 65.[6] Moreover, by the middle of this century, most developed countries will see a decline in the size of their workforces and, later still, an absolute decline in their total populations.

Older populations in rich countries may also mean less vigour in global political pursuits. As one commentator put it, "It's surprising how much 'mature wisdom' resembles being too tired." This may shift the balance of world politics in favour of younger, more dynamic politicians with more energetic and ambitious voters.

Likewise, thoughtful governments of developed countries have recognized the importance of immigration as an invigorating force. Yet there are also economic and political costs to integrating immigrants into a country, and it affects national policies as well. For example, in the United States, the fastest-growing minority are Hispanics. As they grow in political importance, they will change U.S. policies towards Latin America, elevating that area in importance and tempering the traditional "gringo" policies of the near-colonialism of the past.

As for Canada, our birth rate continues to drop, which will present us with all the problems of an aging population. However, Canada has actually tackled these problems more aggressively than almost anyone else. Not only have we drastically (but incompletely) reformed the financing of the Canada Pension Plan, but the Canadian government moved towards an aggressive immigration policy in the 1980s, and is now aiming to increase immigration until it reaches 1 percent of current population a year.

Water

Water, along with population, has been one of the primary historic causes of war. It's a necessity that we take for granted. You can see the growing conflicts over water in North America, although I very much doubt that it will degenerate into armed conflict. Instead, water wars in North America are more likely to be settled with lawyers at 30 paces than with guns. Or, in the coming U.S.–Canadian conflict over whether Canada should export its abundant freshwater supplies, the weapon of choice will be economic and political pressure. The same may not be true elsewhere, especially in the parched Middle East and parts of Africa. So watch for news of disputes over water, and watch how they are being disputed: with guns or lawsuits. Both will create ripples.

The Major Players

The United States

This is the colossus of today's world, comparable in some respects to Rome or Britain in their heydays. Yet, unlike Rome or Britain, the United States is much weaker in some crucial ways, because power is not one-dimensional.

The United States dominates global military power. It spends more on its military than the next eight nations combined.[7] Moreover, not only does the United States possess the world's greatest quantitative military force in terms of raw firepower, but qualitatively the sophistication of its information-based weapon systems towers over that of any other nation on Earth. Furthermore, because of the amount of R&D the U.S. military performs, and the technological lead that the U.S. economy has over other nations, U.S. military dominance is likely to remain or increase for a long time, probably for decades to come.

Yet, partly because of the idealistic nature of Americans and the country's history of honour and fair play, the United States chooses not to exercise its power in a totally arbitrary manner, no matter what its critics say. Any of the Caesars of Imperial Rome would have laughed at the thought of consulting the conquered territories about foreign policy. And the British Parliament would have been haughty and offended if other countries had presumed to criticize the manner in which it shouldered what Kipling so eloquently called the "white man's burden." For all the rhetoric about the United States as a lone gunslinger, since the end of the Second World War the country has worked as hard as anyone—with recent exceptions—to create a system of global laws, and to behave by a code of conduct rather than arbitrarily. It has not always acted with the purest of motives (as when it supported Saddam Hussein in his war against Iran), or with the most carefully thought-out plans (as in Vietnam or Somalia), but its lapses have been just that—exceptions.

If part of the reason for this is idealism, another part is pure pragmatism. An open economy outperforms a controlled one. The United States makes more money through open trade than it would through colonialism or imperialism, so its idealism dovetails very neatly with its own self-interest (politically inspired protectionism notwithstanding).

Moreover, economically the United States does not dominate. Although its economy is larger than the next four countries combined, it is only first among equals in the global marketplace, with more power to arm-twist than anyone else, but without the power to dictate terms.[8] The European Union is almost its equal, Japan is a power that the United States must reckon with, and China's economy is not only important today, but will be the source of much of the growth in world markets tomorrow.

But beyond military and economic power, the rise of what has been called soft power, being the powers of protest, political action, economic boycott, financial markets, and global communication and coordination, works against the military and economic might of the United States, or, indeed, any nation or group of nations. The clearest illustration of this (although not exactly soft) is international terrorist groups. They can communicate and coordinate actions across global distances, without the need to gather in a single room. Nor are terrorists the only ones who make use of soft power. When the U.S. government slapped new tariffs on steel imports in 2002, the European Union threatened to counter with tariffs on selected U.S. exports manufactured in the electoral districts of powerful U.S. congressional leaders. Global environmental groups routinely lobby the U.S. Congress to change federal environmental policies.

What, then, is likely to happen with and because of the United States, and what should a planner watch most closely?

The United States will almost certainly maintain its dominant position militarily, as well as its pre-eminent position economically, for a long time. China, the fastest-growing large economy in the world, would have to grow at an average rate of 6 percent a year for more than 50 years, compared with 2 percent a year for the United States, to equal the size of the U.S. economy.[9] No one else is even close.

But the key factors to watch relate to things that could limit or restrain U.S. power, and the most important of these are internal. If American public opinion swings violently isolationist (as it has on several occasions in the past) or protectionist (if the petty politics of local greed finally triumphs over common sense), then the United States might withdraw from international affairs, producing geopolitical turmoil and global economic chaos.

Finally, and in some ways most threateningly, the United States is in danger of losing its way if it does not soon repair the damage being done to its schools. Everything I've said throughout this book points to the primacy of knowledge workers and the steadily rising importance of education, thoughtfulness, creativity, and innovation. Yet American schools are clearly in decline, not everywhere and in all ways, but in general. I view the other developments that could change U.S. policies and attitudes as less likely, but the debasing of the U.S. education system is well established and must be reversed if Americans—and the world—are to avoid dire consequences. Ignorant people do not make enlightened leaders.

China

After the United States, China is the most important country of the future. Not only is it changing the global economy with its immense workforce and rapid growth and modernization, but it will be the cause of a significant shift in the balance of global power.

Put simply, I believe China has designs on supplanting the United States as the world's dominant economic, diplomatic, and military power. Clearly it cannot do this overnight. Its intentions are aimed at a more distant horizon, coming decades from now but shaping today's policies. I doubt if China intends to confront the United States. Instead, China's leadership intends to do everything it can to promote economic growth, build up its financial and economic clout, and gradually expand its sphere of diplomatic and military influence. It is already expanding its claims to unpopulated islands and mineral rights in the South China Sea, even though such claims are well beyond any recognized international boundaries. Meanwhile, it is using other tools to bully, blackmail, and pressure its neighbours, such as permitting privateers to operate, or threatening to allow a flood of illegal Chinese emigrants into Indonesia, Thailand, and other Southeast Asian countries.[10] In the short term, though, China will work for prosperity, and since prosperity cannot be created in isolation, this means that China's trading partners will also prosper. Its long-term geopolitical ambitions are probably not cause for immediate concern.

Of greater concern is that while China appears to be an awakening giant, it is also a terribly fragile one for it is beset by enormous internal problems. These problems represent a greater source of concern for the world, for they may throw China into chaos, revolution, or create other crises that the world will be forced to deal with.

Let's start with demographic problems. China's pursuit of the one-child-per-family policy has been very successful at slowing its population growth, with salutary economic benefits. But these benefits come at a cost. First, because of the strong cultural preference for male children, the one-child policy has produced one of the largest cases of genocide in history. It's been estimated that there are roughly 30 million more men in their 20s in China than women, which means that through abortion and postnatal murder, that number of females has been eliminated from the population. Edward Tu, a demographer at Hong Kong University of Science and Technology, estimates that for at least the next 40 years there will be a

China's rulers are faced with the enormous dilemma of what to do with the large majority of their workers, for whom there is no economic future.

million more excess bachelors per year.[11] None of this is government-sponsored or -sanctioned, but historically, countries with large numbers of unmarried young men tend to be more warlike, and while 30 million is a small number in a population of (officially) 1.3 billion, it's a significant number of men in that age group.

Beyond that, the one-child policy is exacerbating the differences between Chinese cities and the countryside. Children are an asset in a rural setting, because they represent free labour. Moreover, when the parents are too old to work, they are supported by their children. Accordingly, the one-child policy has been impossible to implement in rural China. The unofficial policy of China is to leave the rural areas alone, but enforce the one-child rule in the cities. As a result, China not only has the problems of a young, industrializing society, but also the problems of an aging society with insufficient pension assets, as *Globe and Mail* writer Miro Cernetig has outlined:

> As China's countryside grows younger . . . the cities are graying at the fastest rate on the planet. Each passing day, there are simply fewer and fewer young urbanites to pay for the burgeoning numbers of old people. . . . Today's young Chinese are becoming increasingly Westernized, hoping for their own apartments and liberty from the tradition of looking after aging parents. And they are often so spoiled from being raised in single-child families, which has created the egocentric Little Emperor Syndrome, that more and more of them feel no guilt in expecting the state to pick up the tab.[12]

Yet, the biggest problem China faces is that it can't find enough work for its people. Traditionally, a country moves from agriculture to manufacturing to services as it develops. Today, about two-thirds of China's workers are still stuck on farms in the impoverished interior, which prevents China from adopting more efficient farming techniques. At the same time, Chinese factories are automating, with the result that urban China has no place to put the massive inflows of workers from the hinterlands seeking a better life. China's rulers are faced with the enormous dilemma of what to do with the large majority of their workers, for whom there is no economic future.

All of this is aggravated by China's lack of land. Although China has one-fifth of the world's population, it has only about one-twelfth of the world's land, much of which is mountainous or uninhabitable. This creates enormous population pressure—and, again, population pressure has historically been one of the major causes of war. So watch China carefully. It is trying to solve its problems peacefully and economically, but history implies it is being pushed towards war.

The Middle East

Samuel Huntington, chair of Harvard's Institute for Strategic Planning, is the author of a book (*The Clash of Civilizations and the Remaking of World Order*)[13] that foresees a new global struggle. No longer will it be the free world versus the communist countries, but a clash of cultures. This clash of cultures is, of course, particularly evident in the Middle East, which seems destined to be unstable for many years to come. Yet this may be too localized an outlook. Over the last 30 years, Arab countries have gradually come to accept that Israel has a right to exist, and, in the Oslo accords, there has been one serious attempt to settle the problems of the Palestinians. I suspect that this area will gradually become more settled, and less contentious, over the next 30 years, as time passes and all concerned push for solutions to the current unpredictable, dangerous, and expensive situation. However, between then and now, there will be further eruptions of violence, and the potential to initiate global conflict. For years yet to come, the Middle East will be a flashpoint that planners need to watch.

Everyone Else

Clearly, there are more countries and geopolitical powers in the world beyond China and the United States. Europe is the most obvious example. But while Europe is roughly equal to the United States economically, it does not dominate like the United States, innovate like it, and cannot seem to speak with one voice diplomatically, much as that vexes the French. Its influence, then, will likely be categorized as "more of the same" rather than "significant factor for change."

This is patently unfair, because there are many innovative and competitive companies in Europe. But given that I have only a few thousand words, and not a few thousand pages, to discuss the future of geopolitics, Europe doesn't merit much attention.

Japan is an economic powerhouse, the second-largest economy in the world, but is in clear decline. It has a democratic government on paper, but is beset with cronyism and vote-buying on such a scale that it is effectively an autocracy. Moreover, the power-brokers that prop up the government are preventing Japan from cleaning up the problems that have resulted in a decade-long recession. Yet Japan's biggest problem is that its population is getting old, having not had the baby boom that Europe and North America did following the Second World War. Soon it won't have enough workers for its factories, and its culture militates against large-scale immigration. So Japan's geopolitical influence, after cresting in the 1980s, is waning.

The other Asian tigers—Taiwan, Singapore, Hong Kong, Thailand, Malaysia, Indonesia, and so on—have been players of growing importance in the past 30 years, imitating Japan's success and foreshadowing China's. Yet today they are rapidly losing ground to the Chinese dragon. Indeed, two of the tigers, Taiwan and Hong Kong, may eventually be absorbed into China and cease to exist as independent entities. So the tigers will continue to grow, and, ironically, China will be their major customer, but their importance will be eclipsed by China.

India would be next on my list. Indeed, India has the potential to do what China has done, in spades. By the middle of this century, India will have surpassed China as the most populous country in the world. Beyond this, it has a tradition of education, and a history of talent in mathematics, engineering, and warcraft. Moreover, virtually all of the most educated people in India speak English, the universal language of business, giving them an enormous advantage over the Chinese. Yet India has major problems. First, it, too, suffers from too little land, and too many people. It, too, has to worry about what kind of work its people can find. But, unlike China, India's government is largely ineffective. It is difficult for any party to develop the stable ruling majority necessary for a country that runs by rule of law. In this, China's communist despots have a major advantage— as long as they can hold power. As a result of India's weak central government, its attempts to open its economy to international trade—in the way that China has—have been half-hearted. Accordingly, India hasn't reaped the enormous economic benefits that China has. For all of these reasons, India has enormous potential, but is lagging far behind its eastern neighbour. If it can correct these shortcomings, it, too, could become an economic giant—but I doubt this will happen quickly.

Russia comes to mind next, and I suspect Russia will become a significant economic and geopolitical player. At present, Russia is not a major economy, having a GDP roughly comparable to that of Belgium. It does, though, have geopolitical clout because of its political past, notably its veto power in the UN Security Council, and because of its future economic potential. It must first overcome its own lawlessness, though, or else it won't be able to attract foreign capital, and its economy will lag. However, most people forget that under the czars Russia was, for a time, the leading exporter of wheat in the world, and remains a treasure trove of natural resources. Moreover, the Soviet Union successfully created an education system that opened up opportunity to every class. If Russia can create economic, legal, and governmental stability—all unproven possibilities at this point—its educated workforce will turn out to be its greatest asset.

Latin America has a great deal of potential, including proximity to the United States and potential free-trade access to the American market. But before any of that potential can be realized, Latin American countries will have to produce stable governments and economies, and attract foreign investment through enforceable laws that protect properties. Those that do will prosper. Those that don't will lag behind. Brazil is an example of a country that could become a major player but is hobbled by its financial and political instability. And some countries in Latin America, such as Mexico and Colombia, may be harmed by internal disputes, potentially leading to secession movements in Mexico and warlords in Colombia (which has arguably already happened with the cocaine drug barons). As a whole, then, Latin America will not be a major force of change because of its lack of stability and cohesiveness as a region.

With a few notable exceptions, Africa is largely a write-off, and, unfortunately, is likely to remain so. It is cursed by geography (too much land in the tropics, too few navigable rivers for inexpensive transport, too little arable land) and by the rampant ethnic tensions that national boundaries merely paper over. Add to this the vicious cycle of poverty, population growth, and diseases that rich-country pharmaceutical companies don't care about, and it's difficult to make a case for Africa being anything other than islands of progress surrounded by a sea of poverty.

Finally there's Canada. Geopolitically, Canada is largely irrelevant. It is a middle power, whose greatest influence comes through its historic ties to Europe; its proximity to and relationship with the United States; or its reputation as an honest intermediary. We will prosper, and we will contribute—but, except for the occasional innovation by some exceptional Canadians, Canada is not, and is unlikely to be, a force in global politics. What happens abroad will affect us. What happens here is unlikely to have much effect on others.

Hope

Most of this geopolitical stuff is pretty depressing. Unfortunately, the nature of looking at the future generally makes it easier to see bad things than good. But I don't expect an apocalyptic future, punctuated with gloom and disaster. Indeed, if you look back over the 20th century, you can see why. People often think immediately of the disasters and hardships: two global wars, plus dozens of smaller ones, the Great Depression, epidemics, and social conflict. But when I look back at the 20th century, I see the emergence of a global system of laws and economic rules that make it easier and more profitable to negotiate than to invade. I see the emergence of widespread modern health care that has almost doubled average life expectancy, and a blueprint that almost any country can follow to achieve prosperity and health for its population. I see advances in science and technology that are beyond the dreams of our forebears, and that have produced lives of affluence that were impossible for even the wealthiest of earlier centuries.

Good things tend to happen gradually and progressively through the compounding of wealth. But watching the wheat grow or stocks inch up doesn't make headlines. And history books tend to be filled with big problems more than with small successes. The same is true with anticipating the future.

It's easy to see potential problems, which is why a discussion of geopolitics comes off as so gloomy. But I believe the 21st century will end with more substantial, widespread progress than the 20th. Nations will work together to produce a world that runs by laws, and where terrorists and lawbreakers of all persuasions are hunted down, even as murderers and bank robbers are today. Our ability to prolong life and to offer opportunities that never existed before will be the most dramatic change.

The end of the 21st century will not see an end to humanity's problems. But it will see a dramatic lessening of humanity's traditional scourges: war, famine, plague, and death—the Four Horsemen of the Apocalypse. In the meantime, you will need to watch the drama unfold carefully, or be savaged by events that catch you by surprise and unprepared.

Which leads us to the final secret, and the one I've been building towards through the entire book.

Create Your Desired Future

"The truth waits for eyes unclouded by longing."

—BUDDHIST APHORISM

13
Making It Happen

Tomorrow hasn't happened yet.

I just thought I'd mention that because so many companies behave as if tomorrow's events were given, and have a highly predictable outcome. As I mentioned at the beginning of the book, the biggest single barrier to thinking clearly about tomorrow is contained in the phrase "the future." It implies that there is only one possible future, which should, therefore, be knowable if you're just smart enough. Even though people instinctively feel that the future is uncertain, there's an intellectual bias towards assuming that it will unfold in a linear, predictable way.

But the future is more like a fog of probabilities than a clear road into a known country. There are trillions of things that can happen, and you can strongly influence many events in your own future. To maximize your influence over tomorrow, though, requires that you think clearly about the wide range of possibilities, and plan carefully to deal with the most likely ones, as well as make provision for less likely, but more dramatic, futures.

I'm not trying to imply that you don't already plan, but in my experience the two greatest failures in planning, regardless of the size of the organization, are: (1) people don't plan far enough ahead; and (2) they plan only for "the" future, rather than a range of possibilities. Whether your organization is big or small, such tunnel vision is like trying to play grandmaster chess while looking only at the next move.

You Can Think about the Future Only in Specific Terms

How, then, do you think coherently about the fog of possible futures? Well, first, you can't think about the future in vague, general terms. The question I dread most is: "What's going to happen in the future?" My answer is: "What's going to happen in the future *of what?*" So, for instance, better questions would be, "How will the aging of the baby boomers, and their move towards retirement, change the nature of corporate senior management? And how will that lead to changes in corporate policy among your clients?" Or how about: "If the Internet is creating a global culture, and young people are more likely to be immersed in it than older people, what will happen in domestic politics when young people think more like their peers in other countries than older people in their own country?" Focused questions suggest specific themes and avenues for investigation.

So planning for the future is about coming up with the right kinds of specific questions that will lead you to new insights. From such insights you can start shaping plans for a range of possibilities, and identify the indicators you should be watching to determine which set of possibilities will actually coalesce into the future. I summarize this process as the 10-5-2 Rule, which says: look out 10 years, take aim at 5 years, and plan for 2 years. Looking out 10 years means being aware of the long-term major forces that are moving and shaping the world, and positioning yourself to exploit opportunities as they unfold. Aiming at 5 years means developing an internally consistent and useful set of possible futures about what the world, the economy, the marketplace, your industry, and your company will be like 5 years from now. Finally, take this 5-year outline and create a detailed plan of what actions you are prepared to take during the next 2 years. This structured approach cuts through much of the fog, challenges your preconceptions, and opens up new avenues of thought. And it fits well with a specific tool I'd like to introduce that helps you create a coherent spread of possible futures.

An Introduction to Scenario Planning

Of the many tools that can be useful when thinking about the future, I'd like to focus on one of the most powerful and flexible. Scenario planning is a deliberate approach to considering possible futures, and it accomplishes two major goals. First, it helps break the "one future" mindset by creating a range of alternative futures. If done properly, it will challenge your hidden assumptions about the way the future is going to unfold. And second, it gives you specific mental equipment that you can use to anticipate problems and opportunities as well as consider the actions you might take.

Scenario planning as a tool for structured thought is something that U.S. military planners created following the Second World War to anticipate what their Communist counterparts might do. Herman Kahn of the Hudson Institute, most famously in his seminal 1960s work *On Thermonuclear War: Thinking the Unthinkable,* further developed scenario planning as a systematic tool for studying the future. Kahn also started applying it to business, which attracted quite a lot of interest among a select group of forward-thinking companies.

The late Pierre Wack was one corporate planner who picked up on Kahn's work and institutionalized it into his firm's planning. Wack worked for Royal Dutch/Shell in London and is generally credited with leading a group that anticipated the Organization of the Petroleum Exporting Countries (OPEC) oil embargo in October 1973, as well as the advent of the Soviet policies of *perestroika* and *glasnost.* These led to the subsequent collapse of the Soviet Union, which produced a sell-off in the prices paid for Russian oil fields. Both of these coups were considered wild, unjustified flights of fancy by contemporaries and conventional planners, and both turned out to be right. More to the point, both made Royal Dutch/Shell quite a lot of money, allowing the company to outmanoeuvre its competitors.

Scenario planning can be much more than a toy to amuse the troops at company retreats. It can be a life-and-death tool that saves your company and lets you prosper when others are suffering.

But for my money, Wack's greatest triumph was playing a part in the demise of apartheid. After Wack retired from Shell in the early 1980s, he was retained by Anglo American, South Africa's largest company and one of the biggest mining companies in the world, to create a range of scenarios about the future of apartheid and South Africa. He later turned these scenarios into a series of public lectures and a best-selling book. Among the scenarios included was one that created a road map of how white South Africans could end apartheid without being victimized by the black majority. It's said that F. W. de Klerk, who became president of South Africa in 1989, took the scenarios quite seriously, including the ones about violent upheaval and the persecution of the white minority, and that they led him to approach Nelson Mandela about mapping out a peaceful road for South Africa's future.[1]

Scenario planning is a skill that improves with practice. In a moment I'll provide a rudimentary introduction to get you started. Doing a scenario-planning exercise just once will be useful, because, assuming you've done it properly, it will challenge your current thinking and give you a sense of the potential of this tool. But to gain the full benefits of scenario planning, it should become an ongoing exercise that you perform and update regularly. First, though, let me give you an idea of how and why such an institutionalized process can be valuable.

Jim's computer genie switches on the video screen as he walks into the kitchen. It had woken him early that morning with the warning that something important was happening: China was firing missiles

into the sea near Taiwan's principal shipping ports, effectively closing them. This happened apparently in response to the inaugural speech of Taiwan's new, firebrand president, who had run on a platform of declaring independence from mainland China, against the advice of the United States and most of its major allies. Now, despite strenuous efforts on the part of the international community, hostilities have broken out—albeit in a token fashion so far.

Jim stands looking at the news, thinking through some of the implications, then tells his genie to call his company's CEO and owner, Marjorie Lamontaigne. When the connection has been made, Jim asks if he can see her this morning. "I'm already in the office," she replies. "How soon can you get here?"

When Jim reaches the company's plant in Mississauga, he stops off first at his own office and picks up a file titled "Armed Conflict—Asia." He walks into Marjorie's office, where she has the vice-president of production with her. They both look worried. Jim says, without preamble, "We've planned for this, Marjorie. I think we're going to be all right."

Marjorie looks surprised, then thoughtful. Over the next 15 minutes, Jim walks her through the scenario that the company's executives and other key thinkers created two years ago, and which Jim had twice updated with his planning committee—a group of particularly enthusiastic employees from all levels of the company. That the company's two top executives had forgotten that they'd ever been involved in such an exercise doesn't surprise Jim, although he feels a little hurt. However, he also feels a fierce sense of pride and satisfaction in the work he's done to push the company into doing this kind of planning and in the subsequent work his planning committee has produced.

Most of the company's product is being manufactured in China, with some of the parts coming from Taiwan, ironically enough, shipped through Hong Kong. But, partly because of their "war

MAKING IT HAPPEN   225

gaming" of this kind of scenario, the company has options on manufacturing capacity in third-party factories in Mexico and Brazil, where it also has a modest level of production as a backup for exactly this kind of development. From Jim's studies of past conflicts, he knows that even a diplomatic settlement would take months or even years. Meanwhile, production and supply could easily be disrupted, and customers might look for other suppliers. Since many of their competitors are relying on China for production too, this is an opportunity to eat up market share. The only downside is that it will increase costs by about 4.5 percent, but that seems like cheap insurance.

Marjorie looks at her two subordinates, and asks if they feel it's too early to trigger the options on the Mexican and Brazilian facilities. They agree it's time. Marjorie gives the order to taper off production at the factories in China immediately, and to notify the Mexican and Brazilian suppliers to gear up production levels as soon as they can get raw materials.

In the months that follow, the company's planning allows it to keep its customers supplied, with only the smallest of hiccups, and, as Jim had predicted, it manages to pick up market share from competitors who are trapped into Chinese production with no fallback. The company is even able to pass on a small price hike to compensate for the higher production costs, which is almost unheard of in today's economy. Because the company's executives had planned for it, this crisis became an opportunity.

As you can see, scenario planning can be much more than a toy to amuse the troops at company retreats. It can be a life-and-death tool that saves your company and lets you prosper when others are suffering. So, if you're going to attempt scenario planning without outside assistance, here's how to go about it.

Step 1: Create a Thinking Environment

Select a group of people who are from, or related to, your organization. Take them off-campus outside of normal working hours to get away from the business-as-usual mindset. Dress should be casual, and titles should be left outside the door. Ban all cellphones (including yours), watches, and clocks for anyone other than a designated facilitator. It's almost impossible to be creative on a strict timetable, or with outside interruptions.

Next, foster an accepting atmosphere. This means that all ideas—no matter how wild, woolly, or apparently impractical—are worth listening to, and no one is allowed to criticize. Critiquing ideas comes at a later stage. Criticism at this stage will cause people to shut up and play it safe.

Have people work in groups of no more than six. If your group is small, have people work in twos or threes. It's best if they sit together, say at a round table, so they can talk among themselves. Equip everyone with writing implements. Supply flip charts for notes that the entire group can see for thoughts that they want to share. Appoint a facilitator, someone who can act as traffic cop to keep ideas flowing and to prevent any one person or group from hogging the proceedings. The traffic cop probably shouldn't be the CEO or a top executive, but someone else that everyone respects, someone who's not afraid to stand up in front of a group, and someone who can keep the proceedings moving.

Step 2: Set the Time Horizon

You need to think about a specific period of time, and it's important to get it right. Depending on what you're trying to accomplish, you need to pick a horizon that is relevant, but further out than your normal thinking. If you are doing a broad-brush first attempt at anticipating the future, go for the 10 years I described above. If you are attempting to do something much more concrete, such as coming up with specific new product ideas for a particular market segment, then the time horizon will be shorter. The key in setting the horizon is that it has to stretch your outlook beyond your everyday thought and planning cycles, but it can't be so far into the future that it seems to be an irrelevant fantasy. For instance, thinking about the next 100 years would strike most people as a waste of time (although it's something I do with fair regularity). And doing scenario planning for the next 18 months is likely to be overkill, like using an elephant gun to swat a fly, unless you are approaching a particularly difficult period. If your normal planning horizon is, say, 3 years, then 5 would be a good stretch without being too fantastic.

Step 3: Break the One-Future Mindset

Start by creating three simplistic future scenarios that are deliberately different from each other. The first one is titled "If This Goes On . . ." and describes the future that you expect. Start by asking everyone to answer the question: "What do you think will happen to our organization, our community, and our suppliers and clients by the end of [the selected planning horizon]?" This should include thoughts on what's going to happen with the global, national, and local economies; the geopolitical situation; the marketplace and consumer attitudes; company executives; competitors, suppliers, and clients; technology, especially computers and communications; health care and health-care spending; the demographics of the society you function within; and anything else that anyone thinks will be relevant. Encourage people to think broadly.

Everyone should start by thinking to themselves. There should be no talking or exchanging of views. That comes later. Give everyone between two and five minutes (which is not a lot of time, but will seem like forever) to think and jot down notes. You can also ask people to think about this scenario before they arrive, and bring notes with them.

Then have people each take one minute to summarize their thoughts to the other members of their group, hitting only the high points. Appoint a scribe for every group to jot down notes. Make sure everyone gets a chance to speak.

Next, have the scribes report the highlights to the entire gathering, with the facilitator calling on each group, one at a time, and summarizing and repeating the thoughts relayed by each scribe to ensure she understands them. Members of each group can supplement the scribe's comments if they feel that something important has been missed. The facilitator jots a summary of each point on the flip charts, with the heading "If This Goes On . . ." at the top of the first page.

When all the points from all the groups have been noted, you will have a grab bag of individual events of one possible future world. These should be torn off, kept together, and eventually typed up and circulated.

Now repeat the process with a very different kind of future, called "Your Worst Nightmare." Here your objective is to embody Murphy's Law in your anticipated future: anything that can go wrong will go wrong, and at the worst possible moment. You can make this even more convincing by appointing different groups to play the role of a set of people that affect your organization's future. Hence, one group can role-play government regulators; another, suppliers; a third, customers; a fourth, competitors; and so on. Each group is asked to think of things it could do by the end of the projected time horizon if that group's only purpose was to do as much harm to your organization as possible. One or more groups are given a slightly different task: to role-play the people in your own organization. Their task is to do everything they can to sabotage the efforts of the organization *without getting caught.*

Again, give everyone time to think to themselves, then share within their groups, then provide the highlights to the facilitator, who writes them on the flip charts under the title "Your Worst Nightmare."

Finally, go through the same process with a third simplistic scenario, titled "Your Fondest Dreams." Here the object is to imagine a world where everything goes right, and all the luck breaks your way. You can keep the same groups as for the previous scenario, but this time have them focus on what they could do that would help your organization improve its market position, standing with clients, and so on. Note that everything discussed should be possible, and that fairy godmothers are not allowed—although you get all the breaks.

You now have three separate scenarios of the future, only one of which is the consensus future that most people probably walked in with. Even that's articulated in more detail than would otherwise have been the case. More to the point, you have accomplished two major things: conditioning your participants to consider more than one kind of future (even though the other two scenarios are not especially realistic), and creating ammunition for the next step.

And, incidentally, you will have accomplished two lesser things as well. First, from "Your Worst Nightmare" you will have a list of recognized bad-management practices from the group representing your employees. Any time any of these things show up, it's an indication that your organization is getting into trouble. And second, the "Your Fondest Dreams" scenario should get you thinking about how to exploit good luck if, as, and when it happens.

Step 4: Identify the Major Forces That Will Affect Your Future

With the three alternative scenarios you've just finished in hand, ask the group to identify the key forces that are going to shape your future. These may be the same in all three scenarios, as with demographic factors, or they may vary, as with the effects of technology on your marketplace. Where possible and appropriate, combine similar or related forces under a single category. However, wherever there's disagreement over combining factors, leave them separate.

Once you have a list of the factors that are going to cause or provoke change, ask your group to rank them in terms of importance. Which force is going to produce the most momentous changes for your organization over the selected time horizon? Ask anyone to suggest a candidate and to then give a brief explanation as to why this is the one. Once you have a series of candidates, vote, asking how many people think each of the factors proposed is the most important, then tally the votes. Ask each person to vote for only one factor.

By now you'll have a ranking of the most important forces, ranked by the number of votes each one received. Note that you have to vote only once. The force with the most votes is deemed the most important, the one receiving the second-highest tally is the second-most important, and so on. Now ask which factors of those identified as important are the most predictable. Hence, demographics are highly predictable, but fashion trends among the young are highly unpredictable. Here all you need is a general consensus on which factors are highly predictable.

Once you've identified the most predictable factors, pick the two most important factors that are deemed unpredictable—that is, they are not on the predictable list. These are pivotal, because the *most important, least predictable* forces are the ones that create the greatest uncertainty and the highest level of threat (and opportunity) for your organization.

Step 5: Create More Realistic Future Scenarios

Let's suppose, for instance, that you selected "acceptance of new technologies by clients" as one of these forces, and "strength of economic growth" as the other. You are now going to create four new, more realistic scenarios using these two factors. You do this by creating a square, divided in quarters, as shown in the figure on the next page.

Hence, in Scenario A you have a future predicated on high economic growth and a slow client acceptance of technological change. I've labelled this "Conventional Warfare" because it's probably similar to what you've experienced in the past. On the other hand, Scenario B, "The Terminator Future," assumes that there will be a high rate of economic growth, and a fast pace of client acceptance of new technologies. This scenario would lead to a completely different kind of marketplace clash, which I've likened to the Schwarzenegger *Terminator* films. Low growth and slow technological acceptance create Scenario C, where nothing much changes. Scenario D—

Four Possible Future Scenarios

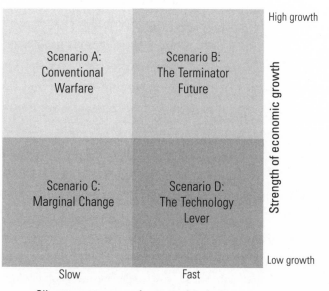

Client acceptance of new technologies

fast technological acceptance in a low-growth world—creates a situation where you can use technology as a lever to gain market share.

There are two things to note here. First, and of lesser importance, is that you need to come up with simple, memorable names that everyone can then use as shorthand to describe each scenario. Thus, when one person refers to "The Terminator Future," everyone immediately knows which scenario is meant, and the assumptions on which that scenario is based.

The second, and more important, point is that you have now created four possible scenarios based on your own assessment of the key forces shaping tomorrow. These scenarios should resonate with you and your people. They should seem plausible and even likely. And they give you the tools to create specific alternative futures, instead of the vague uncertainties you wrestled with before. I'll come back to this in the next step.

Despite the visible and transparent process you've followed to get here, if you've created a successful set of future scenarios, at least some of your people will have difficulty accepting one or more of them. This will be

People tend to want scenarios that validate their beliefs, or that promise higher incomes, or give them more status or influence, just as oil-company executives tend to believe scenarios that point to higher oil prices.

doubly true for people outside this group that were not involved in this process. When I've facilitated groups in this kind of exercise, there are almost invariably some people, for instance, that have rejected the scenarios indicating difficult or harmful changes, and others who have rejected outcomes that were too optimistic. This is natural, and is more a reflection of the psychology or desires of the individuals than the value of the scenarios you've created. Indeed, when you get this kind of emotional rejection to the scenarios you've created, what the scenarios are really doing is *challenging the prejudices and preconceptions of your people and your organization!* This is extraordinarily valuable, because these are blind spots that can cause you great harm. People tend to want scenarios that validate their beliefs, or that promise higher incomes, or give them more status or influence, just as oil-company executives tend to believe scenarios that point to higher oil prices.

One of the biggest problems that Pierre Wack and the futurist planning group at Shell had with the scenarios that anticipated the Arab oil embargo of 1973 and the collapse of the Soviet Union in 1991 was that Shell executives and outside experts refused to believe these things were possible. They were way out in the wild blue yonder, and it was difficult for hard-nosed, common-sense executives to believe in such ridiculous fantasies, even if the scenarios were predicated on reasonable assumptions and backed with impeccable logic. Yet they proved to be correct, and helped Shell weather two very turbulent periods for oil companies.

Step 6: Develop Each Scenario

At this stage, you've created the skeleton of a group of possible planning scenarios. Now you need to flesh it all out to make it useful. First, step back and ask if you've picked the two most important, unpredictable forces, the ones most useful in capturing the uncertainty of the future. Having created four scenarios with the two forces you picked, ask whether other pairings would be interesting or useful. If so, go back and redo your scenarios. Be careful in making such changes, though, that you are actually moving to scenarios that will be more useful, and not merely giving in to your prejudices. You're trying to create scenarios that will help you navigate an uncertain future, not flatter the egos or titillate the interests of your participants.

Next, consider whether the ranges you've chosen for the scenarios are appropriate. For instance, suppose instead of only two options for client acceptance of technology, you allowed for three—slow, moderate, and rapid—which would create six scenarios rather than four. Would that be more useful to you in anticipating probable futures? If so, go with it. If not, stick with the simpler model.

Once you've got a group of scenarios that seems to offer the greatest utility to you for planning purposes, consider the scenarios one at a time. As you consider them, assume that they've already happened, that you are looking back to today from the end of your selected planning horizon, and that the selected scenario is the one that actually happened. Now start to think about and describe what this world will be like. If it's 10 years into the future, how old will you be? How old will the organization's senior executives be? Will they still be working with you, or will they have retired? If you're a salesperson, how old will your principal clients be? Think through all the obvious, simple things that are going to happen, and describe each of them as best you can, accepting that some details, such as who will replace a retiring CEO, may be unknowable. In fact, such uncertainties will become useful in creating action plans later on.

Next, look at the list of major forces you created in Step 4, starting with the most predictable ones, and consider how they will create change in the scenario you're working on. How will demographics, for instance, affect the marketplace, political regulation, consumer demand, housing, interest rates, stock markets, and so on? How will increasing foreign competition affect the market, your clients, the products and services available, etc.?

Work your way down to less predictable factors, always keeping in mind that you're assuming the conditions of that particular scenario. How will e-commerce change in a slow-acceptance future? What will be the major things that help one market player and hurt another? Think through the various aspects of the scenario as best you can, trying to create a storyline. Indeed, the concept of a storyline is important, because when you report back to people not involved in this process, you are literally going to have to tell them a story about what this world will be like. Otherwise they won't understand what you're talking about.

Then go back and repeat the process for each of the other scenarios, one by one, building detailed future histories of the world as it would be under the assumptions of those scenarios. To expedite matters, you can ask different groups to develop different scenarios. This also allows people to select the ones that interest them the most. If there are scenarios that no one wants to work on, ask yourself why. Is it because the scenario represents disaster for your organization (and therefore should be of great interest to you), is it because no one believes it's possible (in which case you should consider whether you've hit a blind spot, or whether it's just not useful), or is it just a boring scenario? If it's the last, that's no reason to discard it. It just may not be as much fun.

Once everyone has finished with elaborations, participants should present their storylines to the entire group one by one, eliciting additional ideas and thoughts, and asking for disagreement or discussion. Here the object is to reach some sort of consensus about what the world, your market, and your company will be like in each potential future. You don't have to like the scenario, just to agree that it's a possibility you should prepare for.

Step 7: Decide on Action Plans for Each Scenario

As you flesh out each scenario, start thinking about what would be the most advantageous actions you could take if it occurred. What would help you most with containing your costs? How could you find and retain the best people? What public positions could you take that would reflect favourably on your organization? How would clients behave, and how could you anticipate their needs if you knew, ahead of time, that this scenario was the one that was going to happen?

Then, once you've developed the storyline for the scenario, work on developing an outline of the strategy you would pursue that would help your organization make the most out of this future.

Once you've done this for all of your working scenarios, you'll find that there are some actions that will make sense no matter what happens. These you should highlight and initiate immediately. For instance, with one group from the federal government that I facilitated through this process, it became clear that no matter which scenario proved to be true, they were going to have to increase their levels of training, for both team management and new technologies. Once they realized that this was a constant, and that it didn't depend on how the future unfolded, they stopped hesitating about whether to invest in it, and started immediately.

The other actions, the ones that are different for each scenario, should be held in reserve until you know which way the world is tending. This was what Jim did in the earlier vignette. When military conflict broke out in China, he pulled out his notes from the relevant scenario and used the defined strategy as a blueprint to help his senior executives decide what to do. And because his company had taken the time to think through a range of possibilities, it had already invested resources to have a backup plan in case production in China was disrupted. It had, in short, a strategy already worked out that helped it respond decisively to events that caught others with their pants down.

Step 8: Develop a DEW Line for Each Scenario

Remember the DEW Line—Distant Early Warning system of radar stations—that was developed to warn Canada and the United States of an incoming aircraft or missile attack during the Cold War? That's what you want to develop for each one of your working scenarios. If Scenario D, "The

Technology Lever," turned out to be the one closest to reality, what warning signs would you be able to see that would indicate that events were moving in that direction? What economic indicators would you watch? Which technologies would experience rapid growth, and which companies would prosper as a result? After the fact, looking back on events, what signs would people have seen that would have told them that the world was heading towards Scenario D? Develop a list of such signs and portents as indicators. You may not see all of them, but if you see enough of them, they'll tip you off as to what's coming.

And, by the way, if too many of the indicators are the same among the different scenarios, it may be that the scenarios are not different enough from each other to be useful.

After Scenario Planning

By the time you've reached this stage, having gone through one complete scenario planning cycle, you'll be painfully aware of how much you've left out. True, you've captured a small number of possible futures, tied them down, branded them, and prepared for them. But you've also become aware of how many more possibilities there are, and of all the gaps that are leaving you vulnerable. This is wonderful news. Before you started, you probably would have had a hard time describing one reasonable alternative to the consensus future that everyone assumes will happen. Now you realize what's possible, and how valuable it can be. You've successfully broken the one-future mindset, and can now consider a wide range of possibilities.

However, this is also dangerous. You don't really want to wind up with 37 flavours of future. Not only would that take an inordinate amount of time and resources to create (although it would probably pay for itself many times over), but it's difficult to keep all the alternatives straight.

The primary reason for giving scenarios memorable, catchy names is to make them easier to bring to mind, to refer to them with other people, and to quickly grasp all the assumptions and implications. If you get up to six or more major scenarios, you're going to find it difficult to keep them straight, let alone to work with them. Moreover, if you wind up with a hatful of scenarios, I wonder how much difference there will be between them, at least in terms of their value in helping you prepare and think through the future. The Law of Diminishing Returns applies as much to scenarios as anything else. Two scenarios are a tremendous improvement over one. Thirty-seven scenarios are a marginal improvement over twenty-six, or twelve.

Then again, the number of scenarios itself presents different kinds of problems. If you have two scenarios, people will reflexively label them optimistic and pessimistic, or best-case and worst-case. If you have three, you wind up with optimistic, pessimistic, and realistic, and people tend to pick realistic. This is simplistic thinking that can drain much of the intellectual value of creating the scenarios in the first place. You're not trying to be optimistic or pessimistic. Nor, really, are you trying to be realistic, whatever that means. What you are trying to do is to explore possible futures that have a high probability of happening, and prepare for them. Avoid knee-jerk labelling, because it inhibits this kind of possibility planning.

Revisiting Your Scenarios

Arthur Burns, the former chairman of the U.S. Federal Reserve, was once asked if there was any way to forecast the economy accurately. "Yes," he replied, "forecast frequently." By this he meant that accurate forecasting was probably impossible to do without regular course corrections. The same is true with scenarios. They should be living documents that are re-examined and updated on a regular basis, not only by how many months have elapsed on the calendar, but also as events conspire to make them obsolete. So, rather than trying to create a range of super-scenarios that will cover all possibilities and endure for all time, create a handful of the best working models you can come up with, and then modify them when you learn more as the future unfolds.

Having once worked through the mental discipline of creating scenarios, you won't need to go through the entire exercise repeatedly.

So, rather than trying to create a range of super-scenarios that will cover all possibilities and endure for all time, create a handful of the best working models you can come up with, and then modify them when you learn more as the future unfolds.

Instead, you can start with Step 4, and work on from there. Or you can go back and revisit the two forces you chose to construct your scenarios to see if they still resonate as being the best choices to work with. If so, then read through the conclusions you came to, and update, challenge, or change any and all aspects of the resulting scenarios to see how they can be improved in light of new knowledge. You can create a working group that is particularly keen on this process, and the members can meet intermittently or regularly to top up your working cases, keep them current, and monitor outside events to see if any of the DEW Line indicators have been tripped.

And every once in a while, you can reconvene a large group, go through the whole process again, train some new people in how it works, and see if they come up with similar conclusions or striking new insights. Moreover, when major, new, unforeseen events take place, you can re-examine your scenarios, and have a working structure that will help you decide how to navigate the newly roiled future from there. Remember, for instance, how lost everyone felt following September 11, 2001? I spoke to a group of insurance people shortly after that, and presented a series of scenarios to them to help them deal with the new uncertainties by breaking the unknown elements down into manageable pieces and analyzing each one. Again, scenario planning is a method of getting away from a hazy, unwieldy future, and dealing with a specific, definable future. Which brings me to two useful extensions.

Wild-Card Scenarios

A wild card is a low-probability event that, if it occurs, will produce dramatic change. September 11 was a wild card. And if a wild card occurs, there's nothing you can do beforehand, right? Not at all. In fact, some of the greatest gains in business occur when you're prepared for the unexpected and your competitors are not. There were several people in different organizations who had correctly anticipated terrorist attacks on the United States, some who had specifically anticipated attacks on the World Trade Center in New York, and a few who had actually discussed attacking buildings with planes. Some of them were academics, some were military analysts, some were futurists. None of them were listened to, and none were planners for the major corporations whose people were killed and businesses harmed by the attacks. How much did those companies spend on recovering? How much will the insurers lose in settling claims? How much better off would all involved have been if they'd thought about the unthinkable?

Coming back to Royal Dutch/Shell, Pierre Wack's group anticipated the collapse of the Soviet Union, and Shell was prepared for the consequences. Hardly anyone else even considered the possibility that it could occur, including the Central Intelligence Agency (CIA), with which Shell shared the observations. To the CIA, not only did the collapse of its principal adversary seem fantastic, but because part of the agency's mandate was to monitor the USSR, the disappearance of the Soviet Union would imply a downsizing of operations. Since individual careers and bureaucratic power depended on expansion, not contraction, the organization was institutionally disposed to avoid thinking about a collapse.

So, if it's possible to "think the unthinkable," how do you go about doing it? Fundamentally it's quite simple: you reverse-engineer the future. By that I mean that you ask one simple question, in many different variants, and then follow the answers to a logical conclusion, even when that conclusion seems preposterous. And the fundamental question is: "What unexpected events or developments would have a dramatic effect on our business if they happened?"

Since Shell is in the oil business, that question became: "What events or developments would have a dramatic effect on the price of oil?" Pursuing answers to this question would lead you to all kinds of possibilities that you might not otherwise consider, such as:

- "What if the Saudi government were overthrown, and a Muslim fundamentalist government put in its place that was hostile to the West?"
- "What if a new technology emerged that dramatically lowered the cost of extracting oil from the Alberta tar sands?"
- "What if hybrid car engines, which get substantially more kilometres per litre (or miles per gallon), were to come down in price so that they were competitive with normal gasoline engines and became wildly popular within the next 10 years?"
- "What if erratic weather patterns create a groundswell of public demand for an end to greenhouse gases, leading governments to legislate a carbon tax and use the proceeds to fund research on creating economically feasible alternatives to fossil fuels?"

As you can see, by asking the kinds of questions that emerge from this simple query—"What could dramatically affect our business?"—you can start to identify wild cards that could change everything about your life and the prosperity of your operations, and you can start to prepare against the possibility that they might happen.

Try it right now. First identify the crucial elements of your business, as important to you as oil is to an oil company. Then ask yourself what could dramatically affect the price, availability, demand, or supply of these elements. Such questions are best if they are as specific as possible to the things that affect your business and your industry, although you can also ask the same kind of question about the national or global economy, or almost anything else. What could dramatically change the global economy? What could dramatically affect life on Earth?

Clearly, there's enormous opportunity here to prepare for an uncertain future. And, again, you're probably wondering where you're going to find time to handle all these new questions, to define where the point of diminishing returns is. That's a healthy question, because it means you're starting to see possibilities that would otherwise never have occurred to you.

The Desired Future

What kind of future would you create for your company if it were up to you, if you could control how events occurred and new developments emerged? This scenario is described as the "desired future," and I'd like to focus on it for a moment.

When Pierre Wack created a scenario for South African society in which it could make the transition from the unstable suppression of a majority by a minority to an egalitarian society without bloodshed, that was a desired future scenario. The creation of such a scenario, along with the elaboration of the steps necessary to make it happen, created hope among people on all sides of the racial divide. By demonstrating that it was possible, it gave people both the energy to undertake it and a blueprint of how to do it. That's what I propose that you do for your organization: first, define the desired future, and then elaborate the blueprint that will allow you to achieve it. Isn't that the point of planning in the first place?

And if you do it within the context of scenario planning, you can simultaneously prepare for possible roadblocks along the way, anticipating them and preparing contingency plans to deal with them. As Henry Ford said, "Obstacles are those frightful things you see when you take your eye off your goal."

To help define your desired future, use statements such as "It would be really great if . . ." then fill in the blanks. For the moment, accept all the wild, unrealistic things you'd like to say, such as "It would be really great if our major competitor voluntarily left the business," but also go for things that are a little closer to today's reality, such as "It would be really great if our clients thought we were just better than anyone else."

From such statements you can start to create an outline of the future the way you'd like it to be, such as "The desired future is one where our clients think we're just better than anyone else," and "Our desired future is one where our major competitor decides to leave the business." Once you've got such statements, you can start to ask simple, pertinent questions, such as "What could cause our clients to decide that we're just better than anyone else?" or "What could make our major competitor decide to leave the business?"

Remember: you can't hit a target if you don't aim for it. Know what your target is.

Is It Worth It?

This all sounds like a lot of work. It is. It sounds as though it costs money and takes time and effort away from other, more immediate, things. It does. Is it worth it? You can certainly carry on as you have in the past. It's got you where you are today. But as sales trainers say, "If you always do what you always did, you'll always get what you always got." In other words, if you want more, you need to do something different.

There's a lot more to scenario planning than I've described, so let me recommend two books that I've used and learned a great deal from. The first is a wonderfully optimistic and deceptively enjoyable book called *The Art of the Long View: Planning for the Future in an Uncertain World,* by Peter Schwartz (New York: Doubleday, 1991: 258 pages). Schwartz, who worked with Royal Dutch/Shell for a time, documents some of the company's triumphs. This is not so much a how-to book as a why-should-you book, and I think you'll find it quite readable. The other is more nuts-and-bolts, and nowhere as much fun to read. It's called *Scenario Planning: Managing for the Future* by Gill Ringland (Chichester, U.K.: Wiley, 1998: 407 pages). It can be a bit overwhelming, and it describes a tremendous range of things you can do with scenario planning in sometimes bewildering detail.

But at the end of the day, scenario planning is a tool, and it should be one that helps you, not overwhelms you. In particular, it should be an adjunct to your current planning, not a replacement for it. There are other kinds of planning and brainstorming tools that I've used, but this is the most directly useful and adaptable for business. In addition to helping organizations anticipate the future, I've used scenario planning for such specific tasks as assisting health-care workers to decide how to prepare a lobbying campaign; helping educators decide what technologies they should introduce into the classroom; and working with a marketing group to design new products for a narrowly defined market segment. It can be a wonderful tool, once you're comfortable in wielding it.

Scenario planning is hard work, even though it can often be fun. But look at the results. A tool that was used to anticipate the collapse of the Soviet Union and helped South Africa make a historic transition without bloodshed should surely be of some interest to you and your organization. You can keep doing what you've done in the past—or you can aim higher.

So the real question is not whether scenario planning is worth it. The real question is: Can you afford not to use it?

Who Owns Tomorrow?

*"A man will never do everything he dreams,
but he will never do anything he doesn't dream."*

—PHILOSOPHER WILLIAM JAMES (1842–1910)

Success is hard. Failure is easy.

Actually, failure isn't easy, but it is simple. In fact, failure is much harder on you than success, to the point where it can ruin your life and even kill you with stress. Success, on the other hand, produces a sense of elation and achievement. It calls forth the best from you and those you work with, and makes you eager to do more. Success builds on itself, moving from strength to strength. Failure hurts. So which would you rather choose: hard-to-achieve success or simple-to-achieve failure?

That sounds like a dumb question, but I'm the champion of dumb questions because they often lead to powerful truths. In Chapter 3 I said that in business, the opposite of "smart" wasn't "dumb," but "lazy." It takes effort, and more importantly, careful, systematic thought to peer into the future and find the most successful strategies.

What does it take to be successful? Ray Kroc, who created one of the greatest success stories of the 20th century, the McDonald's restaurant corporation, said:

Nothing in the world can take the place of persistence. Talent will not;
nothing is more common than unsuccessful individuals with talent.
Genius will not; unrewarded genius is almost a proverb. Education will
not; the world is full of educated derelicts. Persistence and determination
alone are omnipotent.[1]

While I agree that persistence is crucial, in a world that is changing as rapidly as ours, persistence is no longer enough. You now need the willingness to make a systematic study of the future, the ability to inspire other people to achieve, the wits to transform information into wisdom, the grit to act decisively on your understanding, and the courage to change your mind when you're wrong. If you can persist in doing this, you will own tomorrow.

Just as an organization works best when everyone shares the same values and works towards the same goals, so, too, do people pull together best when they share a common vision of the future that excites and inspires them. Too many organizations have no vision, and their only goal is to make some money, somewhere, somehow. There's nothing inspiring in trying to achieve a 3-percent increase in revenues or in dodging the next round of layoffs. You don't call greatness from people by praying you'll survive against new competition.

At the beginning of this book I said I didn't think it was possible to accurately and consistently predict the future. Alan Kay, one of the great technological visionaries of our time, disagrees with me. He once said, "The best way to predict the future is to invent it." We can't control what's going to happen in the world around us, but we absolutely control how we respond to what happens. So it is up to us to invent the kind of future we want for our companies, our communities, our families, our country, and for humanity as a whole. We can achieve far more by planning and working than by stumbling into an unexamined future and hoping things turn out okay.

How high can you reach? No one knows. But when you're supported on the shoulders of your colleagues, with your eyes wide open and your arms outstretched, your reach is substantially greater than if you're working alone, eyes squeezed shut, ignorant and fearful of the future. You cannot control tomorrow, but you can influence it. How much you influence it depends as much on how *well* you try as how *hard* you try.

I wish you good luck, and Godspeed. Tomorrow beckons.

What Did I Miss?

Anybody who talks about the future is giving you an opinion and will be wrong some of the time. That includes me, which is why I say that I don't predict the future but instead try to help people plan intelligently for the future.

Accordingly, I'm sure I've made mistakes, overlooked some things, made too much out of others, and that there are a lot of things I just don't know. If you know of something I've got wrong or overlooked, let me know. You can reach me through my website, **www.futuresearch.com**, or care of the publisher. I will reply if I can.

If you wish to discuss hiring me to work with your organization, please contact me through my website as well. The only work I do for free is speak to high school students, when my schedule permits.

If you want to find out more about having me speak to a group or conference, please contact my agent:

The Lavin Agency
4th Floor
77 Peter Street
Toronto, Ontario M5V 2G4
416-979-7979 / 1-800-265-4870
e-mail: info@thelavinagency.com

And thank you for your interest. I do appreciate it.

Thank You

No book is the product of one mind alone, so to those people who helped me create this one, I'd like to offer my thanks and acknowledgment:

- Jacky Simmons, my wife, assistant, and first editor, who tells me when I'm getting boring or going off track, and keeps me honest.
- Chris Worzel, my son, who was studying molecular biology and genetics at the time of writing, and who contributed ideas to this book.
- David Lavin, Nikki Barrett, Michael Downes, Cathy Hirst, Paul Maroney, Bryce Moloney, and the other professionals at The Lavin Agency, for their support and belief in my work.
- Beverley Slopen, whose guidance as a literary agent has helped me shape my writing and my career.
- Kelly MacDonald and Derek Sweeney, for past support, friendship, and encouragement.
- Andrea Crozier of Penguin/Viking Canada, with whom I felt an immediate meeting of the minds, who made me welcome to a new publishing house, and helped shape this book.
- Susan Folkins, my editor at Penguin/Viking, who lightened the burden of editing with insight, grace, and a sense of humour.
- To the many unseen people who help produce, market, stock, and sell books. Without them there would be an awful lot of frustrated writers.
- And to you, dear reader, for as Spider Robinson once said, "When you stop applauding, I stop eating." The opportunity to write books is a privilege, not a right. I appreciate your interest in my work.

Thank you.

Notes

1: The War for Talent

1. "Have a Nice Day." *The Economist* 2 Mar. 1991: 64.

2. Ibid.

3. "Labours Lost." *The Economist* 13 July 2000. Economist.com accessed 31 Oct. 2002. <www.economist.com/displayStory.cfm?Story_ID=5988>

4. Ibid.

5. Drucker, Peter. "A Survey of the Near Future." *The Economist* 3 Nov. 2001: 16.

6. Costa, John Dalla. "Getting It." *Report on Business Magazine* April 1998: 104.

7. Hymowitz, Carol. "Using Layoffs to Battle Downturns Often Costs More Than It Saves." *The Wall Street Journal* 24 June 2001: B1.

8. "Unthinking Shrinking." *The Economist* 9 Sept. 1995: 70.

9. "A Matter of Choice." *The Economist* 22 Dec. 2001: 74.

10. Drucker, Peter. "A Survey of the Near Future." 8.

11. *Webster's Seventh New Collegiate Dictionary.* Springfield, MA.: G. & C. Merriam, 1972. 273.

12. Stayer, Ralph. "How I Learned to Let My Workers Lead." *Harvard Business Review* Nov./Dec. 1990.

13. "Service with a Smile." *The Economist* 10 July 1997. Economist.com accessed 31 Oct. 2002. <www.economist.com/displayStory.cfm?Story_ID=370506>

14. Ibid.

15. "Labours Lost."

16. "Movable Ladders." *The Economist Review* 15 Dec. 1997: 10.

17. "Nicely Does It." *The Economist* 19 Mar. 1994: 84.

18. Petzinger, Thomas Jr. "Talking about Tomorrow: Peter Drucker." *The Wall Street Journal* 1 Jan. 2000: R24.

19. "Labours Lost."

20. Johnsonville.com. Johnsonville Foods, Inc. website accessed 22 May 2003. <www.johnsonville.com/jville.nsf/PressRoom>

21. Stayer, "How I Learned to Let My Workers Lead."

22. Ibid. 8.

2: HR and the Human Cost of Change

1. Stinson, Marian. "Assembly-Line Robots Taking Workers' Jobs: UN report." *The Globe and Mail* 8 Feb. 2000: B6.

2. Jordan, Miriam, and Hilsenrath, Jon E. "American Talks, India Types up the Transcript." *The Wall Street Journal* 16 Mar. 2000: B1.

3. Swisher, Kara. "U.S. Tech Town Rises in India." *The Wall Street Journal* 7 Jan. 2002: A13–15.

4. Collier, Paul, and Dollar, David. "Globalization, Growth and Poverty: Building an Inclusive World Economy." World Bank website accessed 14 Nov. 2002. <econ.worldbank.org/prr/structured_doc.php?sp=2477&st=&sd=2857>

5. "The Myths about Globalization (5)." *The Globe and Mail* editorial 17 Apr. 2001: A16.

6. "World's View of Multinationals." *The Economist* 27 Jan. 2000. Economist.com accessed 14 Nov. 2002. <www.economist.com/displayStory.cfm?Story_ID=276872>

7. Little, Bruce. "Economy Has Been Dishing Up Very Good Jobs, Indeed." *The Globe and Mail* 31 Aug. 1998: A6.

8. "Career Evolution." *The Economist* 29 Jan. 2000: 89.

9. Ibid.

10. Wessel, David. "Temp Workers Have Lasting Effect." *The Wall Street Journal* 1 Feb. 2001: A1.

11. Ibid.

3: The Opposite of "Smart" Is Not "Dumb"

1. De Geus, Arie. *The Living Company: Habits for Survival in a Turbulent Business Environment.* Boston: Harvard Business School Press, 1997. 1.

2. "The World's View of Multinationals." *The Economist* 29 Jan. 2000: 22.

3. "A Matter of Choice." *The Economist* 22 Dec. 2001: 75.

4. Ibid. 74.

5. Pritzinger, Thomas, Jr. "A New Model for the Nature of Business: It's Alive!" *The Wall Street Journal* 26 Feb. 1999: B1.

6. "Making a Meal of Mergers." *The Economist* 10 Sept. 1994: 87.

7. See, for example, my comments about telecommunications in *The Next Twenty Years of Your Life* (Toronto: Stoddart, 1997) on page 40.

8. "The Vision Thing." *The Economist* 9 Nov. 1991: 81.

9. De Geus, Arie. *The Living Company*. 8.

10. Ibid.

4: Assassin Marketing and Jigsaw Sales

1. Reflect.com website accessed 14 Aug. 2002. <www.reflect.com/servlet/ReflectSessionServlet?NEXTPATH=aboutus/&NEXTPAGE=aboutus_main.html>

2. "A Long March." *The Economist* 14 July 2001: 64.

3. Morra, Bernadette. *The Toronto Star* 15 Aug. 2002: D2.

4. "Enter the Ecosystem." *The Economist* 9 Nov. 2000. Economist.com accessed 14 Aug. 2002. <www.economist.com/displayStory.cfm?Story_ID=417060>

5. "Hi Ho, Hi Ho, down the Data Mine We Go." *The Economist* 23 Aug. 1997: 47.

6. Brooks, Rick. "Unequal Treatment." *The Wall Street Journal* 7 Jan. 1999: A1.

7. Ibid.

8. "Introducing PeopleSoft CRM for Financial Services." Advertisement in *The Wall Street Journal* 17 Dec. 2001: B5.

9. Pigg, Susan. "Diaper, Drinking and Data." *The Toronto Star* 16 Aug. 2002: B1.

10. "Direct Hit." *The Economist* 7 Jan. 1999: 56.

11. This actually happened to Jeff Bezos. In public. Fishman, Charles. "Face Time with Jeff Bezos." *Fast Company* February 2001. Fastcompany.com accessed 16 Aug. 2002. <www.fastcompany.com/online/43/bezos.html>

12. Sheff, David. "Net Life." *Yahoo! Internet Life* Jan. 2000: 91.

13. Ibid. 88.

14. "You'll Never Walk Alone." *The Economist* 24 June 1999. Economist.com accessed 14 Aug. 2002. <www.economist.com/displayStory.cfm?Story_ ID=215676>

15. As quoted, "Who's Wearing the Trousers?" *The Economist* 8 Sept. 2001: 27.

16. Ibid. 26.

17. Connellan, Tom. *Inside the Magic Kingdom: Seven Keys to Disney's Success*. Austin, TX: Bard Press, 1996. 85–86.

5: The Information Swamp

1. Anderson, Curt. "CIA Worries about Data Overload." Associated Press, as reported on NewsOK.com, accessed 26 Nov. 2002. <www.newsok.com/cgi-bin/show_article?ID=950674&pic=none&TP=getarticle>

2. *The Columbia Encyclopedia, Sixth Edition:* "type." Bartleby.com. <www.bartleby.com/65/ty/type.html>

3. As reported in "Consumers Thinking Twice about Buying into Technology." *Trend Letter* 18 June 2001: 3.

4. Kapica, Jack. "How Firms Can Cope with Grip of Data Fear." *The Globe and Mail* 21 Nov. 2002. Globeandmail.com accessed 26 Nov. 2002. <www.globeandmail.com/servlet/ArticleNews/front/RTGAM/20021121/gteinov21/Front/homeBN/breakingnews>

6: Living Naked: The Destruction of Privacy

1. Knowles, Bryan. "Are Employers Violating Worker's Privacy With Electronic Monitoring?" Speakout.com accessed 9 Dec. 2002. <speakout.com/activism/issue_briefs/1300b-1.html>

2. "Something to Watch over You." *The Economist* 15 Aug. 2002. Economist.com accessed 26 Nov. 2002. <www.economist.com/displaystory.cfm?story_id=1280634>

3. "The Surveillance Society." *The Economist* 1 May 1999: 22.

4. Ibid.

5. "Desirable Dust." *The Economist* 31 Jan. 2002. Economist.com accessed 26 Nov. 2002.

6. Tuck, Simon. "Techs Set Sights on Terrorism." *The Globe and Mail* 20 Sept. 2001: B12.

7. Caruso, Denise. "Digital Commerce." *The New York Times* 3 June 1996: C5.

7: Who We Are, Who We Will Be

1. Shirley, M.V., et al. "Population Projections for Canada, Provinces and Territories 2000–2026." Statistics Canada publication 91-520-XIB Mar. 2001: 79.

2. "Re-Engineering Retirement." *The Economist* 14 Dec. 2002: 70.

8: The Gathering Storm

1. "A Critique of Pure Reason." *The Economist* 4 July 1992: 73–74.

2. Bibby, Reginald. "Who Will Teach Our Children Shared Values?" *The Globe and Mail* 3 Feb. 1994: A23.

3. Lasch, Christopher. "Why Liberalism Lacks Virtue." *New Perspectives Quarterly* Spring 1991: 34.

4. Kung, Hans. "The New Ethic: Global Responsibility." *New Perspectives Quarterly* Spring 1991: 44–45.

5. Conlogue, Ray. "Why Pornography Is a Myth." *The Globe and Mail* 4 Jan. 1994: A9.

6. Wattenberg, Ben. PBS website accessed 3 Jan. 2003. <www.pbs.org/fmc/interviews/yankelovich.htm>

7. "America's Decadent Puritans." *The Economist* 28 July 1990: 11.

8. As quoted in "The Enemy Within." *The Economist* 25 June 1994: 92.

9. Ambert, Anne-Marie. "Divorce: Facts, Causes, and Consequences." Vanier Institute of the Family website accessed 2 Jan. 2002. <www.vifamily.ca/cft/divorce/divorcer.htm#True>

10. Valpy, Michael. "The Troubled Children of Families of Convenience." *The Globe and Mail* 3 Nov. 1993: A2.

11. Glossop, Robert. Personal interview 3 Jan. 2003.

12. Stevens, Liz. "The Dying Art of Discipline." *The Toronto Star* 26 Feb. 2000: R3.

13. Glossop, Robert. "Societal Influences." Speech given on 24 May 2002. Vanier Institute of the Family website accessed 3 Jan. 2003. <www.vifamily.ca/PR/speeches/bullye.htm>

14. Leake, Jonathan. "Violent Games Beget Violent Teens: Study." *Halifax Sunday Herald* 6 Aug. 2000: A1–A2.

9: The Economy's Wellspring

1. Heinlein, Robert Anson. *Time Enough for Love.* New York: Ace Books, 1988. 241.

2. "Working Miracles." *The Economist* 4 July 2002. Economist.com accessed 29 Jan. 2003. <www.economist.com/displayStory.cfm?Story_ID=1200215>

10: You Need to Be Good

1. *Adbusters* website accessed 7 Feb. 2003. <adbusters.org/creativeresistance/spoofads/fashion/nike/>

2. "Ethically Unemployed." *The Economist* 28 Nov. 2002. Economist.com accessed 6 Feb. 2003. <www.economist.com/displayStory.cfm?Story_ID=1469387>

3. Ibid.

4. Henderson, David. "Misguided Virtue: False Notions of Corporate Social Responsibility." New Zealand Business Roundtable and the Institute of Economic Affairs, June 2001. Accessed 10 Feb. 2003. <www.nzbr.org.nz/documents/publications/publications-2001/misguided_virtue.pdf>

5. "Doing Well by Doing Good." *The Economist* 20 Apr. 2000. Economist.com accessed 6 Feb. 2003. <www.economist.com/displayStory.cfm?Story_ID=304119>

6. Ibid.

7. Ibid.

8. Drucker, Peter F. *Managing for Results.* New York: Harper and Row, 1964, rev. 1986: 96.

9. Port, Otis. "Dueling Pioneers." *Business Week* 25 Oct. 1991: 17.

10. Connellan, Tom. *Inside the Magic Kingdom: Seven Keys to Disney's Success.* Austin, TX: Bard Press, 1996. 17–26.

11: Governments Become Dangerous

1. "Spend, Spend, Spend." *Economist World Survey* 20 Sept. 1997: 7.

2. I counted these phone listings myself, with an error of estimate of ±4 percent.

3. "The Cost of a Vote." *The Economist* 2 Sept. 1995: 26.

4. Melloan, George. "A Canadian Jurist Challenges a President's Powers." *The Wall Street Journal* 1 June 1999: A23. (Emphasis is his.)

5. Skyvington, Stephen. "Taking the Bull by the Horns." Speech for Coalition of Family Practitioners, Inn on the Park, Toronto, 22 Feb. 2003. (Skyvington's company, PoliTrain, trains organizational leaders to lobby governments.)

12: The Rising Importance of Geopolitics

1. "Echoes of the 1930s." *The Economist* 5 Jan. 1991: 18.

2. Pearce, Fred. "Global Population Forecast Falls." NewScientist.com accessed 27 Feb. 2003. <www.newscientist.com/news/news.jsp?id=ns99993444>

3. Drucker, Peter F. *Post-Capitalist Society.* New York: HarperBusiness, 1993. 153.

4. Nye, Joseph. "The New Rome Meets the New Barbarians." *The Economist* 23 Mar. 2002: 25.

5. Wessel, David. "Immigration's Attraction Lies in Its Boost to Economic Vitality." *The Wall Street Journal* 27 Feb. 2003: A2.

6. Ibid.

7. Nye, Joseph. "The New Rome Meets the New Barbarians." 23.

8. Ibid.

9. Ibid.

10. Xiaokang, Su. "China's Population Pressure Blackmail." *The Toronto Star* 15 Dec. 1995: A31.

11. Marshall, Samantha. "They Don't Say 'I Do,' These Kidnap Victims Taken from Vietnam." *The Wall Street Journal* 3 Aug. 1999: A1.

12. Cernetig, Miro. "Mao's Birth Control Creating Crisis for the Elderly." *The Globe and Mail* 29 Sept. 1999: A16.

13. Huntington, Samuel. *The Clash of Civilizations and the Remaking of World Order.* New York: Simon and Schuster, 1996.

13: Making It Happen

1. Schwartz, Peter. *The Art of the Long View: Planning for the Future in an Uncertain World.* New York: Doubleday, 1991. 210.

Who Owns Tomorrow?

1. Kroc, Ray. *Grinding It Out.* New York: Berkley, 1978. 201.

Index